THE NEW
IRISH SETTER

by WILLIAM C. THOMPSON

ILLUSTRATED

1973—Eighth Printing

HOWELL BOOK HOUSE

730 FIFTH AVENUE,
NEW YORK, N.Y.   10019

*To my wife, Helen, who for years has patiently
put up with the whims of a Setter man,
I affectionately dedicate this book.*

Ch. Milson O'Boy 850620 (Ch. Higgins Red Coat-Milson Miss Sonny).
Also cover photo.

Contents

Foreword

IRISH *Setter in Word and Picture,* published in 1954, is out-of-print. A continuing demand for it and for its updating has resulted in this new edition, entitled *The New Irish Setter.* Although some of the illustrations and numerous pages of text have of necessity been deleted from the original book, much new material and many photographs of recent champions have been added. Emphasis has been placed on the notable progress of the Irish Setter in the categories of field, obedience and bench, especially during the last decade. I have also included a chapter on the accomplishments of the Parent Club, the Irish Setter Club of America. The gracious reception of the first edition is deeply appreciated and it is my hope that the Irish Setter fancy will also enjoy this volume.

Minneapolis, Minnesota   WILLIAM C. THOMPSON

Setters in 1800—from a painting by G. Morland.

Setters in 1805—from a color plate by Sydenham Edwards.

8

1

Early Development

THE origin of the Irish Setter is not known. It is reasonable, however, to suppose that he was evolved for a certain purpose from older breeds by natural or by artificial selection. Records show that the breed was definitely established as early as 1800; but its history prior to that time relies mainly upon tradition, scattered writings and old sporting prints.

While most investigators believe that the foundation stock of the Irish Setter was the setting spaniel, there is a difference of opinion as to what crosses were used. The Bloodhound, Pointer, Irish Water Spaniel, Gordon Setter, English Setter and/or their progenitors have been variously named as possible ancestors. As the early-day sportsmen generally kennelled several breeds, it would seem not unusual for them to interbreed their dogs occasionally in order to improve utility.

Whatever the crosses may have been, the transition from spaniel to setter was apparently very gradual. Sporting illustrations of the period depict setters which resemble spaniels, as in W. Ward's engraving (1806) of G. Morland's painting. A close connection between the breeds is further indicated by the existence in Ireland about 1770, of a variety of setters called red spaniels (in Gaelic, *Modder Rhu*).

A Red Setter—from a painting by H. B. Chalon, 1816.

Pointing a Hare—an engraving by T. Landseer, 1824.

10

By 1800, setter type had become so well established that one has no difficulty in recognizing the Irish Setter in pictures of that era. Take, for example, the plate, "Setters in 1805" by Sydenham Edwards, showing the three varieties of setters; or the painting, "A Red Setter" (1816) by H. B. Chalon. Then there is also the famous painting, "Pointing a Hare" (1824) by Edwin Landseer.

During the period from 1780 to 1850, the Irish families took special pride in the purity of their own strains of setters and upon the number of years they had possessed them. A word in passing about some of the noteworthy strains might be of interest.

One of the first Irish sportsmen to rent shooting moors in Scotland (1779) was Maurice Nugent O'Connor, whose red setters had a trace of white on them, but no black. At his death in 1818, Robert LaTouche acquired the dogs, described as being large, dark red, light boned, well furnished and producing white-marked progeny. The French Park strain was owned in succession by three generations of the Lord de Freyne family (1793–1879). Then there were the strains of the Marquis of Waterford, Mr. Mahon, Lord Clancarty, Lord Anglesey, Lord Lismore, Lord Dillon, Lord Rossmore, Lord Forbes, Lord Howth, Sir Frances H. Loftus, Sir George Gore, Earl of Enniskillen, Yelverton O'Keefe, the Misses Lidwell and many others. John G. King was known as the "Father of the Breed" and Harry Blake Knox was the first to speak of the breed as the "Irish Red Setter."

An interesting description of early setters is given by Henry William Herbert, better known under the nom de plume of Frank Forester, who hunted in Yorkshire in 1825 over "Cynthia and Phebe, a pair of orange and white, silky Irish Setters with large, soft eyes and coal-black muzzles, feathered six inches deep on the legs and stern."

The distinguishing mark of the Irish Setter through the years has been his color, which is likened to that of a freshly opened horse chestnut burr. It has been variously described as red, mahogany, chestnut, blood red and indeed almost every shade between yellow and brown. According to Mrs. M. Ingle Bepler, in early Ireland three distinct color strains were known, the solid red predominating in the north, the parti-colored red and white in the south and west, and an attractive "shower of hail" variety along the northwest coast. The last-named setters were typical of the breed

11

Macdona's Rover 6193 KCSB (Beauty-Grouse).

Setters—an engraving by Martin T. Ward, 1829.

in points and color, but were sprinkled with uniform, quarter-inch, white spots about an inch apart.

Color was long a bone of contention among breeders, some claiming red as the proper color and others insisting upon red and white, although both strains probably originated from much the same parent stock. The opinion has been expressed that the red-and-whites had superior noses, were more tractable, faster and more enduring in the field, easier to see while hunting, less interbred with other breeds and possessed of longer sterns. They were characterized as having black noses and good feathering. White predominated in their coats and the red was preferably entirely surrounded by white. The red "islands," which could be large or small, were in about equal proportion to the white. Even the so-called red dogs probably carried a little white.

At Mount Loftus, County Kilkenny, Ireland, there was an oil painting of three red-and-white setters, painted in the early half of the nineteenth century. The Dublin bench shows of 1874 and 1875 had separate classes for red setters and for red-and-white setters. Both varieties were described by Anna Redlich in *The Dogs of Ireland* (1949). Even as late as 1964 in Ireland, the red-and-white blood was occasionally infused with that of the solid reds to improve style and head carriage.

The first dog show was held in the Town Hall at Newcastle-on-Tyne, England, in conjunction with a poultry show on June 28 and 29, 1859. It was for pointers and setters only, there being sixty entries. Next came the Birmingham, Leeds, Manchester and London shows, which included other breeds as well as gun dogs. Prizes were frequently withheld for lack of merit or for lack of competition. There seemed to be considerable uncertainty as to what constituted true type in Irish Setters, each owner claiming that he alone possessed the ideal dog. Apparently from the description of the entries, the setters were far from uniform in appearance.

Major Hutchinson's Bob, whelped in 1859 and shown four years later, was said in one reference to be "a wide-fronted, thick-shouldered Suffolk cart horse" and in another reference to be "good all over, formed in exact proportion, and with substance as well as symmetry." Be that as it may, it is known that the breeders of that day sought the bloodlines of this dog.

In 1860, there was a famous bench dog called Carlo, said by

13

A British Field Trial Meeting—from a painting by George Earl, 1882.

Idstone to be "pug-headed." Carlo was a red setter with black ear tips, indicative of a Gordon cross. About the same time Captain Allaway's Shot and Dr. Stone's Dash were exhibited. The latter was from stock twenty years in the doctor's kennels. It was said that Dash had white on the head and feet and a white "snake around the neck," but was of good contour.

The celebrated Irish Setter field trial winner, Plunket, whelped in 1868, combined the La Touche and the Hutchinson strains. He was sired by Plunket's Beauty out of Macdona's Grouse, she by Hutchinson's Bob. Although Plunket was small and bitch-like, he possessed speed, endurance and exceptional style on point. He had field trial wins at Shrewsbury, Vaynol and Southampton. Macdona sold Plunket for 150 guineas to R. Purcell Llewellin, who exported him to America, where he was used to improve native stock.

Plunket's success in the field trials brought to mind George Earl's famous composite painting of an early British field trial meeting (1882), in which eighty-five prominent sportsmen were shown with thirty-three of their dogs. The artist was most faithful in reproducing true likenesses of each man and dog. Portrayed were such well known field trial patrons as W. Brailsford, the father of field trials; Edward Laverack, founder of the modern English Setter; R. L. Purcell Llewellin, originator of the field trial strain of English Setter; Vero Shaw, author of *Illustrated Book of the Dog,* the first standard breed book of dogs; Dr. J. H. Walsh, better known as Stonehenge; William Arkwright, of Pointer fame; R. K. Armstrong, noted field trial handler; Reverend Robert O'Callaghan, Irish Setter breeder, and many others. Plunket, the only Irish Setter in the painting, was shown with his owner, Reverend J. C. Macdona, who was the first Englishman to judge an American dog show.

Although Stonehenge rated Plunket highly as a field dog, he chose his brother, Rover, to illustrate the ideal Irish Setter in his *Dogs in the British Islands.*

From 1875 to 1880, Ch. Palmerston reigned supreme; his name is in the pedigree of almost every Irish Setter and he has been credited with serving more bitches than ever possible. He was often referred to as the fountainhead of Irish Setter stock because of his profound influence on the breed. He was bred by Cecil Moore, County Tyrone, about 1862; and his quality was not fully appreciated in his early years as his owner kept dogs chiefly for shooting and seldom exhibited at bench shows. When he was first shown at five years of age, he was offered for sale at five pounds. Since Palmerston was considered too delicate for the field, even though he possessed a good nose and was diligent, Mr. Moore gave orders to drown him because he did not want him used for breeding. T. M. Hilliard, according to the story, intercepted as the drowning was about to proceed and begged for the dog, which was given to him providing that the setter would be kept for bench purposes only. So Palmerston, already along in years, was transferred to a show career. At Belfast in 1875, E. Sandell, a judge called "Caractacus," recognized his type and bought part interest in him. Palmerston was a grand 64-pound dog with good color and an abnormally long, narrow head. A thin strip of white on his forehead started the rage for the "Palmerston snip," which was the fashion for several years.

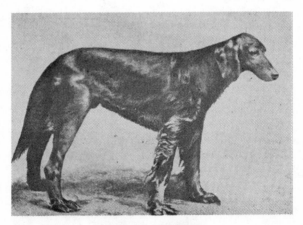

Palmerston 5138 KCSB.

Head Study of Palmerston.

The Kennel Club Stud Book (1876) gives Palmerston's pedigree as: "By Old Shot out of Cochrane's Kate; Shot by Mr. Evans of Dungannon's Grouse out of Juno, late the property of Mr. Hammington."

Palmerston died on September 9, 1880, and his head was mounted and displayed in the Waldorf-Astoria Hotel, New York City, where Hilliard's son was manager. In 1918, the head became the property of the Irish Setter Club of America.

Only a few of Palmerston's sons and daughters came to America. One of the best known of them was Rose, imported by Dr. William Jarvis, Claremont, New Hampshire, in 1877. It was Dr. Jarvis who discovered the nick between the Palmerston and the Elcho strains that had a pronounced effect upon Irish Setter history in America.

17

2

Importations
to America

I N order to obtain a true picture of the early history
of the Irish Setter in America, one should consult the first volume
of *The National American Kennel Club Stud Book* (1878). Only
sporting dogs were registered therein, an English Setter called
Adonis being number 1 and Admiral 534 being listed first among
the Irish. Although the pedigrees of most registrants were recorded
for two generations, frequently the data were incomplete. Of considerable interest to Irish Setter fanciers were the phrases used to
describe some of the dogs, as red with white feet, red with white
frill, and red with white blaze on the face—all of which testify to the
common occurrence of white in the Irish breed. Furthermore, colors
other than red were listed for a few so-called Irish Setters, indicating crosses in the not-too-distant past. Tom (660) was lemon, Van
Clark (663) black and Speed (650) black and white.

Only imported Irish Setters or their progeny could be registered
as Irish Setters, the American strains being referred to as Native
Setters, which were classified in a separate section entitled "Cross-
bred and Other Setters," explained as follows: "Owing to the indefi-

nite character of some pedigrees it was impossible to decide to what breed certain dogs belonged. They were included in the present class to save discarding them altogether." The practise of mating different breeds together was not unusual, as evidenced by the registrations of Irish-Gordon and Irish-English cross-bred setters.

Were the names ever confusing! For example, there were no less than sixteen well known Irish Setters called Dash. Then there were Fisher's Belle, Palmer's, Humphrey's, Ducat's, Moore's, Tileston's and Von Culin's Belles. Whenever a dog was transferred to a new owner, his registered name was probably changed. It can be readily realized that it must have been a colossal task to initiate the registration of purebred dogs.

The first bench show on record in the United States, held by the Illinois State Sportsmen's Association in Chicago on June 4, 1874, was "an exhibition of dogs without any attempt at testing their hunting qualities." Out of twenty-one entries, six carried Irish blood. The show committee hoped that the Association would have future meetings of this nature and "give the Great West a prominence in other branches of sportsmanship."

Next came the New York Sportsmen's Association show at Oswego on June 22, 1874, followed by the Mineola show in October of the same year.

On January 26, 1876, a bench show was held at the Exposition building in Chicago with classes for imported red or for red-and-white Irish Setters or their progeny; and there were similar classes for native red or red-and-white setters called Irish. The latter dogs were judged according to the standard of the Irish Setter, which incidentally was that of Stonehenge published in 1867. Early day shows usually had three classes for Irish Setters: puppy, open and champion.

Prize money was good, $50 values being frequent. Since sporting dogs predominated at the shows, it was appropriate that in addition to the cash prizes in the regular classes, there should be offered special prizes to appeal to sportsmen. For example, the Baltimore show of 1877 listed the following specials: eight bags of chilled shot, a Nichols and Lefever shotgun, a Bussy Gyro pigeon trap, two quarter-kegs of the best Hazard duck powder no. 4, a Holabird shooting coat and a case of Green Seal champagne.

After the Chicago show came St. Louis, Baltimore and then the

Westminster Club House, Babylon, 1884.

Westminster Kennel Club Show, Madison Square Garden, N.Y., May 6–9, 1884.

first Westminster show held at Gilmore's Garden on May 8 to 11, 1877. The New York show, long an annual February fixture, has represented the supreme event of American dogdom through the years. To win at Westminster was the culmination of things hoped for! This is the second oldest sporting event in America, the Kentucky Derby being first.

What gala occasions these early dog shows must have been, even if they were few and far apart! Just imagine crating your dogs, transporting them to the railroad station in horse-drawn vehicles, travelling many miles on slow, non-air-conditioned trains and exhibiting almost a week, following which came the long trek homeward. Perhaps there were recompenses for this in the good fellowship at the shows and in the pride of ownership of great dogs.

It was under these conditions in the decade following 1870, that the Irish Setter gained a foothold in America. Many dogs that made history were then imported from Ireland and England. As they were evidently superior to our native setters in type and certainly in purity of blood, they more or less set the standard of the era.

One of the first importations was Plunket, famous as a field and bench dog in England. Although he sired more than a score of litters from bitches in this country, only a few of the resulting offspring made names for themselves, perhaps because of the paucity of bench and field events at that time. It is noted that many of his puppies carried considerable white, either as a frill or on the feet.

The common practise of crossing breeds is exemplified by the Plunket-Carrie (Irish-English) and the Plunket-Nell (Irish-Gordon) matings. Apparently, Plunket sired good puppies, because a number of repeat matings were made. On three occasions, Kitty (Plunket-Knight of Kerry's Kate) was bred back to her sire. Other well known setters mated to Plunket were: Diffenderffer's Bess, Devlin's Moya, Jarvis' Kathleen and Hudson's Stella.

A sister of Stella, called Friend, was imported from England by E. Fowler Stoddard, Dayton, Ohio, in February 1875. She was a deep red bitch with white on the chest, toes and tip of the tail. In addition to winning on the bench at Memphis and St. Louis, she placed first in a field of thirteen starters in the All-Age Stake of the Minnesota Field Trial Club in 1878. Arnold Burges, Hillsdale, Michigan, acquired Friend and bred her to his imported Rufus, which resulted in a litter of four bench winners.

21

Rufus, a deep red dog whelped in 1873, was imported from Ireland at two years of age. Records show that he won at seven bench shows and that he sired litters from twenty-two bitches, three of which were native Gordon Setter stock.

A word of digression here concerning Arnold Burges (1839–1888) might not be amiss. An ardent outdoorsman and a prolific writer, he contributed a large share of his life to the betterment of sportsmen in America. For many years he was editor of *American Sportsman* and in 1876, he wrote *The American Kennel and Sporting Field*, which book contained pedigrees of 332 early-day field dogs. It was Burges who originated the term "Llewellin Setter" for the field trial breed of English Setter first bred by R. Purcell Llewellin of England.

No less than nine Irish Setters were imported between 1873 and 1876 from J. M. Niall of Ireland that were sired by Going's Bob (Hutchinson's Bob–Hutchinson's Lilly) out of Niall's Fan (Lord Waterford's Ponto–Miss Warburton's Venus). Included in this group were: Bess, Dash, Derg, Eileen, Fan II, Grouse, Guy, Kathleen and Red Hugh. These dogs must have possessed quality or so many of the same breeding would not have been imported over a three-year period. Probably the American breeders were attempting to secure the blood of Hutchinson's Bob.

In the fall of 1875, Charles H. Turner of the St. Louis Kennel Club, imported Sullivan's Rose, Erin, Frisk and Elcho. Erin won the Greenwood Plate Trophy for Irish Setters at the Memphis field trial of 1876. Although he was an excellent dog afield, he had a bad temper and once attacked his trainer, C. B. Whitford, who in self defense had to knock the dog down with a fence rail. Erin sired Bob, represented as "the best snipe dog that ever lived," and Duck, noted for her outstanding show record—she was defeated only once.

Unquestionably, the greatest bench-winning bitch of her time was imported Lou II, which won first at three Westminster shows and was widely exhibited with her famous son Berkley. Her pedigree traces back to the early days in Ireland when some of the setters were unnamed, being designated as "Lord Lismore's dog" or "Delaney's bitch."

During the 1870's in America it was customary for kennel clubs to own and campaign dogs. Elcho, Erin, Lou II, Thorstein, Sting II and Berkley were owned by the St. Louis Kennel Club; Ben and

Fannie Fern by Chicago; Colleen by Westminster; Derg by Baltimore; Doll by Toledo, and Irish Kork by Emporia Kennel Clubs.

A sportsman and the guiding spirit of the St. Louis Kennel Club, Charles Turner, imported Elcho from J. C. Cooper, Limerick, Ireland. The following letter to Mr. Cooper from his trainer relates Elcho's background:

November 6, 1875

Dear Sir:

I give you particulars of my red Irish Setter Elcho. He is by Charlie out of Nell, both of which were especially purchased for their good pedigree and sent out to Russia for breeding purposes. They are the property of Mr. Oppenheimer of St. Petersburg. Charlie was by Pat out of Juno, by Grouse out of Ina, by Derg out of Rhue. Nell was by Heather out of Nance, by Dane out of Loo; Loo by Bone out of Quail. The dog and the bitch both came directly from the strain of Lord Waterford and Marquis of Ormond, and were originally owned by Captain Irwin; you can' get no better blood in Ireland. Elcho was pupped May 1, 1874. I trained him myself and he is the best first season dog I ever had. . . . In case you should send him to America it will probably be of interest to whomever may get him across the Atlantic to learn that he is called after the Elcho Challenge Shield, which came to Ireland by the last shot which was fired by me at Wimbleton this year. By this victory the American Rifle Team is supposed to have thrashed creation, having beaten Ireland, Ireland then beating England and Scotland.

(Signed) Robert S. Greenhill

Ch. Elcho, the first Irish Setter to become a bench champion in America, won prizes in shows at Chicago, St. Louis, New York and Boston. To him belongs the honor of being the best Irish Setter of his period in America, not only because of his own awards, but also because of the success of his progeny on the bench and in the field. He was regarded as a great producer and was often referred to as "The Prince of Stud Dogs." Although some thought Elcho's own field qualifications were disappointing, he sired seven field-trial winners: Joe Jr., Berkley, Raleigh, Leigh Doane, Jessie, Yoube and Bruce.

The Campbells of Spring Hill, Tennessee, who were related to C. H. Turner, bred their native setter, Buck Jr., to Elcho, thereby producing the cross-bred red setter, Joe Jr. The bitch escaped from Mr. Turner's buggy on the trip to the kennels for the mating with Elcho and nearly had an affair with a Newfoundland. Joe Jr. thus might have been a water dog instead of the conqueror in a match race with the famous field trial English Setter, Gladstone.

23

More than 50 bitches had litters sired by Elcho, litters which included 30 bench show winners. He imparted quality, symmetry and refinement to his puppies, which characteristics predominated for several generations.

Although Elcho improved the breed in America as Palmerston did in England, he did not compare as an individual with that superlative specimen, being too low on his legs and much less impressive in head qualities. Elcho was said to have possessed a very dark red coat, a clean-cut 11-inch head, well placed ears, lean neck, good shoulders, deep chest and properly curved quarters. He measured 24 inches at the shoulder and weighed 56 pounds.

In the spring of 1877, Dr. William Jarvis, Claremont, New Hampshire, acquired Ch. Elcho and kept him for many years as his own private shooting dog. He imported Rose (Palmerston-Flora) and Noreen (Garryowen-Cora) from Ireland. The matings of these two Palmerston bitches to Elcho gave America the finest Irish Setter foundation stock. The Elcho-Rose mating was repeated nine times and the Elcho-Noreen mating five times.

Perhaps one should say a few words concerning Dr. Jarvis, who, in addition to being a successful breeder and importer of Irish Setters, was a sportswriter of high merit. After being graduated from Boston Dental College in 1876, he practised his profession in Claremont and later became president of the New Hampshire Dental Society. He kept his Irish Setters and other blooded livestock on his farm three miles from town. Dr. Jarvis was eminent for his activities as a breeder and judge for more than a quarter of a century and for his steadfast support of the Irish Setter.

In this chapter have been mentioned the outstanding imported Irish Setters of the early days. Credit should be given to the men who brought them to America, as these setters were the nucleus from which the breed in this country has developed.

3

Elcho Era

MATINGS among the imported dogs were common and frequently repeated in the decade prior to 1880. Resulting therefrom came the first pure-blooded, American-bred Irish Setters. During the next decade, importations were few; and to satisfy the increasing demand for top quality dogs created by the then flourishing dog shows, many trial matings were made among the American-breds, very few of which were repeated. For studs, the breeders fluctuated from winner to winner, usually without regard for bloodlines or for systematic breeding. In spite of the variation in type and the decided lack of uniformity in the puppies, some good dogs were produced, the most consistent winners of the era being descendants of the famous Ch. Elcho.

Perhaps the ten best known of Ch. Elcho's 197 puppies from 51 different dams were: Ch. Elcho Jr., Ch. Glencho, Bruce, Leigh Doane, Ch. Berkley, Ch. Yoube, Ch. Hazel, Raleigh, Lady Clare and Norwood.

By far the greatest of them was Ch. Elcho Jr. The early American writers seem to be of one accord in acclaiming him to be the foremost individual of his breed ever seen in the United States, a statement which is confirmed by his show record. He was exhibited at more than forty shows, ranging from the puppy class at Boston in

Ch. Elcho 579 (Oppenheimer's Charley-Oppenheimer's Nell).

Ch. Elcho Jr. 3881 (Ch. Elcho-Noreen)

26

1882 to Irish Setter Specials at Chicago in 1891, without a single defeat.

A critical description of this dog, as given by C. H. Mason in *Our Prize Dogs* (1887), reads like the breed standard:

> Red, of the most beautiful shade, being neither too dark nor too light. White spot on breast. . . . Skull well formed and showing prominent occipital protuberance. Forehead a trifle too prominent. Muzzle excellent. Color of eyes a shade too light. Ears, lips and expression very much better than average. This is a good head. Neck sufficiently long. Chest deep and rather narrow as it should be. Shoulders free and well placed. Back, just behind tops of shoulders, not quite right; it should be filled in and not showing the slightest approach to slackness. Loin flat, but strong. Quarters muscular and powerful. Hocks should be nearer the ground and well bent. Elbows would be better if set lower; they are rather too far under the body. Legs straight and strong down to the knees. Pasterns apparently strong, and not too long, but there is a tendency to knuckle over. Feet well formed, being thick through the pads, well arched, not too wide, and having the toes closed and well clothed with hair. Tail in good position and nicely fringed; it should be carried lower. Coat on neck and quarters not quite flat. A dog of nice size, showing strength, character and quality.

From this and other accounts, it would seem that Ch. Elcho Jr. was an upstanding, rangy dog of harmonious proportions, in which the "extreme limit of refinement" had been attained. He produced five bench champions: Duke Elcho, Edna H, Kildare, Seminole and Kildare Glenmore. Even though he was not a field trial winner, he was a good shooting dog; and his owner did most of his winter shooting over him in the Carolinas where birds were plentiful. Dr. Jarvis was induced to part with Ch. Elcho Jr. at nearly ten years of age for $1000 to head the Killarney Kennels of George H. Covert, Chicago. The new owner died within a year of the transfer and the dog's death occurred shortly afterward on November 8, 1891.

B. F. Seitner listed the most successful Irish Setter sires in order as follows: Ch. Elcho, Plunket, Rufus, Ch. Glencho, Berkley, Erin, Ch. Elcho Jr., Biz, Norwood, Ch. Chief, Rory O'More and Stoddard's Bob. Certainly Ch. Glencho, a litter brother to Ch. Elcho Jr., was entitled to high rank, having been the sire of litters from fifty-five bitches. Although he was considered to be somewhat too big according to the standard of his day, nevertheless he had much quality. Widely shown by his owner, W. H. Pierce, he won seven champion classes.

One of the first bitches bred to Ch. Elcho upon his arrival in this

Ch. Kildare 18140 (Ch. Elcho Jr.-Red Rose).

Ch. Duke Elcho 14587 (Ch. Elcho Jr.-Maid).

28

country was imported Lou II, owned by the St. Louis Kennel Club. From this mating came Berkley, the field trial winner and the standard of perfection for several years. His bench record was excellent with wins in the champion class at twelve shows. There were some who discounted Berkley, saying that he was English Setter-like and that his coat was tinged with black. A show critique stated that he was "a shapely little dog, would do better with more range, had a black nose and too dark a coat, and was a little fine before the eye." It would appear, however, that he was an extraordinarily good specimen because he won at the New York show three years and brought $1000 when sold to A. H. Moore, Philadelphia. Alexander Pope, Jr. published a color lithograph of him and also one of Ch. Elcho and Rose.

Max Wenzel's Ch. Chief (Berkley-Duck) was a well made, symmetrical dog with perfect coat and color, but he was coarse in head and shoulders and light in eye. Regardless of these faults, he was the popular sire of more than 42 litters in his long life of 12 years. He sired six field trial winners.

Incidentally, Wenzel was one of the founders of Fisher's Island Field Trial Club, which figured in the history of many an early day bird dog. He was actively interested for more than a score of years in Irish Setters as a breeder, exhibitor and judge; and did much to further the practical use of the breed.

Slow to mature, Ch. Tim (Biz–Ch. Hazel) won little in the show ring until after he was six years of age; and then he was very successful except when he met Ch. Elcho Jr. Tim won at Westminster on four occasions, the last time when he was eleven years old. He was described as a stylish, vigorous, 58-pound dog, having good depth of chest and excellent running gear; but he lacked spring of rib and length of muzzle. Even though he was mated to forty bitches, he produced no champions. He headed the Seminole Kennels of Dr. L. C. Sauveur, Philadelphia, for many years and died when he was thirteen.

While there were other dogs of note in the first generation from Ch. Elcho, such as Brush, Nimrod, Norwood and Race, little information about them was available; so it would be of interest to turn to the second generation of his descendants. Those bloodlines through Ch. Elcho Jr. and Ch. Glencho were the most prominent.

Ch. Kildare (Ch. Elcho Jr.–Red Rose) was owned by W. L. Washington (Kildare Kennels) Pittsburgh, later by F. C. Fowler (Oak Grove Kennels) Moodus, Connecticut, and finally by Joe Lewis, Greenwich. This outstanding setter acquired fifty-three first and special prizes at shows in the decade following 1888. Even though he was only 23¾ inches at the shoulder, pictures made him appear to be sturdily built and quite masculine. Mated with twenty-seven bitches, Kildare was the sire of two champions, Ch. Red Rose III and Ch. Queen Vic. The latter was a good specimen, placing best Irish Setter Bitch at Westminster six years straight.

W. L. Washington commented on his own dogs:

> In my kennels were no less than seven champions at one time: Laura B, Ruby Glenmore, Kildare, Molly Bawn, Winnie II, Finglas, Dick Swiveler, which was a beautiful dog but a duffer in the field, and that old duffer, Sarsfield, which, I believe, did great injury to the breed. I discarded him as soon as I discovered the shortcomings of his progeny. I ran him in the Eastern field trials when he was an old dog, but his nose was gone, and he simply flushed every bird he came upon.

Ch. Laura B (Ch. Glencho–Daisy) was considered better than either Ch. Norna or Ch. Edna H as a show dog. With regard to her sister, C. H. Mason stated: "Structural defects in the body and limbs of a sporting dog must not be overlooked for a sweet face." Ch. Ruby Glenmore (Ch. Glencho–Magg) took over the show laurels where Ch. Laura B left off. A. F. Hochwalt described Ruby as "one of the best show bitches of her day," which statement is supported by her record.

In 1889 and 1890, the challenge class at Westminster was won by Ch. Dick Swiveler (Bruce–Leigh Doane), a dog that set the style for the period. Although Dick won consistently, he was no match for Ch. Elcho Jr., which at nine years of age defeated the younger dog at Buffalo and New York; and at ten years took the challenge class at Chicago. It seemed that Irish Setters were slow to mature; they were long-lived and improved with age. Dick was still being shown at eleven by his later owner, A. B. Truman (Elcho Kennels) San Francisco. He was a short dog with a 10¼ inch head. On the West Coast he headed a whole family of Swivelers, including Ch. Mike Swiveler T and Ch. Lady Swiveler.

Other well known Irish Setters and their owners should be mentioned. Ch. Kildare Glenmore represented the Oak Grove Kennels of F. C. Fowler; Belle of Orange was bred by Samuel Coulson; the beautifully coated Ch. Mollie Bawn was raised by W. Dunphy; the three field trial winning Leigh Doanes were owned by I. H. Roberts, and Ch. Gerald was in the kennels of Jean Grosvenor. Gerald was said to be a long legged dog with too much daylight under him and with light eyes. Evidently this last-named fault was fairly common in those days, for one-third of the bench show winners of 1887 were criticized in that regard. W. N. Callender's Rory of More headed a long strain of O'Mores continuing to Ch. Rory O'More VIII. It is unfortunate that the blood of Ch. Mack N was permitted to die out, because he was reputed to be one of the best field dogs of any breed.

That the red dogs of the Elcho era were good field dogs is substantiated by Dr. Gwilym G. Davis of Philadelphia, who from 1887 until his death in 1918, was an energetic supporter of the breed and who for many years was president of the Irish Setter Club of America. His field trial winners Currer Bell III, Currer Bell IV and Currer Maud were run fearlessly in the trials. Dr. Davis expressed the opinion that Irish Setters ran high-headed, possessed good noses and were wide rangers; but that late development and lack of staunchness on point were the main drawbacks to the unqualified success of the breed in the field.

The decade following 1880 saw a rapid rise of the Irish Setter toward popularity, both on the bench and afield, chiefly due to the Elcho-Palmerston bloodlines.

4

Gay Nineties

THE term "Gay Nineties" is probably best known for its association with the stage; but it is also quite appropriately applied to the field of sport. Football, hockey, cricket, baseball, curling, tennis, yachting, canoeing, fishing, hunting, camping, horse racing, taxidermy, trapping, fencing, photography, mountaineering, pigeon flying, rowing, golfing, exploring and cycling furnished unlimited entertainment for millions. Such periodicals as *Forest and Stream, Outing, Sports Afield, Breeder and Sportsman, Shooting and Fishing, Turf, Field and Farm, Wildwood's Magazine* and *The American Field* helped to create enthusiasm. There were sportsmen's exhibitions to display the latest equipment for each pastime. Of course, bench shows and field trials prospered during the era. About twenty-five dog shows per year were held in the United States, many of which were of four or five days' duration. What a time the fanciers must have had at those meetings! Perhaps the Madison Square Garden shows most nearly approach those early events in atmosphere and good fellowship.

The Westminster Kennel Club shows were held in May of each year until 1888, when they were scheduled for February. Sometimes two or three persons would judge a breed. In judicial roles were the names of Davidson, Glover, Taylor, Pierce, Dalziel and Mason.

Originally, the breed classes for dogs and also for bitches were: champion, open and puppy; but in 1889 challenge classes replaced champion and novice classes were added to stimulate the exhibition of previously unshown dogs. The year 1898 saw the advent of junior and limit classes; also local and field trial classes. In the following year, a system of breed classes with winners and reserve winners placings was instituted.

That the big winners among the Irish Setters at the turn of the century did not show the quality of those in the previous Elcho era, was perhaps due to a lack of unity of effort among the breeders. The fact that each considered his own strain as the "standard of perfection" led to a wide divergence in type, the effect of which was evident for a long time. There were many "in and outers" in the dog game, meaning that certain individuals after a few years of activity in Irish Setter affairs, lost interest completely. Were it not for some of the older breeders carrying on at that time, the breed would have suffered greatly.

Another factor that helped to maintain the breed was the importation of dogs from the British Isles. Ch. Winnie II and Desmond II were imported by Charles T. Thompson (Chestnut Hill Kennels), Philadelphia, from Reverend Robert O'Callaghan, England. They were the same breeding as the English champions Aveline and Shandon II. Their sire was Frisco, a grandson of Ch. Elcho, and their dam was Grouse II, a Ch. Palmerston daughter. Here again was the Palmerston-Elcho combination of bloodlines that had contributed so much to the early American strains.

Ch. Aveline "the beautiful" mated to her brother Fingal III, produced Coleraine, a field-trial bitch imported by E. B. Bishop, Hutchinson, Kansas.

A litter brother of Coleraine, Ch. Finglas, was imported in 1891, by S. L. Boggs of Pittsburgh. Apparently, this brother and sister mating was successful, for Ch. Finglas was a bench champion and field trial winner; and also the sire of three bench champions and seven field trial winners. His name occurs in the pedigree of almost every American-bred Irish Setter. His champion daughters were: Bessie Finmore, Red Bess II and Red Bud Finglas. Ch. Finglas was the Absolute Winner, All-Age Stake, American Field Trial Club, Columbus, Indiana, 1892.

The imported Irish Setters were well distributed in this country.

Ch. Finglas 21569 (Fingal III-Aveline).

Shamrock—from a painting by Thomas Blinks, 1895.

34

F. H. Perry, Des Moines, Iowa, imported from Ireland a half-brother of Ch. Aveline, called Claremont Patsy (Frisco–Nellie IX). Nellie was a granddaughter of Ch. Palmerston. Patsy was best known as being the sire of Chief Red Cloud, one of the forefathers of the Law strain.

C. M. Rounds, San Antonio, Texas, imported Princess Royal, a bitch of Palmerston lineage. More of this blood was brought over from England with Inchiquin (Ch. Shandon II–Iona) by J. J. Scanlon, Fall River, Massachusetts.

A well known breeder of Irish Setters in the Nineties was J. Gibbons Hawkes, Kenmore, Ireland, who was said to have had twenty-six field trial winners in his kennel at one time. Among them were the famous Muskerry and nine of his field trial winning get. Three of the latter were imported to America: Blue Rock, Signal and Tearaway. Although Blue Rock was widely advertised at stud by Dr. William Jarvis, his record in America is not impressive.

On the other hand, Signal figured in the pedigrees of many Irish Setters, especially since his bloodlines seemed to nick well with those of the Finglas bitches; and the word "Signal" appeared in dogs' names over a ten-year period. He sired Signora, Sig's Girl, Signal Jr., Shamrock Signal, Red Signal, Young Signal and many others. His daughter, Clare P., was a pillar of the Law strain.

Tearaway was noted for one litter he sired from the field trial winner Tillie Boroimhe Boru, because it contained two winners in the Irish Setter Club Trials of 1892, Sagax Tearaway and Tillie Boru II. These dogs were owned and handled by George E. Gray, Appleton, Minnesota, one of the major circuit handlers of the early days.

Another dog from J. G. Hawkes' kennels was Henmore Shamrock (Muskerry-Avoca), imported by F. L. Cheney (Onota Kennels), Pittsfield, Massachusetts.

The importation of these sons of Muskerry to America had the effect of contributing ruggedness and field ability to the Palmerston-Elcho strain. Although Palmerston was in the fourth and the fifth generations of Muskerry's pedigree, the preponderance of other blood served as an outcross for the American stock.

The Gay Nineties in America brought forth many new breeders of Irish Setters. Kennel prefixes like Lismore of the Wall Brothers and Shamrock of the Carmichaels became famous around Chicago.

35

L. L. Campbell and A. B. Truman upheld the Irish standard in California and Samuel Coulson did likewise in Montreal, Canada. A jumbling of the letters in the name of F. M. Thomas made a distinctive prefix for the "Thasmo" dogs. Then there were the Finmores—Bessie, Blanche, Cora and Ruby—a quartet of bitches exhibited by W. H. Eakins, Columbus, Ohio. About this time other kennels were established by F. H. Perry, G. O. Smith, Dr. J. S. Laycock, A. W. Pearsall, F. P. Kirby, George Kunkel, Michael Flynn, Joseph Lewis and others.

The bench laurels in this period were usurped by the champions Kildare, Queen Vic, Norna, Tim, Seminole, Laura B, Edna H, Bessie Finmore, Pride of Patsy and Duke Elcho. On the West Coast Dick Swiveler, Lightning T, Lady Swiveler and Queen of Kildare were the big winners. It is significant that most of these dogs were descended from Ch. Elcho.

5

Law Strain

IT has been stated that the Law suffix originated with old Shan Law in Ireland, a point which has not been substantiated. Nevertheless, in America the fountainhead of the Law strain was Ch. Ben Law (Chief Red Cloud–Nancy Finglas), whelped August 22, 1896, and owned by Charles A. Gale, Rutland, Vermont. Although Ben's three-year bench show career was not a straight string of victories, he had sufficient merit to win at Westminster in 1901, thereby defeating among others, imported Prince Victor and Ch. Rockwood Jr. Mated to a dozen bitches, he sired sixty dogs, including the following seven champions: Conn Law, Hibernian Ben, Gael Law, Shan Law, Pat Law, Shandon Ben and St. Cloud's Lorna. These six sons of Ch. Ben Law and their offspring played a prominent role in the development of the Irish Setter in America over a forty-year period.

Ch. Conn Law, noted for his beautiful head, was a very popular sire in the East. J. S. and T. Wall (Lismore Kennels) of Brooklyn, must have liked Conn as a sire, because they bred their lovely Ch. Lismore Colleen to him thrice. M. G. Heim of Kansas City shipped his Ch. My Irish Rose half-way across the continent to be bred to him. Ch. Sheila O'Brien, owned by Charles Esselstyn, Hudson, New York, raised a litter bearing the "of Kelt" suffix sired by the same dog. Conn also sired Ch. Lismore Freedom, Ch. Lismore Brendan and Ch. Mike Law. In the show ring Ch. Richwoods Roy and Ch. Riversdale Red Guide furnished too much competition for Conn.

His brother, Ch. Hibernian Ben, was not very successful at bench shows, being consistently defeated by Ch. St. Cloud III. However, Louis Contoit (St. Cloud Kennels), Greenwich, Connecticut, seemed to prefer Ch. Hibernian Ben to the other Law dogs, for he mated five bitches to him. He sired the field-trial winner, Brimstone, and Ch. St. Cloud's Ruby.

Perhaps the best known of the Law dogs in the East was Ch. Shan Law, whelped August 31, 1901, and owned by Dr. William Jarvis. He had no significant record on the bench until he was four years old; but in the succeeding years, he was Winners Dog 21 times at shows from Milwaukee to Bar Harbor, including New York on two occasions. Although defeated by Ch. St. Cloud III and by Ch. Dermond a few times, he placed over them at others. He also won over Ch. Duke of Gloucester, Ch. Borstal Rock, Storm Cloud, imported Daerig Prince, Ch. Gael Law and Ch. St. Cloud's Blarney.

A critical description of him was given by A. F. Hochwalt:

> Shan Law was a beautifully colored dog with a well-made, long head of typical quality, character and expression. His neck was long and clean, shoulders well set, ears properly hung, forelegs straight, ribs well sprung but just a shade long in body and a trifle faulty in quarters and stifles, which defect he was prone to show more in action than in repose. . . . He was a broken field dog, and while he lacked the pace and range of most English Setters and Pointers, there was a certain amount of attractiveness about his points that was superior to the average of his breed.

Shan sired four champions: Heir-at-Law, Patricia, St. Lambert Doris and St. Lambert Phyllis. The St. Lambert Kennels were owned by Samuel Coulson of Montreal and Dave Ward of Toronto. Among the bitches bred to Shan were Ch. St. Lambert Kathleen, Roma, Ch. Lady Dakin II and two Culbertsons. While he did not rate with his brother, Ch. Pat Law, as a producer, he doubtless was superior in bench show points. He died in the spring of 1910, just a few weeks before his master.

Ch. Gael Law, owned by N. M. Emerson, Boston, apparently left no registered offspring. It was not easy for him to win his championship when competing against such dogs as Shan Law, St. Cloud III and Heir-at-Law.

Perhaps the greatest producing sire in the Midwest in the early part of the twentieth century was Ch. Pat Law, whelped June 20, 1903, and owned by Walter McRoberts, Peoria, Illinois. He sired 82 puppies in six litters, which is probably a record for a stud:

Date	Dam	Puppies
12–20–07	Nell of Culbertson	15
12–22–07	Aileen of Culbertson	10
6– 6–08	Biddie Finglas	13
7–14–08	Nell of Culbertson	18
7–15–08	Aileen of Culbertson	13
9–29–14	Richwoods Gretchen	13

Between 1909 and 1914, McRobert's favorite bitch, Ch. Holly of Culbertson, had six litters by Pat that contained six champions. The same dog sired half a dozen litters from Rosa Rathclane, a bitch known for having almost human intelligence. With this kind of production, Walter McRoberts soon had his Richwoods prefix on the names of over 100 Irish Setters, eight of them champions. In passing, it might be noted that McRoberts, who was a bachelor, had his kennels in the suburban section of Peoria called Richwoods and that his kennel name derived therefrom was neither possessive nor plural. Whenever he sold a dog, he demanded the privilege of first purchase in case the animal was resold. He had high regard for his setters and upon his death left $4,000 for their care.

Many of Ch. Pat Law's 160 sons and daughters were of national importance to the breed. There were Otto Pohl's famous Ch. Drug Law and Ch. Pat-A-Belle. Another good dog was Chieftain Law, which carried on his sire's reputation as a producer. He was first shown at Omaha at nine years of age. Then there was Red Law, considered a fine specimen of the breed, which did not become a champion because his owner refused to exhibit in closed halls on account of distemper. Five bitches sired by Ch. St. Cloud's Blarney were bred to Pat, the best dog resulting therefrom being Ch. Richwoods Glenroy. McRoberts also mated his two field trial bitches, Ch. Virginia Belle and Hurrah, to Pat. In general, it was said concerning his offspring, that the dogs were inclined to be coarse and the bitches rather small.

Ch. Pat Law was campaigned about the Midwest from 1906 to

Ch. Drug Law 150134 (Ch. Pat Law-Hurrah).

Ch. Drug Law 150134 (front); Ch. Pat-A-Belle 150135.

40

1910, at shows with only mediocre competition. Ch. Shan Law, a bigger dog, defeated him at Pittsburgh and Detroit; and Ch. St. Cloud's Blarney placed over him at Cincinnati. Pat was a grand dog nevertheless, a credit to the Irish Setter breed.

After winning at four shows in the East in 1903, John J. Scanlon's Ch. Shandon Ben was sold to Paul Peipers, Los Angeles, thus to represent the Law strain on the West Coast. He was Winners Dog at Los Angeles three years straight—in fact, he never was defeated in the breed classes. He produced no get of exceptional merit from the five bitches bred to him.

The six champion sons of Ch. Ben Law, living in various parts of the country, served to distribute the Law strain widely; in fact, more than half of the dogs registered in 1920 had some of that blood in their veins. The Law strain flourished with such representatives as Judge Law, Ch. Heir-at-Law, Ch. Drug Law, Ch. Mike Law and Ch. Max Law. As time progressed, it gradually faded and became practically extinct in pure strain. However, some of this blood regained prominence with the field trial Irish Setters of the 1950's.

The Law setters were great shooting dogs. They were the choice of the market hunters in the early part of the century when prairie chickens were shot by the thousands on the Minnesota prairies and shipped in barrels to Chicago. In those days, hotels and railroad dining cars served upland game and wildfowl regularly on their menus. Perhaps these Law dogs were preferred for market hunting because they were bold, rugged "good-doers," sturdy and tireless, and possessed of sure bird finding ability.

Much has been written about Otto Pohl and his dogs, some of which were of the Law strain. At his untimely death from Spanish influenza in 1918, this Fremont, Nebraska, druggist and sportsman owned an aggregation of Irish Setters that had established an enviable reputation in field trials and bench shows around the Midwest. Several imported dogs were in his kennels too, which he had included in an extensive breeding program. His passing was a serious loss to the Irish Setter fancy and he will long be remembered for his efforts to combine bench and field qualities in the breed. In his pamphlet *The Irish Setter* (1917), he wrote:

> If faith in the breed and the right bloodlines will do it and the assistance of a few of my friends, I am going to produce field-trial winning Irish Setters and they will be good looking dogs too.

Ch. Rheola Clanderrick 183598 (Clancarty Rhu-Rheola Ronda).

Ch. St. Lambert's Caltra M, 190637 (St. Lambert's Larry-Ruby T).

Probably the first record of Otto Pohl in canine affairs was the registration of a dog called Drug in 1899. From all accounts Old Drug, in addition to possessing almost human intelligence and being a retriever par excellence, was "the finest flower in the canine field" in his master's opinion. Is it not frequently the case that glamour and romance color the memories of the first owned setter? Mated with Red Belle, Drug sired some locally renowned shooting dogs.

In 1909, Pohl bought Ch. Drug Law and Ch. Pat-A-Belle from Walter McRoberts and trained both dogs thoroughly for prairie chicken and quail shooting. Two years later when he became interested in bench shows, he exhibited them throughout the Midwest. At that time they were much publicized in the dog literature by a lovely brace picture.

Pohl's first importation was Morty Oge (pronounced Augh), representing English field trial blood. Although this son of Dunboy and Alizon died about a year after his arrival in this country, he was used at stud with fifteen bitches; consequently, he figures in the pedigrees of many American-breds of that period. He was a large, coarse, dark mahogany dog with a wide head. He sired only one champion, Ch. Richwoods Gretchen. His best known son was Donegal's Morty Oge, out of Ch. Pat-A-Belle. This dog was not very successful in the show ring, chiefly because of his mediocre head. However, as he was superb in the field, Pohl did most of his shooting over him. The seventeen bitches mated to him during his long life of nine years flooded the Midwest with Morty Oge breeding, which accounted for many good bird dogs. Among them were Morty Oge's King, Elcova's Kinkie, Pocahontas Red Jacket, Donegal's Morty Oge II, Patrick Kenmore and Lingo-dell's Morty Oge.

The second import was Mrs. M. Ingle-Bepler's young dog, Ch. Rheola Clanderrick (Ch. Clancarty Rhu-Rheola Ronda), which came over from England in 1914. Shortly after his arrival in this country, he won his championship easily and was widely used at stud. He was a very popular sire and the name of Clanderrick was carried along for more than forty years. His best known sons and daughters were Duke Clanderrick, Major Clanderrick, Rheola Morello, Erin's Fairy, Shamrock Clanwood Pat and Withrow's Duke Clanderrick.

Two more Rheola dogs were imported in 1915, the dark, pro-

Kennard 295405 (Ch. Midwood Red Jacket-Ch. Carntyne Clodagh).

Ch. Lismore Freedom 218154 (Ch. Conn Law-Ch. Lismore Colleen).

44

fusely coated Rheola Pedro (Galahad-Leverton Lass) and the small
Rheola Judy (Rheola Bo'sun-Sh Ch. Ypsilanti), both tracing back
to Ch. Clancarty Rhu. Pedro, an excellent field dog, seemed to pass
along to his offspring this field ability as well as his magnificent dark
mahogany coat.

Although Rheola Judy was not a show dog because of her lack of
size and desirable head character, her chief claim to fame was that
she was the dam of the noted field trial winner, Donegal's Alizon,
and the bench winner, Ch. Donegal's Judy Law, litter sisters sired
by Ch. Drug Law.

While Otto Pohl derived much pleasure from the bench wins of
his dogs, he greatly enjoyed his field trial dogs. His biggest thrill
must have been in January 1918, when his Donegal's Alizon,
handled by J. M. Avent, placed third in the Derby Stake, All-
America Field Trial Club, Grand Junction, Tennessee, in competition with three English Setters and three Pointers. This was a signal win for the breed, which had been hopelessly outclassed in field
trials for the previous twenty-five years. Alizon whelped litters by
Donegal's Pat II and by Donegal's Morty Oge.

McKerry (Nebraska Ranger-Lyon's Kathline) was another Irish
Setter that Pohl entered in the big time trials. He received favorable
comment and got as far as the second series in the All-Age Stake,
All-America Field Trial Club, Aberdeen, South Dakota, September 1, 1914, in competition with 20 English Setters and eight Pointers. McKerry changed hands three times, finally going to Fred J.
Lefferdink, Hickman, Nebraska, who offered the dog at stud until
his death in 1923. A general description of this dog implied that he
had strong running gear, a well muscled back and loin, a wide,
square, poorly chiselled head, and plenty of substance. He possessed
intelligence, speed, endurance and the nose required of a field
trial dog. McKerry sired 30 litters and produced two field trial winners, McKerry's Pat and McKerry's Queen. The pedigrees of several
American Irish Setter field champions have been traced back to
him.

At the San Francisco Exposition in May 1916, Pohl purchased
Ch. St. Lambert's Caltra M (St. Lambert's Larry-Ruby T) at the reputed figure of $750 from J. J. Mitchell. From all accounts this dog
had a beautiful, long, lean head with oval skull, pronounced occiput, low hung ears, medium sized eyes and moderately deep muzzle.

45

In fact, it was supposed to be the ideal head, the closest to the Irish Setter standard. Pohl believed that Caltra M could contribute many desirable qualities to his stock. But the dog was not long at stud for he was killed in a kennel fight early in 1919. Only five bitches were bred to him. His well known progeny were: Donegal's Pat II, Caltra M's Ruby, General Foch and Bird-A-Rosa.

From this account of Otto Pohl's dogs, it can be readily seen that here was an Irish Setter enthusiast who had the best interest of the breed at heart. He had assembled a nucleus in his Donegal Kennels for a promising breeding program; and it is to be regretted that he was not permitted to complete it. Several types as well as bloodlines were represented. After his death the kennels were transferred to Dr. L. C. Adams, Dayton, Ohio, and a year or so later to D. J. White, Decatur, Illinois. Both of these men mated some of the dogs together, but no one carried on a systematic scheme of line breeding to fix the good qualities of the Pohl dogs.

Contemporary with McRoberts and Pohl were the bachelor brothers, Joseph and Thomas Wall, of Montreal, Chicago and later Brooklyn. Their prefix which was derived from their ancestral home at Lismore, County Waterford, Ireland, was prominent in Irish Setter cycles for forty years. Joseph was an officer in the Irish Setter Club of America and also a dog show judge. Well known dogs in their kennels included Ch. Lord Lismore, Lord Lismore Jr., Ch. Lismore Colleen, Ch. Lismore Deirdre, Ch. Lismore Macree, Ch. Lismore Brendan and Ch. Lismore Freedom. The consensus of opinion was that Colleen was the best setter the Walls ever owned. Of the two litter sisters, Deirdre and Macree, the former had the better show record. Ch. Lismore Freedom (Ch. Conn Law-Ch. Lismore Colleen) has been described as large, masculine, of good color, somewhat rough in shoulders, light eyed and a poor mover. In spite of his faults, he won his share of ribbons at bench shows from 1916 to 1921, and was a popular stud. He sired six champions and that wonderful bitch, Craigie Lea Mona, the dam of Ch. Higgins' Red Coat and Ch. Higgins' Red Pat.

Ch. Lismore Freedom and Ch. Midwood Red Jacket, a brother of Ch. Lismore Colleen, were close competitors in the show ring. These two dogs were of different stamp. Freedom was rugged and very masculine, whereas Red Jacket was smooth and refined. Both dogs won twice at Westminster.

46

The history of the Irish Setter in this country would not be complete without mention of the brothers, Louis and S. A. Contoit, St. Cloud Kennels, in the New York Area. From 1889, when Louis registered St. Cloud (Ch. Elcho-Noreen), until his death about 1930, this man (to use his own words) "owned at least 5,000 Irish Setters," many of which carried the St. Cloud prefix. His forty year career involved numerous champions, a multitude of acquaintances and a profound knowledge of Irish Setters. He preferred type and refinement in his setters and often expressed his opinion about "red Newfoundlands" and "red Dalmatians" in most uncomplimentary terms.

The Contoits were among the first to establish a modern strain of Irish Setters by line breeding. One of their favorite systems of breeding was to mate several sisters to the same sire and then to cross the offspring. They usually retained the bitches and sold the males in the litters. Most of the St. Cloud dogs trace back to Elcho-Noreen or to Elcho-Rose matings. Outstanding among their early sires were Ch. St. Cloud III and Ch. St. Cloud's Fermanagh, both beautiful type setters. The former was Winners Dog 35 times in 39 shows and the latter 10 times with no defeat. Other St. Cloud dogs to win the purple ribbon consistently were St. Cloud's Lorna, Kathleen, Laddie, Lurline, Rosamonde, Ruby, Shanmore, Star and Vida. The Contoits also used the Law dogs and the St. Lamberts in their breeding programs.

Ch. St. Cloud's Blarney (Elcho Ranger-Ch. Red Rose III) was the mainstay of the kennel of working setters owned by Clemer Bell and John H. Chappell, Oakland City, Indiana. Blarney ran in three field trials, was shown 15 times and sired litters until he was 13 years old. Ch. Virginia Belle and Rob Rollo, both field trial winners, were among his 160 get.

F. A. Johnson, Detroit, owned Ch. St. Cloud's Kenmore (Ch. Heir-at-Law-Daisy Law), said to be a good field dog and popular stud. Cushbawn Desmond was imported from England by F. A. Walsh, Winnipeg. In Oakland, California, Peter N. Hanrahan had several champions named with the suffix "H," as Ch. Pat H, Ch. Jim H and Ch. Margaret H, which traced back to the Glenmore setters of L. L. Campbell. Other Irish Setter fanciers of the period included Stacey B. Waters, Michael Flynn, Fred Kirby, George Thomas and Ben Lewis.

47

After the turn of the century an increasing number of women became interested in the red setter. There were Mrs. Walter Simmons
with Ch. Midwood Red Jacket, Miss E. L. Clarkson with Ch. Lans-
downe Red Rose, Mrs. R. W. Creuzbauer with Ch. Lady Dakin II,
Miss Elise Ladew with Ch. Carntyne Clodagh, Mrs. E. B. Chase
with Ch. Bob White Red Storm, Mrs. E. Alban Sturdee with Ch.
Richwoods Roy, Miss Marie Louise Welch with Ch. Barney O'Flynn
and Mrs. Helen M. Talbot with Ch. Muskerry Fen. Miss Welch
wrote a little book *Your Friend and Mine* (1934) about the beauty,
courage, affection and intelligence of the Irish Setter.

6

Roaring Twenties

IN the decade following World War I, there was an unprecedented increase in the number and popularity of Irish Setters. At least 200 of them were imported then from Canada and the British Isles. Interbreeding the many unrelated strains led to wide variations in breed size and type—as far apart as Spaniels, Whippets, Pointers, and St. Bernards except in color. Even among the champions there was a decided lack of uniformity. Before the decade passed, however, there emerged from this "melting point' a new, stylish, streamlined Irish Setter destined to set the type of the modern dogs. The old Law strain was on the decline, while the Boyne family originated by J. A. Carbery, Drogheda, Ireland, was ascending.

One characteristic of the era was the valiant attempt of Irish Setter owners to reinstate their breed in field trials. In the old days the red dogs had competed on even terms with other gun dogs. They had always been considered to be reliable shooting or "meat" dogs, but for one cause or another they lost caste in the trials. Various reasons were advanced for this, including breeding solely for the bench, slow maturing of puppies, lack of style and staunchness on point, the color handicap and loss of interest among owners.

Although the red setter seemed hopelessly outnumbered in field trials, there were some staunch backers of the breed as a field dog. One of them was G. O. Smith, Wheeling, West Virginia, who had imported the field trial winner, Young Signal, back in 1893. Thirty years later he was still interested to the extent that he imported several well known stud dogs, including Tipperary Eamon, Billy Palmerston, Bran of Boyne and Raneagown. The first named of these dogs with twenty field trial winners in his pedigree was imported in July 1920. He made the name "Tipperary" famous for several years through his numerous sons and daughters, many of which were run in field trials. Some of the field trial champions of the 1950's trace back to him. After his death of ptomaine poisoning on November 24, 1923, an attempt was made to find among his sons a stud to replace him. Several of them were advertised as "Tipperary Eamon's best son"; Tipperary Eamon's Tip, Tipperary Eamon Jr., Tipperary Brownie Law, Tipperary Irish Duke and Tipperary Eamon's Ghost.

In 1922, Smith imported a litter brother to J. Horace Lytle's Demon of Boyne, called Raneagown. Of this setter, Smith said, "I have been shooting ruffed grouse since I was a boy and I don't think I ever shot over a dog superior to Raneagown." The dog sired two champions, Belle's Anniversary and Raneagown's Proud Peggy, both from Horn's Queen.

Smith was not in sympathy with the practise of close breeding as was followed by Llewellin breeders. Both Tipperary Eamon and Raneagown, of course, represented bloodlines quite foreign to any in America. The famous English Ch. Gruagach sired Raneagown and also the later importations, Sarsfield, Liam, Tadg and Domnal MacGruagach. Typical of this strain was great size and coarseness.

An ardent supporter of the Irish for his bird-finding qualities was H. A. Wisher of Philadelphia, whose advertisements in the dog magazines of the period remind one of something a sportsman journalist once said. He stated that a newspaper can stretch a point now and then in describing hunting conditions, game bagged, size of fish caught, etc. Not to be outdone, the dog fancy reacted similarly and some of the stud cards of the Roaring Twenties really glowed. Nevertheless, these cards make interesting reading and in some ways it is to be regretted that such means of advertising have long been discontinued. One of Wisher's advertisements in *The American Field* read:

imported Bob of Down
imported Shantallow's Mick
imported Mack of Gortin
imported East Galway Pat

Four of the best Irish Setter field dogs living, bar none. These dogs were all heavily shot over by my scout, John Bradley, one of the best sportsmen and judge of dogs in Northern Ireland; when Mr. Bradley lands a dog for me it has to come to him on trial. . . . Each of my dogs is a new strain in this country.

Of these good gun dogs, perhaps the best known was Ch. Wisher's Bob of Down, a broken shooting dog as well as a bench champion. Although more than thirty bitches were mated to him, only one champion was produced, Lady Gregory.

The Irish Setters of Dr. John D. DeRonde (Palmerston Kennels), New York City, were in the forefront for about ten years. This enthusiastic breeder, judge and President of the Irish Setter Club of America kept approximately sixty dogs in his country kennels, from which he sold setters to almost every state in the Union, even as far west as California. Mary Pickford, the famous movie star, owned one of his breeding.

DeRonde's first big circuit winner was imported Tyrone Larry (Tyrone Terry-Sonora Norma), whelped in 1917 and purchased at three years of age from E. C. Howard, Montreal. This dark red, typey, 56-pound dog soon became a Canadian and American champion. His head was rather plain and his chief fault was quite straight stifles. In spite of this he built an enviable reputation during his long life. Widely advertised at stud, he was the sire of more than 140 registered offspring, many of which were exhibited at shows or run in field trials.

Ch. Palmerston Connemara Grand, Ch. Palmerston Jerry and Ch. Palmerston Red Mike also were owned by DeRonde. It is said that he refused a $10,000 offer for the last two-named dogs. Undoubtedly his best setter was Connemara Grand, imported from New Brunswick and the winner of 76 championship points and Best of Breed twice at Westminster.

One of the outstanding competitors of the Palmerston setters was Ch. Londonderry's Legion (Judge Law-Glencho Sally Oge), purchased for $1,000 from John Moroney, Toronto, to head the

Ch. Tyrone Larry 278171 (Tyrone Terry-Sonora Norma).

Ch. Peggy Belle 578414 (Ch. Londonderry's Legion II-Londonderry Flashlight).

Londonderry Kennels of Charles H. Jackson, Forked River, New Jersey. This beautiful, dark red, 65-pound dog was a great favorite with the majority of judges. In his long career on the bench he defeated at times Ch. Palmerston Connemara Grand, Ch. Bergniel Red Helmet, Ch. Bob White Pat Storm, Ch. Old Oaks Garryowen and Ch. Admiration. As Legion was a popular stud, many of the best Eastern Irish Setter bitches were sent to his kennel. He sired six bench champions, including Ch. Kenridge My Dear, Ch. St. Cloud's King and Ch. Londonderry's Legion II.

The last-named dog established a breed record by completing his championship at the early age of nine months and 27 days. He rated high as a sire with such prominent get as Ch. Peggy Belle, Ch. Rascal Red Pat, Ch. Sheila Tullyval and Orchid Lady, the granddam of Ch. Milson O'Boy II and Ch. Milson Top-Notcher.

Other dogs bearing the Londonderry prefix were L. Legion III and IV, L. Sweetheart, L. Flashlight, L. Ambition and a host of others. Ch. Londonderry's Ambition (Ch. Lismore Freedom-Londonderry Kells) was widely campaigned in the East by his owner, A. A. Bell. At the 1926 Aqueduct show this setter was placed over Ch. Higgins' Red Pat, but at the subsequent Sesquicentennial show the decision was reversed. Ambition was a small, heavy-boned dog, noted especially for his remarkable ring manners.

One of his sons from Ch. Lady Betty was Lewis H. Starkey's Redwood Ranger, first registered as Sunny Jim Redjacket. This changing of names, not unusual in the Twenties when transferring ownership of a dog, was most confusing. Ranger, an excellent specimen and one of the pillars of Redwood breeding, was the sire of Ch. Redwood Rita. When he had been shown only a few times, he injured a vertebra, which disfigured him; and his show career ended.

Other cases of confusing nomenclature in the same period were Ch. Richwoods Roy, also known as Corry Law; Ch. Red Boy III, the same dog as Prince of Killarney; and Ch. Raggen of Lanark, called Benmore's Pat.

A contemporary of Legion and Ambition was Ch. Celtic Admiration, later named Admiration quite appropriately because he was greatly admired for his beautiful head. He was owned by Dr. T. Joseph O'Connell, the 1924 New York State Trap Shooting Champion. This dog was the sire of Ch. Elcova's Admiration and the grandsire of the renowned Jordan Farm Abe.

About 1909, the kennel prefix St. Val appeared in the names of some excellent Irish Setters which carried the early Lismore and St. Cloud bloodlines. The profile of one of them adorned in bas-relief the bronze medal of the Irish Setter Club of America. St. Val was the kennel name of Warren Delano, Jr. until his death, when the kennel was dispersed.

In 1923, his daughter, Miss Laura F. Delano, Rhinebeck, New York, decided to continue the strain as a memorial to her father. After considerable search she acquired some of the same strain in Kerry Boy of Knocknagree (Ch. St. Joe Kenmore's Boy of Kelt-Glencho). Starting with this dog she bred setters of traditional Knocknagree quality. Among them were Ch. Duna Girl, Ch. My Duna Girl, Ch. Patricia Girl, Ch. Redleen Girl, Can. Am. Ch. Clondeen Girl, Can. Am. Ch. Cragie Girl, Can. Am. Ch. Lea Girl and Can. Am. Ch. Colley Boy (all of Knocknagree); and there was a whole dynasty of Kerry Boys, continuing at least to Kerry Boy of Knocknagree VIII.

On several occasions, the Knocknagree Irish Setters won the Best Team in Show award at Westminster and at the International. What a thrilling sight it was to see four of Miss Delano's gorgeous red champions moving majestically around the big show ring together as a team!

The Milson prefix, which played such an important role in Irish Setter history, was used by Sidney H. Sonn, Harrison, New York, from 1923 to 1930. Sonn started with three-months-old Milson Peggy (Ch. Lismore Freedom-Ch. Swifty Holden). Although this medium sized, well balanced setter became a popular favorite at shows and won her championship readily, she was probably best known as being the dam of Ch. Milson Sonny, Ch. Sheila IV and Ch. Fetridge's Pat, all sired by Ch. Higgins' Red Pat.

A kennelmate of Peggy, the lovely Milson Colleen (Kennard-Lismore Norna), died young; but in her one and only litter were Ch. Terence of the Cloisters, Ch. Patsy VI and Ch. Milson Tess. The bloodlines of both Peggy and Colleen were represented in Ch. Milson June Blossom.

Sonn's Breeding program involved eight homebred bitches, including three that were not champions: Milson Pat's Girlie, Milson Goldie and Orchid Lady. Later generations proved the wisdom of his choice of brood matrons. Not an advocate of line breeding, he

54

used various stud dogs from outside his own strain. For instance, Ch. Patsy VI produced litters from seven different sires.

About 1930, the Milson bloodlines were transferred to Harry Hartnett, then later to the Caldene Kennels of Dr. Jay W. Calhoon and again to the Knockross Kennels of Welrose I.L. Newhall.

Edwin M. Berolzheimer, President of the Eagle Pencil Company, chose "of the Cloisters" as his kennel suffix, a term quite appropriately applied to his beautiful estate high above the Hudson River at Tarrytown. The architecture of his home with its high vaulted ceilings, enormous fireplaces and walls decorated with coats of mail, contributed to the theme of baronial or cloistered halls.

His first Irish Setter was Comfort, imported from Canada in 1919. As her name implies, there was a firm bond of affection between the Berolzheimers and this bitch, which reveals again the tremendous appeal of the Irish Setter. When Comfort died of distemper at nine years of age she was greatly missed. In those days there were no protective serums and over half of the bird dogs died of distemper.

One of the top show dogs in the kennels was Ch. Terence of the Cloisters (Ch. Elcova's Terence McSwiney-Milson Colleen), noted especially for his beautiful front and exceptionally good feet. At the Cloisters all the dogs were trained to the gun. Berolzheimer became interested in field trials; and until his death in 1949, he energetically championed the cause of the Irish Setter in this competition.

At one time in his kennels there were four generations of field trial Irishers, headed by the first American Kennel Club Irish Setter field champion, Elcova McTybe (Ch. Elcova's Terence McSwiney-Modoc Bedelia). Mac, from field trial winning parents, won the All-Age Stake thrice at Irish Setter Club of America trials; but due to heart worm he ran in only a few trials. Among his noted descendants were: F. Ch. Clodagh McTybe, F. Ch. Shaun McTybe, Tyron McTybe, Brian McTybe and Rufus McTybe (all of the Cloisters).

Mac was bred and trained by one of America's foremost dog trainers, Elias C. Vail, Poughkeepsie, who devoted most of his life in one way or another to the progress of field trials and dog research. His methods of training were aptly described by Ella B. Moffit in *Elias Vail Trains Bird Dogs* (1937). Vail was prominently identified with Irish Setters for many years. Although his Elcova dogs won frequently at shows, their chief renown was in the field. Ch. Elcova's

Ch. Terence of the Cloisters 471648 (left); F.Ch. Elcova McTybe 861800.

Ch. St. Cloud's Fermanagh III 464167 (Ch. St. Cloud VII-St. Cloud's Colleen).

Terence McSwiney, Ch. Elcova's Admiration, F. Ch. Elcova's Mc-Tybe, Elcova's Kinkie and Modoc Bedelia were best known. Vail ran his setters fearlessly in the trials at a time when other breeds were represented in overwhelming numbers and it was an uphill task for an Irish Setter to win.

Just as Colonel Bradley's Kentucky thoroughbreds had names beginning with "B," so the Kenridge dogs were registered with "K." C. C. Stillman, who popularized the Morgan horse in America, built the elaborate Kenridge Kennels in 1922 for his son, Master Elliot. Located on his spacious estate at Storm King Mountain, Cornwall, New York, they were complete to the last detail, including office, kitchen, hospital, grooming room and indoor exercising rings. Redwood walls, electric stove, no-draft windows, food chutes to the kitchen, a setter skeleton, microscope, life-size paintings and statuettes of the dogs were but a few of the special features. Percy Stoddard, who designed the kennels, was placed in charge of the establishment with its Irish Setters, Cocker Spaniels and Pointers.

Initially six Irish Setters were purchased from Dr. DeRonde, including Palmerston Molly Bawn; and from Canada came the foundation brood matron Ch. Kenridge My Dear, winner of the Best Sporting Dog special trophy at Framingham in 1924.

Heading the Kenridge Kennels was Ch. Bergniel Red Helmet (Lord Lismore II-Bergniel Guri), a most attractive dog with pleasing type and flowing gait—a consistent winner on the bench from 1923 to 1928. His most important win was Best in Show over 500 dogs at Paterson, New Jersey in September 1925. Incidentally, Best in Show and Group judging became an official procedure at American shows in 1925. The first Irish Setter to be crowned Best in Show was Ch. Modoc Morty Oge (also called Kildare's Morty Oge) at Des Moines on April 3, 1925. The second Irish Setter to win the award was imported Ch. Tadg at San Francisco and Oakland in May 1925.

Red Helmet was the sire of seven champions, among which were Emily Schweitzer's Ch. Verbu Red Mollie and William R. Lubben's Ch. Rex's Red Don. Ch. Kenridge My Dear had four litters by him. He died in 1928, on the same day that his master, young Elliot Stillman, was killed in an automobile accident in Arizona. Soon afterward the Kenridge Kennels were dispersed. At the time they housed four champion stud dogs, Ch. Terence O'Brien Law, Ch. Kenridge Kinsman, Ch. Kenridge Kelvin and Ch. Kenridge Klondyke. Although the period in which the Kenridge dogs were before the public was relatively short, they established a reputation because of the marvelous condition in which they were shown. They had a notable influence on the breed.

Interested in Irish Setters about this time were two parties of the same name but spelled differently, Mrs. Carl F. (Olga B.) Nielsen (Bergniel Kennels), Laurel Hill, New York, and C. Frederick Neilson (Rosecroft Kennels), Shrewsbury, New Jersey. The former, raising quality stock until 1926, mated her imported Molly of Laurel Hill to Ch. Lismore Freedom to obtain Ch. Bergniel Prince Charming and Bergniel Guri, the dam of Ch. Bergniel Red Helmet. The latter registered his Rosecroft prefix as early as 1905 and it was still current forty years later.

Another long time breeder and judge of Irish Setters, Mrs. E. Alban Sturdee, Albany (later Toronto), obtained her first dogs from Walter McRoberts in 1912. Since then several hundred setters have borne the Glencho prefix, at least a dozen of them champions. Probably the best known stud dogs in the kennel were Ch. Glencho Lanty and Glencho Morty O'Callaghan.

The Irish Setter Club of America, established about 1886, thrived in the Twenties with more than 200 members. A series of annual field days, including a breed field trial and specialty bench show, was inaugurated by the Club in 1927. The first one was held at Albany through the courtesy of Mrs. Sturdee. Ch. Higgins' Red Pat went Best of Breed and Gibbs' Carolina Queen won the All-Age Stake in the trials.

The Second Annual Field Day was held on the beautiful estate of the Sonns at Harrison, New York, in October of the following year. In winning Best of Breed Ch. Terence of the Cloisters defeated the runner-up, his own sire, Ch. Elcova's Terence McSwiney; but the latter acquired plenty of laurels anyway, for he won the field trial All-Age Stake.

In October 1929, the Third Annual Field Day took place at Cornwall, New York, at the invitation of Miss Elizabeth Stillman of Kenridge fame. Best of Breed over the 62 entries went to the famous Ch. Delaware Kate; and in the trials Ch. Cloudburst Red won the All-Age Stake with nine starters.

A noted favorite of the era was Ch. St. Cloud's Fermanagh III, preferred because of his refined type, general balance, grand head, perfect shoulders and deep chest. He was one of the first setters to possess the stylish, streamlined body and the elegant, upright carriage of neck and head so apparent in his pictures. This dog came honestly by these good points, being line-bred from Ch. St. Cloud III and the illustrious old Ch. St. Cloud's Fermanagh. As he had the ability to pass quality to his offspring for several generations, his influence on the breed was noted throughout the country in such kennels as Milson, Knocknagree, Hedgewood, Hollywood Hills, Rosecroft, Ruxton, Wamsutta and others.

Ch. St. Cloud's Fermanagh III was shown under the colors of Mrs. Cheever Porter of New York City, and was an ancestor of her famous Ch. Milson O'Boy and Ch. Rosecroft Premier.

A son of Fermanagh III, called Ruxton's Stop Light, headed the kennels of Ernest D. Levering, Ruxton, Maryland, for several years. These kennels contained several imported Irish Setters, including Ch. Queen of Barrymore, Ch. Sensation Dempsey, Letchworth Daisy, Niall of Aileach, Achler and Sally of Ballybay. Both Niall and Ruxton's Condonderry placed five times in shooting dog stakes at Eastern trials. At the time of his death in 1938, Levering had assembled a fine kennel of working setters. Perhaps his most important contribution to the Irish Setter in America was a litter by Ch. Higgins' Red Coat ex Ruxton's Tadg, in which there were four champions: Ch. Ruxton's Mollie O'Day, Ch. Maggie the Irish Lady, Ch. Ruxton's Wanda and Ch. Ruxton's Sean of Gruagach. He supplied foundation stock for the breeding programs of Jack Spear, Ward Gardner and Warren K. Read, Jr.

Nearly every Irish Setter owner has heard of the "red-headed Irishman," the most literary dog in the world, Rufus H. Phelps, that lived to the venerable age of fourteen years in the home of Professor William Lyon Phelps of Yale University. In this environment the dog was accustomed to meeting great men of letters and paid particular homage to George Bernard Shaw, Joseph Conrad, John Galsworthy, Hugh Walpole, John Masefield and others. Rufus, the favorite pet of the Yale campus, filled the post of librarian and had his own charge account at the meat market. When he died in 1931, the news of his death was chronicled by newspapers all over the world.

One of the most unique personalities in Irish Setter affairs and a man who contributed a large share of his life to the breed was Wil-

Morty Oge's King 362099 (Donegal's Morty Oge-Queen Chicko).

Ch. Modoc Chief 441534 (front); Ch. Modoc Morty Oge 479553.

liam Cary Duncan. He owned gun dogs as a boy, even against his father's wishes. He loved setters—all three varieties—and for a time maintained the Thistlerock Kennels with R. B. Adams. Much of his interest lay in field trials until heart weakness interfered; but dogs proved to be a great relaxation from his intensive profession of writing musical comedies for Broadway. His best known setter was Ch. Elcova's Admiration, which was acquired from Elias Vail.

But it was not as a breeder that Duncan was eminent; he was the Irish Setter Club of America delegate to the American Kennel Club and breed correspondent for at least twenty years prior to his death in 1945. One has only to read his columns touched with Duncan humor and human interest to appreciate his real forte. Then, too, one never tires of reading his *Golden Hoofs,* a story about the famous trotter Goldsmith Maid; and *Dog Training Made Easy.* The sportsmen knew him as dog editor of *Outdoor Life.*

The Twenties will be remembered for their imported Irish Setters. No less than 30 Boyne dogs came from the kennels of J. A. Carbery, Drogheda, Ireland; about a dozen setters sired by Eng. Ch. Gruagach transferred from England; and others representing Gadeland, Glenariff, Ravenhill, Rheola, Sulhamstead and Wizbang strains arrived in America.

The Eng. Ch. Terry of Boyne (Eng. Ch. Brian of Boyne-Young Norah of Boyne) was imported in 1923 at the then record price of $2,600, to head the Woodbine Kennels of F. R. Wingerter, Hurdland, Missouri. Terry was not a big dog as he weighed only 59 pounds but he was well balanced, deep chested and beautifully coated. Afield he was an excellent shooting dog, stylish and staunch on point. He died of pneumonia about two years after he came to America; however, in this short time he sired 259 progeny from 55 dams in 71 litters. Apparently he was not entered in bench shows and field trials in this country. Eight of his sons and daughters were imported from Ireland: Flora, Paddy, Kevin, Lanark, Mattie, Murty, MacQueen and Sean (all of Boyne).

Wingerter got Sheelah from Kingdom, Sable of Ryhill and Donnie Rhu from Ireland. Donnie had just won third place in the Grand All-Aged Stake (20 starters) at the Ulster Gundog League trials in 1923. It was hoped that he would improve the working stock in America; but his record here was not impressive.

Another importer of Irish Setters was Fred J. Lefferdink, Hick-

Ogallala Prince 57108 FDSB St. Lambert's Sam-
Bessie Roque Clanderrick).

Ch. Tim Red Flag 586464 (Orphan Boy Tim-Nora
Red Flag).

man, Nebraska, whose Modoc kennel name graced the pages of sporting journals for more than three decades. Being actively engaged in field sports, he always required that his adult dogs be trained to the gun. Toward that end he acquired and bred utility stock. In 1923, he imported Sean of Boyne (Eng. Ch. Terry of Boyne-Grannie of Boyne) from J. A. Carbery. In America, Sean won only ten points toward a bench championship, because he was considered too large. However, he weighed only 60 pounds and stood 27 inches at the shoulder. Sarsfield and Khan Sahib Bahudur were imported kennelmates of Sean.

One of the first Irish Setters that Lefferdink owned was McKerry, the dog that Pohl ran in the All-American Trials of 1914. Next came Ch. Mike Law (Ch. Conn Law-Ch. My Irish Rose), a level-headed field dog and bench champion. Later there was Morty Oge's King (Donegal's Morty Oge-Queen Chicko), a natural retriever from land and water, "the best duck dog in Nebraska." But the dogs that really established Fred's reputation in Irish Setters were Ch. Modoc Chief and Ch. Modoc Morty Oge (Morty Oge's King-Fan Tan Shaughran). These two litter brothers were campaigned on the Midwest Circuit from Duluth to Tulsa. When shown as a brace, as they frequently were, these mahogany-coated beauties created quite a sensation, because they were as alike as two peas.

Although Lefferdink maintained a kennel of brood matrons tracing back mainly to Pohl's setters, his favorites were his stud dogs. He advertised about a dozen of them, including those already mentioned, Ch. Tim Red Flag, Ogallala Prince, Modoc Mike Law, Modoc McKerry and Ch. Finefield's Invasion.

Other Midwestern breeders included the combination, William F. Davis of Kansas City, L. C. Fauble of Omaha and John W. Collins of Yorkshire, Iowa, who interbred their respective Irish Setters to fix a type similar to Fauble's foundation bitch, Rheola Morello. Best known of this strain were Ch. King Morello Oge, Ch. Betty Clanderrick, Ch. Biddy Clanderrick, Ch. Ruth Lambert Law, Ch. Iriset Kathleen, Ch. Iriset Colleen and Ch. Ogallala Princess. Most of these dogs won their championships under the guidance of Fauble, who was a professional handler. Mention should also be made of R. A. Ferris with Eng. & Am. Ch. Bran of Boyne, J. E. Anderson with Ch. Red Law Redfield, P. I. Appleman with Chieftain Law and J. Frederick Walter with Sir Patrick Redfield.

63

Ch. The Red Comet O'Shagstone with her adopted family of African lion cubs.

From left—Kiltane, Ch. The Red Comet, Ch. The Bronze Baron, Ch. Irish Elegance, Ch. Joan O'Shagstone.

On the West Coast about 1914, Mrs. Nancy Lee Fletcher Nannetti obtained Peggy O'Shagstone (St. Lambert's Larry-Noreen), which traced back to the older California strains. With Peggy as a start, Mrs. Nannetti developed her Shagstone Kennels of home bred champions famous through the years. In the 1920's, there were Ch. Joan, Ch. Irish Elegance, Ch. Copper Nob, Ch. The Duchess, Ch. Chancery Joan, Ch. Fine Feathers and Ch. The Bronze Baron (all O'Shagstone). The last three-named dogs won Best in Show awards. At that time bench shows in the West were few and far apart, so several years were usually required to finish a champion.

Some strange foster mothers are on record, but undoubtedly the oddest combination occurred in Mrs. Nannetti's kennels at Oakland in 1927, when her Irish Setter bitch Ch. The Red Comet O'Shagstone, was entrusted with the care of two lion cubs from the local zoological garden. At five months of age the cubs were taken back to the zoo; but as they did not thrive there and since Red Comet wildly missed them, they were returned to the kennels for a year or more, where it was a most unusual sight to see Irish Setter puppies playing with a grown lion, putting their heads in his big mouth.

Between 1926 and 1931, John M. Colbert of San Francisco, had eight imported Irish Setter bitches in his Shanagolden Kennels, including: Achler, Aryan, Ajmer, Bell O' Erin, Gertrude of Gramsceugh and Mairgread Dileas. He also owned the two imported. brothers, Eng. Sh. Ch. & Am. Ch. Tadg and Ch. Liam (Eng. Ch. Gruagach-Oona of Derrynane). Tadg acquired an American championship in short order, winning 2 Best in Show, 8 First Sporting Group and 10 Best of Breed awards. His most popular win was to top 500 dogs at the 1925 Golden Gate Bench Show by the blind ballot of five judges. His best known get were Ch. Maura of Shanagolden and Ruxton's Tadg. Liam, not as good a bench specimen as Tadg, was said to be short in head and neck, and wide in skull.

The third brother, Eng. Irish & Am. Ch. Domnal MacGruagach, was imported in 1925, by Edward Beale McLean, President of *The Washington Post* and husband of Mrs. Evalyn Walsh McLean, socialite and owner of the Hope diamond. His bench record in this country was not especially impressive, perhaps because American judges did not prefer the heavier stamp of setter represented by these sons of Eng. Ch. Gruagach; but Domnal did become a champion in three countries.

65

To return to the Shanagolden Kennels, John Colbert purchased from the East the famous old campaigner, Ch. Bob White Pat Storm (Ch. St. Cloud's Fermanagh-Ch. Bob White Red Storm) and used him with some of his imported bitches to get Ch. Paddy of Shanagolden, Ch. Emma of Shanagolden and Ch. Duffy of Shanagolden. Paddy was a good sire, producing Ch. Baggage of Shanagolden, Ch. Barrymore of Shanagolden, Ch. Sheik of Shanagolden, Ch. Jordan Farm John and Ch. Wamsutta Cleopatra. In 1931, Colbert sold Emma for $1,500 and Paddy for $2,500 to Warren K. Read, New Bedford, Massachusetts; Sheik for $1,000 to Victor Eisner, Atherton, California; and Ch. Maura of Shanagolden to Robert W. Gerdel (Killbuck Kennels), Wooster, Ohio. These dogs played most important roles in the breeding programs of many kennels. It is significant that the strain represented by Ch. Bob White Pat Storm returned to the East.

In the Northwest were C. G. Jennings of Tacoma with Can. & Am. Ch. Jennings' Mack and Can. & Am. Ch. Jennings' Mike; J. P. Link of Milwaukie, Oregon, with Can. & Am. Ch. Link's Michael and Ch. Link's Molly; and Earl Kreuger of Portland with Ch. Liam and Ch. Red Law Redfield.

7

By Paddy of Boyne
Ex Craigie Lea Mona

I N 1923, William W. Higgins, Charleston, West
Virginia, imported from J. A. Carbery, Drogheda, Ireland, a small
dark mahogany, profuse-coated Irish Setter named Higgins' Paddy
of Boyne (Eng. Ch. Terry of Boyne-Dora of Boyne). Although Paddy
did not compete in bench shows or field trials, he became famous as
a sire and exerted a great influence on the breed in America. It was
not that his offspring from fifteen of the sixteen bitches bred to him
were outstanding, but that his matings with Craigie Lea Mona resulted in a most successful nick.

Craigie Lea Mona (Ch. Lismore Freedom-Clare II), bred by
Maurice Brill of Mount Kisco and owned by Higgins, came from
good old American stock carrying the blood of Ch. Conn Law, Ch.
Lismore Colleen, Ch. St. Cloud's Fermanagh and Ch. Bob White
Red Storm. She was a relatively large, solid red bitch; and not
timid as some rumors would have it. She was professionally trained
afield by O. S. Redman. Although never in the show ring, she was
of excellent conformation; in fact, some people attributed the unusual quality of some of her progeny to her rather than to Paddy

of Boyne. But such did not seem to be the case, because Mona whelped a mediocre litter of eight puppies by imported Bob of Down and then a disappointing litter by Can. & Am. Ch. Tyrone Larry.

Paddy sired four litters from Mona, all bred by Higgins. From this combination came six champions of great renown and importance to the breed:

Ch. Higgins' Red Pat, whelped 4–26–24
Ch. Higgins' Red Coat, whelped 9–30–27
Ch. Sister A. C. F., whelped 9–30–27
Ch. Barney of Boyne, whelped 5–30–28
Ch. Rose of Sharon II, whelped 5–30–28
Ch. Patricia of Boyne, whelped 2–1–29

Paddy was the sire of one other champion, bred by Maurice L. Baker and owned by Jack Spear, called Ch. Tyronne Farm Jerry, out of Ch. Hedgewood Judy. Mona produced only six champions.

It is of interest that Ralph and Irene Hallam of Chicago, at one time owned all six champions together with their sire and their dam —probably the greatest aggregation of Irish Setters ever assembled in one kennel. He is said to have paid $5,000 for Red Pat, $1,250 for Sister and $7,000 for the others. Many believe that Red Pat was the best Irish Setter that ever lived; Red Coat, of course, was the noted sire of 30 champions; Sister had but one litter; Rose of Sharon II never whelped any puppies; while Barney and Patricia were bred together in a brother and sister mating. The progeny of Paddy and Mona almost usurped bench show honors in America for a quarter of a century. Afterward, it became increasingly difficult to preserve a fair percentage of this blood, but nearly every American-bred Irish Setter had some of it in his pedigree.

The strain possessed certain outstanding qualities such as clean, arched necks flowing into beautiful shoulders, extreme depth of chest with accompanying short forearms, and lovely eye and ear placement. When the dog reclined on the bench with body in upright position, the shoulder blades were nearly horizontal, which served to emphasize their length and layback. Refinement even to a fault, breed type exemplified by thin lips and ear leather, blood vessels showing in the muzzle and well domed occiputs—all imparted distinctive Irish Setter quality. The strain has been criticised at times for light eyes, for heads small in proportion to the bodies and for gay tails. It is observed that both long and short coats were found on Red Coat progeny and occasionally some white markings. In spite of these faults which appeared infrequently, the strain was far above average. The dogs were slow in developing, usually requiring more than eighteen months to mature; but they did not grow coarse with age—they were "lasters."

Isn't it true that the popularity of a breed more or less parallels the sensational show wins of some prominent representative of the breed? Red Pat's unusual American Kennel Club record of 24 Best in Show, 43 Best in Group and 74 Best of Breed awards did much to bring the Irish Setter to public favor. A wonderful showman and campaigner, Pat travelled thousands of miles in his career on the bench from the time he was first exhibited in the Novice Class at Westminster in 1926, until his farewell appearance at Madison Square Garden six years later. In his first seven shows, his class wins were not impressive, but thereafter his record was a seldom broken string of victories at the largest shows. He became an American and Canadian champion.

One of the highlights of his career was the 1926 Sesquicentennial show in Philadelphia, where he was the choice of the "Squire of Inglehurst," Charles T. Inglee, for Best of Breed over the superbly conditioned and perfectly ring mannered Ch. Londonderry's Ambition.

It was an award of historical importance when Red Pat won Best in Show at the first Morris and Essex event, a spectacular one day show with 504 entries held May 28, 1927, on the polo field of the famous Giralda Estate of Marcellus Hartley Dodge, Madison, New Jersey. By this splendid win the ringside favorite acquired a leg on the Percy A. Rockefeller Silver Trophy.

Pat was awarded first in the Sporting Group at the second Morris and Essex Show by A. F. Hochwalt; and it was at this occasion that the contest in Irish Setters was between the two past masters of the handling profession, Ben Lewis with Pat and Percy Roberts with Ch. Bergniel Red Helmet.

The Dr. Davis Memorial Cup for Best Irish Setter was won by Pat in 1926, 1927, 1928 and 1930. He also won the Cornwall specialty show in 1930 and Best of Breed at Westminster on three occasions. He placed Best in Group at Worcester County show,

Ch. Higgins' Red Pat 511275 (Higgins' Paddy of Boyne-Craigie Lea Mona).

Ch. Higgins' Red Coat 634787 (Higgins' Paddy of Boyne-Craigie Lea Mona).

September 1, 1930, in an entry of 72 Irish Setters, including 17 champions. It was at this show that the Parade of Champions was introduced. Harry Hartnett handled Pat on the Eastern Circuit and Colonel R. L. Davis guided him in the Midwest. In his career on the bench he defeated even his own brothers and sisters. About the only top-ranking contemporary that he did not defeat was Ch. Delaware Kate; and it seems that these two never met in the show ring.

As a young dog Pat was field trained by O. S. Redman. He and his sister, Ernst Nancy Langhorne, were entered in the Derby Stake (29 starters), West Virginia Field Trial Association, October 1925; but neither dog placed.

Twenty bitches were bred to Red Pat, resulting in 65 registered offspring and including six champions: Ch. Ardmore Ringleader, Ch. Duke of Red Pat, Ch. Cloudburst Red, Ch. Fetridge's Pat, Ch. Milson Sonny and Ch. Sheila IV.

Red Pat died of cancer in the veterinary hospital at the University of Pennsylvania on July 9, 1932; and he was buried near his old home kennel on the Higgins estate, Caldwell, New Jersey, beside his famous dam that died but a few weeks earlier. Thus ended the career of one of the greatest show dogs of any breed in American history.

In 1930, when Hallam purchased the Higgins' dogs, Red Pat was a champion and all the others except Sister had not been shown. Dr. A. C. Foster got Sister A. C. F. (note the doctor's initials) as a puppy from his friend Bill Higgins and easily put eleven championship points on her at big Eastern shows. Hallam speedily finished her championship requirements with a five-point Best of Breed at Greenwich. Thereafter, she was shown infrequently because she was the household pet of Irene Hallam. Sister might well rank as one of the great Irish Setter bitches of America and certainly she was far ahead of her time in type. Her extreme length of neck and well proportioned body combined to produce an unusually stylish appearance. It is unfortunate that the mold in which Sister was cast has been lost. She had only one litter, that sired by the beautifully headed Ch. St. Cloud's Fermanagh III; and in this litter there was only one dog, Sigvale's Captain Costigan.

The literature is scant concerning the first three years in the life of Sister's litter brother, Ch. Higgins' Red Coat. He was first shown under the Hallam colors at Cedar Rapids and at the Western

71

Ch. Rose of Sharon II 749035 (left); Ch. Sister A.C.F. 671720.

Ch. Barney of Boyne 749034 (Higgins' Paddy of Boyne-Craigie Lea Mona).

72

Specialty show in 1930. His next show was Westminster, which stands out as of particular interest in Irish Setter history, because Hallam showed the "Big Six" full brothers and sisters. Mrs. E. A. Sturdee placed Ch. Rose of Sharon II as Best of Breed and Red Coat as Winners Dog. This was really the start of his career under Harry Hartnett's guidance, which eventually totalled to one Best in Show and 36 Best of Breed awards. Although his bench record may not be as good as that of Red Pat, he placed in the Sporting Group twice at Westminster and thrice at Morris and Essex. In 1931, he was transferred to C. Frederick Neilson of Rosecroft fame, who owned him until his death in July 1939. The last eight years of his life were spent in Hartnett's Milson Kennels at Harrison, New York, where he lived the life of Riley.

Red Coat's claim to fame is as the sire of 30 bench champions. He is credited with 220 registered get from 39 bitches, representing 45 litters. The largest litter, whelped September 13, 1934, from Red Pal Mag and bearing the Oakdene suffix of Dr. Gilman S. Currier, contained 14 puppies. Incidentally, the largest Irish Setter litter on record is 23 puppies whelped in 1925 at Waukegan, Illinois. As a rule Irish Setter bitches have little trouble whelping and make good mothers; and furthermore, 15 to 17 progeny at one whelping is not extremely uncommon. H. J. Cooper's Conn of Sonora gave birth to 65 puppies (60 males) in five litters.

Probably Red Coat's most famous litter was that containing four champions, whelped September 4, 1932, from Ruxton's Tadg (Ch. Tadg-Ch. Mairgread Dileas). Then there were three other litters, each containing three champions from Colleen Girl of Knocknagree, Ch. Queen Maive and Ch. Redwood Rita.

In August 1930, Hallam started Rose of Sharon II and her litter brother, Barney of Boyne, on the Midwestern Circuit where the former won consistently Best of Breed and the latter Winners Dog. Handled by R. L. Davis on the Southern Circuit, Rose continued to win; however, at Kansas City she lost to Ch. Delaware Kate. The following year Red Pat, Barney and Patricia were frequently shown in the vicinity of Chicago and in the South, where they usually accounted for top breed honors. The relative ranking of the Hallam dogs varied somewhat under different judges. A summary of their bench records as tabulated from *American Kennel Gazette* follows:

73

	Best in Show	Best in Group	Best of Breed
Ch. Higgins' Red Pat	24	43	74
Ch. Higgins' Red Coat	1	13	36
Ch. Sister A. C. F.	0	3	10
Ch. Rose of Sharon II	4	19	27
Ch. Barney of Boyne	0	1	9
Ch. Patricia of Boyne	5	9	14

At eight years of age Ch. Rose of Sharon II, handled by Hollis Wilson, won two Best in Show and ten Best of Breed awards at Midwestern shows in 1935. She was one of the finest moving Irish Setters of all time, she would literally "float" around the show ring. Rose never had any puppies.

Ch. Barney of Boyne was a strongly built dog of pleasing proportions, but his skull was wide, a fault he passed along to many of his progeny. In brother and sister matings of Barney and Patricia, two litters where whelped, the first of which contained Patricia of Boyne II and Rosemary of Hallamshire.

Ralph Hallam died of pneumonia in November 1935, after which his famous kennel of Irish Setters was widely dispersed. Old Paddy of Boyne died shortly before his owner. Rose was sold to J. O. Black in Michigan; Barney and Patricia went to Ralph Matthiessen in New York; Patricia of Boyne II to Harry Aldrich in Colorado and Rosemary of Hallamshire eventually to H. J. Cooper in Illinois.

This is the story of six champions by Higgins' Paddy of Boyne ex Craigie Lea Mona, that have played such a prominent role in the history of the Irish Setter.

8

Red Coat Family

AFTER Ch. Higgins' Red Pat and Ch. Higgins' Red Coat came their sons and daughters to hold the center of the stage. Red Pat's blood was not especially influential, but on the other hand Red Coat's effect on the breed was tremendous. As the years passed, there was scarcely an American-bred Irish Setter without some of his blood.

Among the six champions sired by Red Pat was Ch. Cloudburst Red, a well proportioned setter that was successful in Eastern bench and field activities.

Another son, Ch. Ardmore Ringleader owned by Kenneth Campbell of Detroit, was admired for his regal bearing, cleanly chiselled head and beautiful flat coat. Every hair was dark mahogany, uniform in color from tip to root. Campbell also owned two daughters of Red Pat and a daughter of Red Coat, called Ch. Ruxton's Wanda. Due to confusion in transfer of ownership, Wanda won enough championship points to acquire the title two or three times. Several champions resulted from the matings of these Glen Ryan dogs.

Ringleader's brother, Ch. Duke of Red Pat, sired a few litters in Illinois; but this line did not survive. Another brother was the Canadian champion, Red Pat of Brimore.

75

Ch. Fetridge's Pat (Ch. Higgins' Red Pat-Ch. Milson Peggy), a field trial and bench winner, was lost when he escaped from his owner's car in 1930. His littermate, Ch. Milson Sonny widely advertised at stud, apparently was not a prepotent producer and left very few descendants. A sister, Ch. Sheila IV owned by Dr. Herman Baruch, Wyandanch, L. I., had two litters sired by imported Colin of Fermanar. As the Baruchs were fond of dogs and sports, they entered their Marobar setters in both bench shows and field trials with some success; but it was short-lived as the kennels were dispersed in 1935.

It was during the early Thirties that Dr. Arthur A. Mitten of Philadelphia, acquired the Smoot collection of setters for his Happy Valley Kennels. Included were four English Setter champions and the famous imported Irish Setter, Ch. Delaware Kate (Ravenhill Phil-Delaware Mill Lass). Kate, a champion in England, Ireland and the United States, was never defeated by an Irish Setter in America—Kate and Red Pat did not meet in competition. She won 8 Best in Show and 21 Best in Group awards. In the show ring she had personality plus—a big, upstanding, magnificent bitch that no judge could overlook. Some ranked her as the top Irish bitch of all time. Her death in 1932 from complications while whelping a litter sired by Ch. Cloudburst Red, brought great sadness to her owner and serious loss to the breed.

The history of the 1930's is one devoted largely to the Ch. Higgins' Red Coat family. Many of the best bitches of the day were sent to Red Coat or to his well known sons. Among these matings certain litters stood out as superlative.

Some branches of the family became especially prominent—those lines from his three sons: Ch. Milson O'Boy, Ch. Kinvarra Son of Red Coat and Ch. Redwood Russet of Harvale.

One of the greatest show dogs of all time was Ch. Milson O'Boy (Ch. Higgins' Red Coat-Milson Miss Sonny), owned by Mrs. Cheever Porter of New York City. If ever a dog had public appeal it was he, and those who saw him will never forget him. Arthur Roland paid him this tribute in *The New York Sun*, July 20, 1945:

> It was at the Garden that one of the most striking demonstrations of O'Boy's appeal to a crowd was given. That was in the final of the 1936 show when the showy Irishman was representing the gun-dog group in the great sextette that came before the late C. Frederick Neilson. O'Boy

76

had captured the crowd when he won his group and they began rooting for him the minute he came into the ring for the best-in-show decision. Every time the judge looked in his direction there was applause and it grew deafening when the big fellow raced up and down the big arena keeping pace with the late Harry Hartnett, who handled him on all his ring appearances.

When Neilson passed over O'Boy in favor of the smart little Sealyham, St. Margaret's Surprise of Clairedale, the crowd made it very clear that it didn't like it at all. It was the first time in Westminster history that its best-in-show award had evoked such a hostile demonstration. What the crowd did not know was that Neilson was one of O'Boy's admirers and that, in giving preference to the Sealyham, he was not following his heart but his responsibility to judge the dogs on comparative show standards as he saw them.

Another great demonstration of the way this dog could capture the hearts of a crowd was given at the Morris and Essex show of 1935. He certainly was a picture as he paced over the velvety turf on the polo field at Giralda Farms, against the brilliant backdrop formed by the evergreens and geraniums which bordered the judging platform and the bright summer clothes of the spectators. This time the gallery was bigger than at the Garden and its tribute to the great dog even more thunderous. When G. V. Glebe sent him to the center of the ring to receive the best-in-show trophy the crowd roared approval.

What won the gallery every time O'Boy appeared in the ring was the fact that this dog made it perfectly clear that he knew what he was in there for. If ever a dog was trying every minute to win it was Ch. Milson O'Boy. He would never sleep with his collar on—to him that was the evidence that there was a show battle to be fought—and once the lead was around his neck it was all that Harry Hartnett could do to keep him quiet. He would race from the crate to the entrance of the ring and fidget around until it was time to go in. There was no relaxing for him until the contest was decided and he was back in the crate again. He would keep his eye as steadily on the judge as would his handler and there was no question but that he ate up the gallery tributes.

There are many other interesting stories about O'Boy, some of which have been recorded in a book by Jay W. Calhoon, M.D., published as a memorial to O'Boy.

In a five-year period, Ch. Milson O'Boy accumulated an impressive list of wins, which included 11 Best in Show, 46 Best in Group and 103 Best of Breed awards. He won Best in Show at Morris and Essex in 1935, over an entry of 3175 dogs of 73 breeds, including 120 Irish Setters. After his retirement at the height of his career in 1938, he led an easy life as a pet devoted to his mistress. On June 29, 1945, he died in his sleep at 13 years of age and was laid to rest in the peaceful quiet of Hartsdale Cemetery.

A well deserved honor was bestowed upon him when the American Kennel Club chose his photograph to represent the ideal Irish

Ch. Milson Top-Notcher 943879 (Ch. Milson O'Boy-Milson Squire's Janice).

Ch. Rosecroft Premier A290869 (Ch. Milson O'Boy II-Rosecroft Fern).

78

Setter in *The Complete Dog Book,* which contains the standards of all recognized breeds.

As time passed, it became apparent that O'Boy was a key producing sire. According to the records he sired 163 puppies in 41 litters. Outstanding among his sons were Ch. Milson Top-Notcher and Ch. Milson O'Boy II. Top-Notcher was owned at various times by Milson Kennels, Rosecroft Kennels, Caldene Kennels and the Honorable Mrs. Katherine St. George, U.S. Congresswoman from New York. Mrs. St. George and Mrs. Allan A. Ryan, her daughter, were co-owners of several noted Irish Setters, including imported Ch. Beorcham Blameless, imported Ch. Red Sails of Salmagundi, Ch. Jordan Farm Lady and Ch. Headliner the Flaming Beauty.

Ch. Milson Top-Notcher was awarded Best of Winners at the 1935 New England specialty the first time shown. During the next five years he acquired 5 Best in Show, 29 Best in Group and 115 Best of Breed awards. He was an excellent show dog and seldom did he fail to place in the Sporting Group. Because of this he was widely and frequently shown, as often as 47 shows per year. As a sire, he was known chiefly for his daughters Beg Pardon Rury Limerick, Ch. Seekonk Judy O'Grady and Ch. Miss Judy Ann Shields. Judy was pictured on the packages of a certain brand of dog food.

Top-Notcher's kennelmate at the Milson establishment was Ch. Milson O'Boy II, which later headed the Knightscroft Kennels of Joseph P. and Henrietta M. Knight, Jr. O'Boy II figured basically in the breeding program of the Knightscroft Kennels from 1938 until his death in 1945. He sired 20 champions. Ch. Rosecroft Kitty Kelly had seven litters by him, Ch. Rosecroft Mona three and Rosecroft Fern four.

The Knight's first Irishman, Loudon Knight's Terry purchased from C. F. Neilson in 1933, was killed by an automobile. Then they acquired the Rosecroft bitches, Ch. Jordan Farm Lady and Jordan Farm Scarlett O'Hara, from which foundation stock came 39 champions bearing the Knightscroft prefix—such famous ones as Knightscroft Danny O'Boy, K. Dollymount Dan, K. Fermanagh, K. Patty Boyne, K. Squire Muldoon and K. Symphony. Dogs from these kennels have been widely distributed to every part of the country. But of all his setters, Joseph Knight's favorite was his de-

Ch. Knightscroft Bliss S17535
(Ch. Milson O'Boy II-Ch. Rosecroft Mona).

Ch. Knightscroft Squire Muldoon S450772
(Ch. Knightscroft Eric-Knightscroft Kerry Dancer).

voted companion and King of the Kennel, the dignified and regal Ch. Milson O'Boy II.

From Ch. Milson O'Boy II (Ch. Milson O'Boy-Milson Vanda) and Rosecroft Fern (Ch. Milson O'Boy-Ch. Loudon Aroon) came Mrs. Cheever Porter's famous Ch. Rosecroft Premier, whelped April 9, 1938, a double cross to O'Boy. Of bold and fiery disposition, Premier cut quite a figure in the show ring where he amassed a record list of wins: 12 Best in Show, 53 Best in Group and 124 Best of Breed awards. He won ten specialty shows, which is most unusual. Outstanding among his progeny were Ch. Seekonk Patty O'Byrne, Ch. Milson Christopher Robin, Ch. Caldene Jamaica, Ch. End O'Maine Luckalone and End O'Maine Sarah Jane.

Ch. Milson O'Boy II was also an ancestor of three Shawnlea champions, bred by May H. Hanley, Rehoboth, Massachusetts. Ch. Shawnlea's Purcell O'Gorman was one of the top ten Irish Setters of 1950. Ch. Shawnlea's Fanfare, a stylish, well balanced Irishman, has a fine bench record, including three Best in Show wins. Miss Hanley bought her first Irish Setter in 1933, a son of Ch. Wild Irish Ringleader. She has owned dogs of Knightscroft, Wamsutta, Charles River and other bloodlines.

The Milson Kennels of Sidney H. Sonn were managed by Harry Hartnett from 1923 to 1930. Then on the death of Mr. Sonn, Harry purchased the kennels and bred and exhibited many fine setters. He handled the four brilliant stars to Best in Show wins: Red Coat, O'Boy, Top-Notcher and Premier. In 1944, when he retired in poor health, the Milson breeding stock was transferred to Jay W. Calhoon, M.D., Uhrichsville, Ohio.

The doctor first became interested in Irish Setters in 1936, when he purchased Judy Legore Colquohoun as a puppy from Dr. Clyde Leeper. She later became an American and Canadian champion. He also acquired Ch. Baggage of Shanagolden, Jordan Farm Patsy, Jordan Farm Molly and the Milson dogs. Next he bred his matrons to the following sires: Ch. The Baron Gore, Ch. Killbuck Red Duke, Ch. Milson O'Boy, Ch. Milson O'Boy II, Ch. Harwale Hero, Ch. Rosecroft Premier, Ch. Seekonk Patty O'Byrne and others. The fusion of Milson and Jordan Farm bloodlines produced excellent results that have had a lasting effect on breed type in America. Among the 20 or more champions carrying the Caldene prefix are: Ch. Caldene Judson, Ch. C. Jamaica, Ch. C. Picardy and Ch. C.

Ch. Caldene Moike A385635
(Ch. Killbuck Red Duke-Ch. Baggage of Shanagolden).

Ch. Hedgewood Plainsman A571703
(Kendare Color Bearer-Goldsmith Flame).

M'Boy. Ch. Caldene Patrice and Ch. Caldene Pixie were considered great brood matrons. At times there were 60 dogs in the kennels and puppies were sold to all parts of the United States. Ch. Caldene Mickey Mischief represented the strain in the West. When the Caldene Kennels were dispersed in 1952, most of the stock, including Picardy, Polly and Rita, went to the Knockross Kennels of Welrose L. Newhall, Coraopolis, Pennsylvania.

The successful breeding program of Dr. Calhoon and the preservation of the Milson bloodlines have been carried on by "Slim" Newhall. For a time Ch. Caldene Mick O'Boy was his foremost stud dog; but in 1960, Mick's son Knockross' O'Boy took over. The former sired nine and the latter 16 champions. Although Knockross' O'Boy obtained points toward a championship, he did not acquire the title because he accidentally became blind in one eye. He is the sire of the Wheatleys' Ch. Caldene Ailene, Mrs. Charles Crawford's Ch. Knockross' Ruby, Mrs. C. E. Holvenstot's Ch. Knockross' Sally, Walter McCoy's Ch. McCoy's Squire of Verbu, Emily Schweitzer's Ch. Verbu Erin and Ch. Verbu Maureen, Dr. H. F. Kinnamon's Ch. Knockross' Red Patti and others. Ruby had a nice litter containing four champions sired by Ch. Draherin Irish Chieftain. One of them, Ch. Shannon's Shawn of Erin, owned by Joseph and Marilyn Slick, became a champion in America, Canada and Bermuda.

Emily Schweitzer, the mistress of Verbu Kennels, Dundee, Illinois, obtained her first Irish Setter from Mrs. E. A. Sturdee in 1923. The dog was Glencho Ruddy Oogh (pronounced as in rouge), which soon became the family guard, pet and showdog. Next came Ch. Verbu Red Mollie (Ch. Bergniel Red Helmet-Palmerston Mollie Bawn), a very beautiful setter professionally trained as a gun dog. Emily had long been interested in the progress of the Irish Setter for bench, field and obedience.

Dog obedience testing, which originated in Europe, was started in the United States by Mrs. Whitehouse Walker, Bedford, New York, in 1935. The following year the American Kennel Club approved the rules and the degrees for this activity. Since then the Verbu Kennels have finished 19 Irish Setters to Companion Dog (CD), 9 to Companion Dog Excellent (CDX), 5 to Utility Dog (UD) and 3 to Utility Dog Tracker (UDT). Ch. Verbu Killeen Oogh was the first Irish Setter recorded as CD and as CDX; further-

Ch. Knightscroft Symphony S17782
(Ch. Knightscroft Erin Elan-
Ch. Knightscroft Aileen).

Ch. Verbu Red Mollie 746022
(Ch. Bergniel Red Helmet-
Palmerston Mollie Bawn).

more Ch. Verbu Norna Oogh was the first of the breed to obtain the UD title.

At one time in the Verbu Kennels there were five obedience-trial winners, three of which were international bench champions:

Can. & Am. Ch. Verbu Killeen Oogh, CDX
Can. & Am. Ch. Verbu Norna Oogh, UDT
Can. & Am. Ch. Verbu Peter Oogh, CDX
Verbu Noreen Oogh, UDT
Verbu Susie Oogh, UDT

In field trials the Verbu setters, represented by Missy, Midgie, Shawn, Maureen and others, have placed in over 50 stakes. Ch. Verbu Missy Oogh, CDX is a likely candidate for the triple crown.

Over the years there have been more than a dozen Verbu bench champions. Five of them also obtained Canadian championships. Of superlative Irish Setter breed type are Ch. Verbu Erin, Ch. Verbu Maureen and Ch. McCoy's Squire of Verbu, all from a litter sired by Knockross' O'Boy ex Ch. Caldene Maura, CD. They represent the Milson bloodlines. Erin is renowned as a specialty show winner and Maureen excelled in the breed at the Combined Setter specialty and at Westminster in 1965.

Other Ch. Milson O'Boy progeny of note included the Oakdene litter from Red Pal Mag, the Milhaven one from Princess Dido, O'Waccabuc from Loughdune O'Waccabuc, O'Flynn from Ch. Cloudburst O'Flynn of Lastery, Kinvarra from Ch. Kinvarra Zoe and Hedgewood from Hedgewood Lea Mona.

Although Mag never became a champion, she produced six champions in three litters. One of her litters by Ch. Higgins' Red Coat contained 14 puppies. Rather exceptional was the fact that all eight placements in the Junior Puppy Classes at the 1935 Morris and Essex Show were awarded to dogs from this litter. Gilman S. Currier, M.D., bred several Oakdene champions, including Ch. Judge Red Pal of Oakdene, Ch. Rosie O'Grady O'Oakdene and Ch. Oakdene's Barbarossa.

In the Princess Dido litter, Serena should be mentioned as the important producing dam of five West Coast champions. The O'Flynn litter contained Ch. Pat McCauley O'Flynn, bred by Marie Louise Welch and owned by Harry A. McCauley of Baltimore. The Independence Day litter from Ch. Kinvarra Zoe will be remembered for Ch. Kinvarra Ensign and Ch. Maggie the Irish Lady II.

Ch. Laurel Ridge Star Rocket S523138
(Ch. Red Star of Hollywood Hills-Ch. Honors Even Rakish Jane).

Ch. End O'Maine Luckalone A902171
(Ch. Rosecroft Premier-Ch. End O'Maine Best Wishes).

The Hedgewood Lea Mona litter, owned by Maurice L. and Beryl Baker, Minneapolis, Minnesota, could well typify what O'Boy did for the breed. There were ten puppies, as alike as ten peas. Domed top-skulls, low-set ears, lovely heads, gorgeous shoulders and great depth of chest were apparent at an early age.

It has been the Bakers' custom to name their setters after famous horses. Starting with the Law strain in 1925, they have line-bred for 16 or more generations to the Paddy of Boyne–Craigie Lea Mona strain with occasional outcrosses, the practise being to select the best bitch in each litter to propogate the strain. They have bred forward using young blood and have not repeated matings. Outstanding among the Hedgewood champions as excellent examples of refined breed type were Ch. Hedgewood Rhea Rita, Goldsmith Maid of Hedgewood, Ch. Hedgewood Plainsman, Ch. Hedgewood Regret and Kendare Color Bearer. Maurice's keen observation of desirable qualities in dogs has been a valuable asset in breeding and showing; and it has led to his competence as an all-breed judge.

The End O'Maine setters of Hollis and Jo Wilson, Amherst, Wisconsin, are known from coast to coast. Hollis hunted over setters as a boy and later owned Irish Setters in partnership with a fellow townsman, J. W. Delaney. About 1924, he established the End O'Maine Kennels. His first Irish Setter champion was Ch. Raggen of Lanark. Next he bought Ch. Belle's Anniversary, bred her to Ch. Golden Dawn of Gadeland and thereby obtained End O'Maine Autumn Leaf. From then on there has been an unbroken succession of End O'Maine bloodlines.

The Wilsons are advocates of breeding to noted sires, as over the years they have had litters by Ch. Higgins' Red Coat, Ch. Milson Top-Notcher, Ch. Rosecroft Premier, Ch. Kinvarra Kermit, Ch. Redwood Russet of Harvale, Ch. Red Sails of Salmagundi, Ch. Charles River Color Sergeant, Ch. End O'Maine Luckalone, Ch. Tyronne Farm Shanahan, Ch. Laurel Ridge Star Rocket, Ch. Conifer's Lance and others.

They raised brood matrons of traditional End O'Maine quality, such as the following champions: End O'Maine Beg Pardon, Kathleen, Burnie Burn, Encore, Refrain and Pigeon; and undoubtedly their favorite female was Ch. End O'Maine Best Wishes. It is of special note that the Ch. Carrvale's Terry Terhune-End O'Maine

Ch. Tyronne Farm Clancy A992502
(Ch. Tyronne Farm Tipperary-Ch. Tyronne Farm Kay).

Ch. Tyronne Farm Shanahan S159581
(Ch. Tyronne Farm Malone-Ch. Tyronne Farm Merriwynne).

Claret litter, whelped 3–14–57, set a breed record in that it contained seven champions: End O'Maine Lady Amherst, E. Morning Bird, E. Red Cloud, E. Yours Truly, Redman, Tarawil's Geronimo and Wautoma.

It is also significant that the End O'Maine dogs have served as foundation stock in many kennels. For instance, Joyce Holzman Nilsen's Ch. Kinvarra Portia, the dam of a dozen champions, made a tremendous contribution to the breed, as did Ch. End O'Maine McCabe, owned by Professor Orrin Evans of the University of Southern California Law School. Then, too, there were the End O'Maine stud dog champions Luckalone, Billboard, Patridge, Lord Bourbon and others.

For many years the Wilsons showed dogs professionally, finishing numerous champions of various breeds for their clients. They exhibited Irish Setters for Hallamshire, Kinvarra, Tyronne Farm, Tattersall, Laurel Ridge, Crosshaven, Tirvelda, Honors Even and other kennels. It would be difficult to estimate the number of championship titles they won or to recall all the interesting experiences of those years—like the time that Ch. End O'Maine Kathleen went from the Puppy Class to Reserve Winners at Morris and Essex or when Ch. Erin's Beau Brummell won Best in Show the first time shown (1941 at Milwaukee). It was a thrilling moment, too, when Jo Wilson took End O'Maine Sarah Jane from the Puppy Class to Best of Breed at Westminster in 1946. Then with a special ceremony at the 1957 International show, the Professional Handlers' Association honored Hollis for his outstanding work over the years in the show rings of America. The Wilsons retired from showing dogs and raising setters in the summer of 1962. Hollis then became a dog show judge.

There is another man who has contributed many years of his life to the progress of the Irish Setter. He is Jack A. Spear, Tyronne Farm Kennels, Tipton, Iowa. Mrs. Spear and the sons have also been interested in the breed. The kennel name was derived from County Tyrone, Ireland, the ancestral home of the Spears.

In 1934, Jack purchased Jordan Farm Nancy and Ch. Tyronne Farm Joan from Jordan Farm Kennels and Ch. Tyronne Farm Jerry from Maurice Baker. It was early in the following year that he bought the famous producing dam and lovely show bitch Ch. Ruxton's Mollie O'Day (Ch. Higgins' Red Coat-Ruxton's Tadg) from

Ch. Tyronne Farm Malone A669668
(Ch. Kinvarra Kermit-Ch. Ruxton's Mollie O'Day).

Ch. Seaforth's Dark Rex S158260
(Ch. Tyronne Farm Malone-Ch. Seaforth's Red Velvet).

E. D. Levering. Spear showed frequently and widely, and soon his setters were well known. In the course of time he obtained Ch. End O'Maine Kathleen (Ch. Higgins' Red Coat-Ch. End O'Maine Beg Pardon) from Jo Wilson. The two Red Coat daughters were mated to Ch. Kinvarra Kermit in what seemed to be two perfect nicks. The Kermit-Mollie Litter of 2–13–39, contained six champions; and the Kermit-Kathleen litter of 8–27–39, had four. Mollie, first bred at seven years of age, had only five litters and 35 puppies in her lifetime; but she produced 14 champions, a breed record. The litters were by Jordan Farm Abe, Ch. Kinvarra Craig, Ch. Kinvarra Kermit and Ch. Tyronne Farm Tipperary. Her daughter, Ch. Tyronne Farm Debutante, a large well proportioned setter, was a universal favorite. Can. & Am. Ch. Tyronne Farm Mollie O'Day, the 1941 Westminster winner, was owned and campaigned for a time by Wilfred S. Kennedy. O'Flare and Collette were best known as field trial winners. One cannot hope to name all the prominent Tyronne Farm field dogs, but some of them stand out, as Merriwynne, Countess, Kay, Frolic, DeEtte and others.

Over the years most of the Spears' setters have been homebreds, some of the champion sires being: Tyronne Farm O'Brien, Tipperary, Malone and Shanahan. O'Brien was a rugged individual, Tipperary was more refined, the grand-headed Malone stamped his get with size and style, and Shanahan threw puppies of nice breed type. Of late years since Jack resigned from judging, Can. & Am. Ch. Wautoma, Ch. End O'Maine Lord Bourbon, Ch. Dix-Mac Mignola, Ch. Tyronne Farm Rex and others have been used in his breeding program.

The Tyronne Farm dogs appear to have their own individuality, difficult to describe, yet easily observed. In the show ring they have been prominent for thirty years, winning fifty or more championship titles and at least fifty Best in Show awards. Ch. Tyronne Farm Clancy, the top winning Irish Setter for 1949, was awarded 19 Best-in-Show ribbons. His most thrilling win was Best in Show at Morris & Essex in 1950 with 2263 dogs in competition. Ch. Tyronne Farm Shanahan after completing his title was never defeated in the breed, always placed in the Group and won five Best in Show awards.

Some of Jack's dogs have been transferred to various sections of the United States where they have served as foundation stock for other kennels. Ch. Tyronne Farm Malone II, owned by Kinvarra

Ch. Kinvarra Kermit A217049
(Ch. Kinvarra Craig-Ch. Kinvarra Mollie of Gadeland).

Ch. Tirvelda Storm Lark A385351
(Ch. Kinvarra Craig-Ch. Kinvarra Mollie of Gadeland).

Kennels, Darien, Connecticut, has had an impressive effect on the breed, even extending for several generations. On the West Coast, Ch. Tyronne Farm Malone through Ch. Seaforth's Dark Rex and Ch. Innisfail Color Scheme has made a great contribution—approximately 75 per cent of the California Irish Setter show dogs have his bloodlines. The Webline, Enilen, County Clare, Lismoro, Glendee, Wildwood, Shamrock, Yorkhill and other kennels have Tyronne Farm stock.

The Kinvarra Kennels of Lee M. Schoen, Darien, Connecticut, were established in 1932. The kennel prefix, derived from the name of a hamlet in Ireland, was said to mean "Community of Kin."

The basic bloodlines stemmed from Ch. Kinvarra Son of Red Coat (Ch. Higgins' Red Coat-Ch. Queen Maive) and imported Borrowdale Yseult of Kinvarra (Rheola Boniface-Eng. Ch. Norna). Lee described Yseult, his favorite foundation bitch, as being not much over 23 inches in height, dark, lustrous and very beautiful to watch in the field. He said that upon her arrival from England, the spirited young setter walked proudly and confidently down the gangplank of the steamship as though she realized her importance to the breed in America. Her numerous champion descendants show that she truly was a great producing dam.

Five generations later in champion line came Lee's other favorite bitch, Ch. Kinvarra Bootsie—she loved human companionship. Not only was she an excellent brood matron, but she was also a field trial winner, trained and handled afield by Mrs. Schoen.

Among the many dogs that Schoen imported from England was Ch. Kinvarra Mollie of Gadeland. Mated to Ch. Kinvarra Craig, a son of Yseult, Mollie produced one of the all-time Irish Setter greats, Ch. Kinvarra Kermit. Beautifully proportioned and well coordinated like a champion athlete, he had wonderful spirit, disposition and showmanship; but unfortunately his show career was cut short by World War II.

As a sire he stamped his get with his own distinctive qualities. Breeders found that the Kermit blood crossed with Red Coat stock was an ideal combination. Two litters sired by Kermit contained six champions each. He sired a total of 29 champions. Without mentioning all of his noted sons and daughters, one must name as eminent: Ch. Kinvarra Portia, Ch. End O'Maine Best Wishes, Ch. Kendare Stout Fellow, Ch. End O'Maine Patridge, Ch. Tattersall

Ch. Redwood Russet of Harvale A95567
(Ch. Higgins' Red Coat-Ch. Redwood Rita).

Ch. End O'Maine Billboard A823016
(Ch. Redwood Russet of Harvale-Ch. End O'Maine Best Wishes).

Tenaj, Ch. Tyronne Farm Debutante, Ch. Tyronne Farm Malone and others. During the last years of his life at the Kinvarra Kennels, Kermit enjoyed his daily run afield. He died at eleven years of age in 1948. His great record as a producer is his memorial.

It was fitting that Kermit's grandson, Ch. Tyronne Farm Malone II, followed in his footsteps at Kinvarra. Indeed Malone II was much like his grandsire, especially in color and size. Both were happy setters with endearing personalities, vivacious and yet gentlemanly. Among the 25 champions sired by Malone II are such prominent studs as Ch. Kinvarra Malone, Ch. General Beauregard, Ch. Draherin Irish Regardless, Ch. Draherin Irish Chieftain and Ch. Tirvelda Aran.

The Kinvarra Irish Setters are widely distributed in the United States and in foreign countries as foundation stock for many kennels.

E. Irving (Ted) Eldredge, Tirvelda Farms, The Plains, Virginia, has owned Irish Setters since he was twelve years of age. At fourteen he imported English dogs of the Ardagh and the Boyne strains. The first litter to carry the Tirvelda prefix was whelped in 1937, by Ch. Kinvarra Craig ex Ch. Kinvarra Mollie of Gadeland, a bitch imported by Lee Schoen and transferred to Ted. Among the thirteen puppies were two that became champions, Ch. Kinvarra Kermit and Ch. Tirvelda Malva. Ch. Tirvelda Storm Lark, Ch. T. Storm King and Ch. T. Storm Lass came in the second litter from the same parents.

When Malva and Kermit were mated, Ch. Tirvelda Raive resulted, whelped on New Years Day 1940; and later when Raive was bred to Storm Lark, Ch. Tirvelda Tiana was produced. Thus for a time the Tirvelda dogs were a closely bred family.

To introduce new blood, the bitches were mated to Ch. Harvale Hero, Ch. Kleiglight of Knocknagree, Ch. Domino of Gadeland and others. Just as Eldredge was beginning to raise Irish Setters again after the war, he lost Mollie, Malva, Raive and Tiana in a series of accidents within a period of 18 months, which left him with only three mature setters.

As tme passed, Tirvelda recovered from this severe loss and Ted acquired such famous dogs as: Ch. Redwood Russet of Harvale, Ch. End O'Maine Billboard, Ch. Faig-a-Baile of Crosshaven, Ch. Kendare Red Dawn, Ch. Hartsbourne Sallyann of Tirvelda and many others.

Ch. Rufus of Hollywood Hills A309658 (Ch. Redwood Russet of Harvale-Penny Tax of Hollywood Hills).

Ch. Red Star of Hollywood Hills A932359 (Ch. Rufus of Hollywood Hills-Ch. Faig-a-Baile of Crosshaven).

Sallyann raised litters from four sires of different strains. Two of her well known progeny by Ch. Kinvarra Malone are Ch. Tirvelda Sybil, a consistent winner on the bench, and Ch. Tirvelda Nutbrown Sherry, the dam of nine champions. Seven of them are from one litter sired by Ch. Michael Bryan Duke of Sussex.

From this account of the Tirvelda background, it is apparent that Ted has had first-hand experience with a wide variety of Irish Setter bloodlines.

Ch. Kinvarra Kermit's progeny formed the basic stock for the Kendare Kennels of Wilfred S. and Clarabelle L. Kennedy, Walled Lake, Michigan. It was about 1940, when the Kennedys acquired Kinvarra Marguerite and Ch. Ruxton's Followmere and mated them to Kermit. Next they obtained Ch. Tyronne Farm Tyrone and Ch. Tyronne Farm Mollie O'Day, both progeny of Kermit, from Jack Spear. From Maurice Baker they bought Goldsmith Maid of Hedgewood and Kendare Color Bearer; and from Ward Gardner Ch. Molly of Crosshaven. Just as the Kendare breeding operations were getting under way, Wilfred died and the kennels were dispersed. Jack Spear obtained Ch. Tyronne Farm Mollie O'Day and Ch. Kendare Topper O'Day, one of the tallest Irish Setter champions. Ted Eldredge bought Ch. Kendare Red Dawn.

In the Forties, Dr. Milton O. Hager, Eggertsville, New York, owned the Honors Even Kennels, which housed Ch. End O'Maine Patridge a son of Kermit, Ch. Red Ranger Pat a son of Jordan Farm Abe, Ch. Kinvarra Portia a daughter of Kermit, and a number of Honors Even champions from these dogs.

Joyce M. Holzman, a high-school girl in Buffalo, obedience-trained Ranger's Red Lass CD, a daughter of Ch. Red Ranger Pat. Then in 1946, just before her father moved the family to California, Joyce purchased Ch. Red Ranger Pat and Ch. Kinvarra Portia, that lovely producing dam of twelve champions that later became the cornerstone of the Thenderin Kennels. From these two dogs came the Thenderin "A" litter of five champions. Portia, also the dam of the "B" and the "D" litters, was chosen Best Brood Matron of 1948, 1949 and 1950. She died at ten years of age while whelping a litter by Ch. Red Star of Hollywood Hills. In history she rates as one of the Irish Setter greats and her descendants are indeed a galaxy.

Joyce also owned Ch. Cill Choinnigh Paganach, which completed his championship at 15 months of age. Later she acquired part in-

97

terest in Ch. End O'Maine McCabe with Professor Orrin Evans. In 1953, Joyce married Athos Nilsen and both became professional handlers of show dogs.

Thenderin Kennels, which have bred more than 100 champions, have had wide experience with Irish Setters of various bloodlines, like Ch. Seaforth's Dark Rex, Ch. Memory of Devon, Ch. Rheola Shaun of Bail-Lo, Ch. Caldene Mickey Mischief, Ch. Margevan's Athos, Ch. End O'Maine Luckalone, Ch. Charles River Blazing Beauty and many others. Some of the Thenderin dogs have been dominant producers like Wind-Warrior which sired seven champions and his son, Drum Hills, which sired the "O" litter with its four champions.

The Thenderin setters have played an important role in Irish Setter history over a twenty-year period. There are more than a dozen Thenderin obedience title winners, several field trial winners and Best in Show dogs. Well known in the show ring are Endorsement, Maximillian, Cayenne, Kismet, Maestro, Nor'wester, Paddy's Hero and others.

Undoubtedly one of the most famous and also the most traveled setter with the Thenderin prefix was Ch. Thenderin Brian Tristan (Ch. End O'Maine Luckalone-Ch. Kinvarra Portia), whelped in California on St. Patrick's Day 1948. He was purchased as a puppy by James R. and Mary Fraser, who lived in 17 different places in 23 years. When Brian came to them at the airport in Cleveland, he burst out of the dog crate with all his dynamic energy. As a young dog he was most unmanageable and willful—he even fought a horse —but as he matured he became obedient, responsive, dependable and dignified. He was an intelligent companion, a marvelous personality and a strong, sound setter.

In the period from 1950 to 1954, Brian won 10 Best in Show, 23 Best Sporting Group and 61 Best of Breed awards. He topped the group at both Westminster and the International in 1953, which is an exceptional achievement.

Although he was a great showman, his most important contribution to the breed was as the prepotent sire of 30 champions. The extraordinarily high quality of Irish Setters in America, particularly in the Michigan–Ohio area, can well be attributed in no small part to Ch. Thenderin Brian Tristan. Ch. Cherry Point Brask, Ch. Esquire of Maple Ridge, Ch. Headliner The Flaming Beauty and Ch.

Michael Bryan Duke of Sussex are good illustrations of this quality. Incidentally, these four dogs are Canadian champions as well as American. They, too, are siring good stock.

The Frasers have owned Irish Setters since 1928, the first one being Braeland Farms Queen. They bought Ch. Kendare Ardri from the Kennedys and bred Ch. Kendare Red Duke. Cu-Machree is the Frasers' kennel name, which is Gaelic for "Dog of My Heart." The Cu-Machree champions are: Tim, Sybil, Mr. Wonderful and Mollio.

A third important branch of the Red Coat family was headed by Ch. Redwood Russet of Harvale (Ch. Higgins' Red Coat-Ch. Redwood Rita). Redwood was the prefix of the late Lewis H. Starkey who lived in New York and later moved to Pasadena. From the half brother and sister mating of Redwood Ranger and Redwood Ruby, Starkey obtained Ch. Redwood Rita, a somewhat masculine, showy bitch. She produced five champions in two litters by Ch. Higgins' Red Coat: Ch. Redwood Regent, Ch. Springbrook Marchioness, Ch. Springbrook Margot, Ch. Harvale Hero and Ch. Redwood Russet of Harvale. Regent, which completed his championship in five straight shows, never was defeated in breed competition. Unfortunately he died as a three-year-old. The two Springbrook sisters were owned and shown by Harold Correll. Hero was a marvelous setter— everyone liked him. He spent several years at Dr. A. C. Foster's kennels and many of the Manorvue dogs trace back to him.

Starkey also owned Am. & Can. Ch. Redwood Rhoda, a Best in Show bitch and the dam of Redwood Rocket. This fine son of Ch. Higgins' Red Coat sired 14 champions, six of them in one litter. Rhoda was known for her charming personality and it was said that she would shake hands with a judge when he gave her a prize ribbon. After her death Rhoda was prepared by the Peabody Museum at Yale as an exhibit of an outstanding specimen of the breed.

To return to Russet, he was shown on the West Coast from 1936 to 1939, was seldom defeated in the breed judging and usually placed in the group. At the 1946 Specialty Show of the Irish Setter Club of Southern California, fifty of his sons and daughters appeared in the ring with the old dog as a "living pedigree" exhibition.

The 16 champions sired by Russet represented Crosshaven, End O'Maine, Kendare, Waterford, Hollywood Hills, Philacre and other

99

Ch. Golden Dawn of Gadeland O'Aragon 824644 (Ch. Rheola Bryn-Lassie O'Murrell).

Ch. Kleiglight of Aragon A380784 (Ch. Redwood Russet of Harvale-Ch. Stardust of Crosshaven).

kennels. His sons, Ch. Rufus of Hollywood Hills, Ch. Munn's Autumn Flash and Ch. Philacre Gentleman Jeff were prominent show dogs. Rufus was beautifully depicted in color in an Eastman Kodak advertisement in 1945. Russet's Crosshaven progeny were especially well known, including Ch. Copper Coat of Crosshaven in the North Pacific region, Ch. Faig-a-Baile of Crosshaven in California, Ch. Cul De Sac of Crosshaven in Salt Lake City and Ch. Kleiglight of Aragon in the Mid-West.

Ward Gardner, Walla Walla, Washington, started his Crosshaven Kennels in the early Thirties with two well bred bitches, Ch. Lady Mac of Shanagolden and Ch. Ruxton's Shannon of Boyne. In 1937, the latter whelped a litter of 11 puppies by Redwood Rocket that included six champions. One of them, Ch. Hinman's Duke of Denver, was said to have had the heaviest coat ever seen on an Irish Setter. There were two magnificent sisters in the litter, Ch. Sally O'Bryan of Crosshaven, the biggest winning bitch in America in 1939, and the runner-up Ch. Stardust of Crosshaven. When they were campaigned that year at 26 shows in the West and Mid-West, they won almost all the honors. Later both of them were mated to Ch. Redwood Russet of Harvale, which represented a famed double cross to Ch. Higgins' Red Coat. Sally produced Ch. Faig-a-Baile of Crosshaven, while Stardust was the dam of Ch. Kleiglight of Aragon and Ch. Molly of Crosshaven.

Ch. Kleiglight of Aragon (1939–1952), one of the truly great Irish Setters of America, was owned by "The Old Maestro" H. Jack Cooper, Franklin Park, Illinois, who bred and showed dogs for over forty years. Although he had many breeds, he always kept English or Irish Setters. Among the early Irish dogs at the Aragon Kennels were Can. Ch. Automatic Red, Ch. Quinn of Aragon and Leona Automatic Betty. Then there were the numerous imports: Conn of Sonora, Patsy O'Flynn, Delaware Phil, Rheola Benjudy, Shemus Og of Boyne and the most famous of all, Ch. Golden Dawn of Gadeland O'Aragon (Eng. Sh. Ch. Rheola Bryn-Lassie O'Murrell). Dawn had probably the longest registered Irish Setter name.

Fresh from his many laurels in the big English shows at Crufts, Crystal Palace and Birmingham, Dawn raced to his American championship in eight weeks in 1932, under seven different judges and then went along to win 4 Best in Show and 15 Best in Group awards.

He was the prepotent sire of 253 registered offspring in 73 litters.

101

There were many repeat matings. Leona Automatic Betty and Patricia of Aragon each had four litters sired by him.

On Fathers' Day, June 19, 1938, 37 of Dawn's sons and daughters, young and old, gathered at Aragon Kennels to pay their respects to him. Five of his eight American champion get acted as hosts. They were Lady, Joan, Norna, Babs and Terry of Aragon. More than 300 persons dropped by during the afternoon to witness an informal bench show of his non-champion progeny. The closing scene of the day was long to be remembered as the sunset glow played upon the burnished coats of Golden Dawn and his children.

Another one of Cooper's setters to achieve wide recognition was Ch. Kleiglight of Aragon, which finished his championship at thirteen months of age, and in seven years' time accumulated 21 Best in Show, 55 Best Sporting Group and 104 Best of Breed awards. He won top honors in the breed at Westminster three years in succession.

Kleiglight, or "Pete" as he was called, was the prolific sire of 595 registered offspring in 131 litters from 94 bitches. Ch. Mahogany Sue O'Aragon had five litters by him and Ch. Charles River All Afire had six. The 30 champions that he sired carried the names of many kennels, including Aragon, Denhaven, Mid-Oak, Flaming Beauty, Knocknagree and others. His bloodlines have had a pronounced effect on Mid-Western Irish Setter strains. Pete died of a stroke in 1952; and when Jack Cooper died the following year, the Aragon Kennels were continued by Mrs. Ethel Cooper.

Richard and Ruth Cooper, who handle dogs professionally, have shown numerous Irish Setters to their championships. Dick has known sporting dogs from his youth. He started handling in 1935, and was honored as the Handler of the Year in 1961. And sometimes when he poses a gorgeous red dog in the show ring, is he reminded of Old Dawn or Pete or Mahogany Sue?

9

Today's Irishmen

THIS chapter is devoted to Irish Setters prominent in the last twenty years. Inasmuch as champions are numerous and space is limited, the material must be concise. It seems necessary, therefore, to emphasize the dogs rather than their owners and to eliminate lengthy anecdotes. In a work of this nature some individuals may be overlooked, but the omissions are unintentional. Moreover, errors occur in spite of one's efforts in behalf of accuracy. It is also true that time flies, litters come and go, old records fade and new champions capture the limelight. The turn-over is rapid and before long today's Irishmen will take their places in history.

ALLEN, WILLIAM B. & DILLY, Menlo Park, Cal.
    Ch. Thenderin Jacynth and Ch. Thenderin Trailblazer.

ANDREWS, CLAIRE (Kimberlin), Providence, R.I.
    While a student at college, Claire obedience-trained Lady Velvet of Hillcrest UDT. She also owns Ch. Kimberlin Brian Boru UDT and Ch. Kimberlin Kinsale. Ch. Kimberlin Encore placed in the Sporting Group at Westminster in 1964.

AVERILL, PAUL B., New Orleans, La.
    His Ch. End O'Maine Pat Hand (Ch. Conifer's Lance-Ch. End

Ch. Tyronne Farm Rex SA129704 (Ch. End O'Maine Lord Bourbon-Ch. Kate O'King Size).

Ch. Cherry Point Brask S982781 (Ch. Thenderin Brian Tristan-Ch. End O'Maine Encore).

104

O'Maine Flyaway), shown widely in the South, has 2 Best in Show and 13 Best in Group awards.

BACIGALUP, WARREN & WALLI, Van Nuys, Cal.
Webline Reverie and Michelle's Copper King CD.

BAILEY, MRS. OSCAR L. (Bail-Lo), Los Angeles, Cal.
Ch. Rheola Sharon of Bal-Lo and Ch. Rheola Shaun of Bail-Lo.

BAINES, ARTHUR S. & AUDREY (Dunguaire), East Longmeadow, Mass.
Ch. Brynmount Maydorwill Brandyson, imported from England, was exhibited at Eastern shows in the Fifties and used at stud as an outcross to American strains. Brandy sired 8 champions, including Ch. Dunguaire Bryson, one of the top sporting dogs of 1956. Bryson won 9 Best in Show, 34 Best in Group and 97 Best of Breed awards.

BAKER, MAURICE L. & BERYL (Hedgewood), Minneapolis, Minn.
See previous chapter.

BALLARD, BURTON L. & CHARLOTTE (Ballarrell), Waukesha, Wis.
F. Ch. Tam of Ballarrell CD is a likely candidate for the triple crown. His sire, Ch. Carrvale's Commodore CD was especially noted for his very beautiful dark mahogany coat.

BAYLESS, HELEN A. & MADELINE (Enilen), Woodland Hills, Cal.
James W. Bayless, a prominent member of the Irish Setter Club of America, died in November 1964. Mrs. Bayless and her daughter have continued the outstanding obedience activities of the Enilen Kennels. They have owned 5 UDT champions: Van Ayl Dennis Jerold, Tyronne Farm McCorkney, Red Barn Rosabelle, Enilen Ginger Snap and Enilen Michael Terrence. Jerold's obedience record has never been equalled. McCorkney, a Best in Show setter, has participated in more tracking tests than any other Irishman. Rosabelle was the dam of 3 champions. Ginger is an American and Mexican champion. Terrence has a Mexican PC (Perro Companero or Companion Dog) and a PR (Perro Rastreador or Tracking Dog) in addition to his

Ch. Flagstones Flame A448648
(Ch. Tyronne Farm Malone II-
Flagstones Erinhyl Copper).

Ch. Flagstones Sabrina Fair
S653109 (Ch. Kinvarra Somerset-
Ch. Flagstones Flame).

American UDT degree. Madeline's latest pupil is Enilen Mc-Corkney's Garmhac, CDXT and PC.

BENTON, CHARLES B. T. & ALBERTA (Aaragon), Farmington, Mich.

The Bentons tell a story about their first Irish Setter, Timothy Shawn O'Dea CDX, an obedience and field trial winner. One hot summer day Tim was in the obedience ring on the long down test at an outdoor show. After Chuck left the ring Tim crept out and sat in the shade of a tree until the command, "Return to your dogs." Then Tim went back to the down position, where he was waiting when Chuck came into the ring. Probably the best known litter at the Aaragon Kennels was that by Ch. General Beauregard ex Ch. Argo Lane's Countess of Cork which contained 5 champions: Aaragon's Empress Sheba, A. General Beau, A. Prince Nichols, A. Raque of Rusthills and A. Rustic Rover.

BERRY, JO ANN (Bangor), Broomfield, Colo.

Ch. Seekays Berry Gay Rhu CD.

BESSONETT, CHARLES K. & ELEANOR, Indio, Cal.

Ch. Weblyn Luminous Lass and Am. & Mex. Ch. Thenderin Valentine CD & PC.

BLAIR, ROBERT L. & ALICE (Dunleary), Vallejo, Cal.

Hunter's Lady Tizzalia and several Dunleary field trial winners.

BOGIE, HARRIET T. (Dariabar), Vincentown, N.J.

Ch. Dariabar Copper Ranger and Ch. Dariabar Range Finder.

BOLGER, COBY B. (Orania), Sewickley, Pa.

Best known of the Orania dogs were Ch. Terry Bumps, Ch. Miss Judy Ann Shields and Ch. Beau Geste of Orania. Starting with Irish Setters in 1937, Coby kept a small kennel where the dogs received individual attention.

BRIDELL, ROBERT J. & AUDREY (Taradell), Roswell, Ga.

When Bob was 12 years of age he obtained his first Irish Setter, Peggy of Aragon II, a daughter of Ch. Kleiglight of Aragon. He showed Peggy in Puppy and Children's Handling Classes; and later on he bred her to a son of Ch. Charles River Color

107

Ch. Shawnlea's Purcell O'Gorman S167431
(Ch. Shawnlea's Marshall Lacey-Knightscroft Gleana Scota).

Ch. Shawnlea's Fanfare S846781
(Ch. Charles River Lance O'Lane-Shawnlea's Jane Barlow).

108

Sergeant. This mating resulted in Ch. Tara's Theme, the foundation brood matron of the Taradell Kennels. She produced 5 bench champions, including the Best in Show winner Ch. Taradell's Bright Future and Virginia Hardin's well known Ch. Runwild Fiona. Theme placed in 5 stakes at field trials.

BRODIE, GEORGE E. & BARBARA (Seaforth), North Easton, Mass.

The Brodies' first Irish Setter, Ch. Seaforth's Red Velvet, was obtained from the Charles River Kennels of John Downs in 1946. Two famous champions came from the mating of Velvet to Ch. Tyronne Farm Malone: Ch. Seaforth's Poetry of Motion and Ch. Seaforth's Dark Rex. Poetry won 39 Best of Breed awards in the East, while Rex won about the same number in the West. The latter, a sire of 20 champions, contributed great quality to Thenderin, Coppercountry and Innisfail bloodlines.

BROOKS, MARIE T., Greendale, Ky.

Marie's husband, James, died in 1957. They owned Ch. Fanny Red Star of Kentucky and Ch. Sharoc's Copper Luster.

BROOKS, MAJ. WM. C. & PATRICIA (Bayberry), Falls Church, Va.

Ch. Tirvelda Cathy O'Rinn (Ch. Michael Bryan Duke of Sussex-Ch. Tirvelda Nutbrown Sherry) produced a nice litter of 9 Bayberry puppies sired by Ch. Kinvarra Malone.

BROWN, CLAUDE & MAUDE (Utehaven), Salt Lake City, Utah.

Ch. Tirvelda Malva's Memory, Ch. Cul De Sac of Crossgaven, Ch. Cul De Sac's Memory and 4 Utehaven champions.

BROWN, DR. EARL H. & NENA (Larne), Lincoln, Neb.

The Browns' first Irish Setter, obtained in 1950, was Princess Panayiota, which means "Princess" in Greek. She was the family pet and a marvelous field dog. They have owned several champions, including Ch. Shamrock Beauty, Ch. Shamrock Nena O'Beauty and Ch. Larne's Sham Sham. The kennel name was derived from "Killarney."

BUCK, HARRY D. & DOROTHY (Buck Acres), Oakland, Cal.

Ch. Baker's Buck-Ette, Buck Acres Clancey the Clown and the field trial winner, Buck Acres Prince Ballyroan.

Ch. Wolfscroft Vanguard S921502 (Ch. Kinvarra
Lord Raglan-Ch. Wolfscroft My Irish Rose).

Ch. Gay Holly O'Dandy S890278 (Ch. Kinvarra Dandy Boy-Thenderin Queen O'Hearts).

BUCK, LT. COL. PEER A. & E. ANN (Muckamoor), Plover, Wis.
The Muckamoor Kennels, established in 1949, were named after
a town in Ireland. While the Colonel was on active duty in the
army, the Bucks moved frequently—East, West and Mid-West—
their setters became national travellers and their stock was
widely distributed. Starting with Kinvarra, Knightscroft and
Hollywood Hills bloodlines, Peer and Ann have bred a dozen
or more bench champions, about the same number of obedience
title winners and several field trial winners. Some of their best
known dogs are Ch. Muckamoor's Silky Sue, Ch. M. Maroon
Marty, M. Michael McGuire, Ch. M. Masterpiece, Ch. M. Marty
McCuhl and Ch. Weblyn Masterpiece.

BURKE, RUSSELL R. & IRIS (O'Farrell), Calumet City, Ill.
Ch. Fergus O'Farrell and Ch. Red Rascal O'Farrell.

BUTLER, ELIZABETH J., Spokane, Wash.
Ch. Red Sails Cavalier, a double cross to Can. & Am. Ch. Red
Sails Michael of Oak Grove, has done considerable winning on
the bench in the Northwest.

BYRNE, E. J. & BEULAH (O'Byr-ne Lane), Del Paso Heights, Cal.
Starting with Shanagolden bloodlines in 1946, the Byrnes have
been interested in field, obedience and bench. They owned Ch.
O'Byr-ne Lane Miss Rosie O'Grady and Ch. Moikel Ann Kathy
O'Byr-ne Lane.

BYRNE, FRANCIS S. & KATHLEEN M., Pacific Palisades, Cal.
Thenderin Luimneach Siege CDX and Ch. Valorous Piper CD.

CALHOON, M. D., JAY W. (Caldene), Fort Lauderdale, Fla.
See previous chapter.

CALL, DR. JUSTIN D. & BARBARA J., Los Angeles, Cal.
Ch. Thenderin Drum Hills and Ch. Thenderin Odyssey.

CARR, DR. HERMAN J. & MARTHA (Carrvale), Palatine, Ill.
The late Dr. Carr, who died in 1962, raised Irish Setters in the
internes' quarters at a Chicago hospital about 1938. His first
dogs were from the Denhaven and the Devon Kennels. Ch.
Carrvale's Sergeant Terrence, a son of Ch. Charles River Color
Sergeant, completed his championship at the age of 12 months
and 9 days. Among the 10 Carr champions were Ch. Carrvale's

111

Ch. Wolfscroft Amaranthus S582177
(Ch. Brynmount Maydorwill Brandyson-Ch. Knightscroft Dixie Belle).

Ch. Hearthstone's High Hopes SA43397
(Ch. Kinvarra Wansdyke-Ch. Gay Holly O'Dandy).

Terry Terhune, Ch. C. Lad o' Lark, Ch. C. Billy Boy and others. Both Terrence and Terry, Best in Show dogs, were prepotent studs.

CASPER, DR. WOLFGANG A. & DR. ANNE F. (Wolfscroft), Staten Island, N.Y.

The Caspers, who have had Irish Setters for more than 20 years, are especially interested in obedience, conformation and judging. One of Dr. Wolfgang's activities is to serve as Irish Setter show chairman at the Combined Setter specialty, which he has done since it began in 1960. This event has become a highlight of the Irish Setter year. A dozen Wolfscroft litters have been bred, starting with Ch. Knightscroft Dixie Belle CD. As time passed other champions came along: Ch. Knightscroft Blitzen, Ch. Wolfscroft Amaranthus CDX, Ch. W. My Wild Irish Rose and Ch. W. Vanguard UD. The Caspers enjoy their setters and have the opportunity to study them closely. In fact, Wolfgang, who is a dermatologist, stated that dogs have many of the same skin afflictions and allergies that humans do. He also said that often there is hope for badly crippled dogs, and sighted Amaranthus' remarkable medical history as an example. One February day in 1957, Randy went for a run in the woods and returned with his left hind foot dangling, the tendons completely severed. Some thought that it was impossible to save the dog's leg, but an orthopedist at the hospital where the Caspers were associated volunteered to operate. The surgery proved successful and Randy finally returned to the show ring to complete his championship and obedience titles.

CHANTRY, DONALD J. & AUDRY (Sean-try), Minneapolis, Minn.

Ch. Oliver Reginald Sean-try.

CHESSER, DR. IAN M. & LUCILLE (Hi-Lu), Tucson, Ariz.

Ch. Coppercountry Claret.

CLEGG, SHARON (Shardmore), Santa Rosa, Cal.

The first love of this veterinary student at the University of California is obedience training and her first Irish Setter is Raferty's Kathleen Magee UD. With regard to her interest she states, "I am convinced that obedience is essential if setter

113

Ch. Tirvelda Sybil SA91892
(Ch. Kinvarra Malone-Ch. Hartsbourne Sallyann of Tirvelda).

Ch. Tirvelda Cathy O'Rinn SA177127
(Ch. Michael Bryan Duke of Sussex-Ch. Tirvelda Nutbrown Sherry).

114

Ch. Tirvelda Aran S504094
(Ch. Tyronne Farm Malone II-Ch. End O'Maine Cartel).

Ch. Tirvelda Nutbrown Sherry SA91894
(Ch. Kinvarra Malone-Ch. Hartsbourne Sallyann of Tirvelda).

115

(left) Riley's Ramsay MacDonald UDT S547303;
Riley's Norman Thomas UD S547304.

Ch. Onesquethaw Star Dancer S950502
(Ch. Thenderin Nomad-Ch. Red Barn Primrose II).

116

owners are to get the maximum enjoyment from their dogs." Kate, mated to Ch. Patrick of Ide, produced Ch. Shardmore Autumn Sheen UD, which had the highest average score (196.8 points) in Novice Class Obedience Tests of any Irish Setter in the United States in 1959. Eight of Kate's descendants are field trial winners, including Ch. Shardmore's Autumn Echo, S. Main Attraction, S. Autumn Flare CD and others.

CLEMONS, ARTHUR E. & ORPHA (Onesquethaw), Selkirk, N.Y.
Onesquethaw, meaning "Good Harvest," is the name of an Indian tribe in the Catskills. The Clemons family has enjoyed Irish Setters since 1949, especially in regard to obedience work. They have owned at least 9 obedience title winners, including Ch. Red Barn Primrose II CDX, Ch. Onesquethaw Star Dancer CD, Riley's Ramsay MacDonald UDT, Riley's Norman Thomas UD and others.

COBLENTZ, WILLIAM & BETTY, Milwaukee, Wis.
Ch. Mahogany's Socair Buacaill CD.

CONLON, FRANK E. & ELIZABETH (Erinhaven), Califon, N.J.
The Erinhaven champions include Moira, Kate and Dennis Muldoon.

COOK, WILLIAM B. & MELISE (Flagstones), Portchester, N.Y.
The beautiful head studies of Ch. Flagstones Flame CD and Ch. Flagstones Sabrina Fair CD have made this mother and daughter the most talked about setters of Irenhyl Avenue. Apparently these two descendants of Ch. Tyronne Farm Malone II showed their interesting personalities in many ways. Flame liked to deliver the mail, especially rolled up newspapers; and she nursed Sabrina's puppies. Moreover, she was a field trial winner and a spirited worker in obedience tests.

CORRELL, HAROLD A. & VIOLET (TERCOR), Bernardsville, N.J.
Harold died of a heart attack on August 8, 1965, at 65 years of age. This foremost authority on dogs, 35 years a handler and holding AKC license #1, twice Dogdom's Man of the Year and a recipient of the Fido Award, will be especially remembered by the Irish Setter folks for his long and loyal support of

117

Ch. Banshee Sharpshooter S848248 (Ch. Knightscroft Ever Reddy-Ch. Knightscroft Lady Vogue).

(left) Ch. Charles River Claudia SS662839; Charles River Dream Girl, S662838.

the red dogs. It was indeed fitting that he was an honored judge at the 1965 Combined Setter Specialty Show. Among the early Tercor dogs were Patricia whelped in 1924 and Red Mike. The Corrells owned the famous Ch. Knightscroft Patty Boyne, the two Springbrook sisters, Margot and Marchioness, Ch. Redwood Rufus of Harvale and Ch. Faig-a-Baile of Crosshaven. From these and others through the years in many litters came numerous "of Tercor" setters as: Timekeeper, Red Coat, Red Jacket, Classic, Red Flare, Fancy, Rita, etc. Some of the Correll setters were not shown extensively, as Harold was showing dogs for others. At Morris & Essex in 1936, he showed 124 dogs. It is said that in his long career he handled 500 dogs to their championships. Among them were such well known Irish Setters as: Ch. Charles River Color Sergeant, Ch. Knightscroft Patty Boyne, Ch. Knightscroft Symphony, Ch. Phantom Brook's Burgundy, Ch. Brazen Bridget of Englewood, Ch. Garden State Reno's Blaze, Ch. Dix-Mac Saintfield, Ch. Dix-Mac Mignola, etc.

CORY, FRANK & DOROTHY (Devon), Arlington Heights, Ill.
Among their first Irish Setters were Wamsutta Dream Girl and Knightscroft Golden Glow, both of which had litters by Ch. Kleiglight of Aragon. When John Downs moved from Massachusetts to Oregon in 1946, he transferred Ch. Charles River Color Sergeant to the Corys who campaigned the dog in the Mid-West. He placed Best of Breed at the Western Specialty in November 1947. It was at this show that a tragic event occurred, when Frank died with a heart attack while showing the English Setter Winners Bitch. In the months that followed Dorothy continued to campaign Sarge; he won 5 Best in Show, 12 Best Sporting Group and 40 Best of Breed awards in his career. His most outstanding achievement was to top all breeds at the 1949 Chicago International with 1890 dogs in competition. It is also of interest that 12 years later his great, great grandson, Ch. Conifer's Lance, became the second Irish Setter to win Best in Show at the International. It must have been a real thrill for Dick Cooper who handled the winning dogs on these two occasions. Color Sergeant sired 250 registered offspring, including 17 champions. Because his progeny were widely distributed from Maine to California, his effect on the

Ch. Charles River Color Sergeant A570236
(Ch. Red Sails of Salmagundi-Wamsutta Susie Q).

Ch. Sergeant Red Sails of Devon S508797
(Ch. Charles River Blazes-Ch. Red Mollie of Devon).

120

breed has been very pronounced. He was chosen as the Best Sire of 1949 and 1950. Being a strong, bold, intelligent dog with a marvelous disposition, he was much sought after as a stud. Some of his progeny have been excellent shooting dogs: Ch. Carrvale's Sergeant Terrence, Mahogany Tim II, Ch. Honey's Roma Sherry, Ch. Captain Red Coat of Devon, etc. Sarge died of cancer at 12 years of age. Dorothy Cory has retained the bloodlines of this great setter through her Ch. Memory of Devon, Ch. Red Mollie of Devon, Ch. Sergeant Red Sails of Devon and Ch. Abbeyleix Cavanaugh.

COTTON, VOLNEY R. & LUTRENNA (Englewood), Ortonville, Mich.

The Cottons advocate planned breeding by pedigree. Their foundation bitch was Betsy Maine of Englewood, which had Ch. End O'Maine Billboard, Ch. Tyronne Farm Tyrone, Ch. Tyronne Farm Mollie O'Day and Ch. Redwood Russet of Harvale close-up in her family tree. Englewood bred several champions, including the noted Ch. Brazen Bridget of Englewood and Ch. Dix–Mac Cobb.

CRAWFORD, CHARLES L. & BETTY (Shannon), North Jackson, O.

Shamrock of Erin, as Irish as her name, was the dam of the Crawford's first champions. Then they acquired Ch. Knockross' Nero and Ch. Knockross' Ruby from W. L. Newhall. In 1962, Ruby was bred to Ch. Draherin Irish Regardless (Ch. Tyronne Farm Malone II-Ch. Thenderin Elixir), resulting in a litter of four Shannon champions: Sharon, Sassy, Shane and Shawn.

CRAWFORD, RALPH E. & WILMA (Sunset), Whiteland, Ind.

Ch. Sunset Emerald CD, Ch. Sunset Brandy, Ch. Argo Lane's Brady Murphy and Ch. Argo Lane's Fancy Feathers CD.

CROSLEY, FLOYD M. & IMA (Shamrock), Fremont, Neb.

At least two dozen Southwestern champions are descended from the Shamrock setters of the Crosleys. Their stud dogs have been Tyronne Farm Chauncy II, Ch. Shamrock Clancy O'Rielly and Ch. Draherin Coronado; and the brood matrons were Ch. Thenderin Keepsake, Shamrock Fancy, Shamrock April An-

Ch. Honors Even Lady Bet S1416
(Ch. Red Ranger Pat-Ch. Kinvarra Portia).

Ch. Carrvale's Terry Terhune A561510
(Ch. Carrvale's Sergeant Terrence-Tyronne Farm Sherry).

122

them and others. These dogs have figured in the breeding programs of other kennels as: Larne, Hartmann, Jo-Ett, Threejay, Arrowwood, etc.

DAFOE, ROY L. & DORIS (Challenger), Burlington, Ont.
The Dafoes started with the Red Barn strain about 1950, and have owned Can. & Am. Ch. Red Barn Red Stardust, Can. Ch. Prince Rory of Kent CD, Can. Ch. Argo Lane Beryllium and others. Three Challenger dogs have Canadian obedience titles: Bronze Knight UD, Irish Lancer CDX and Pride & Joy CD.

DANSIN, SAM & ELEANOR, Milwaukee, Wis.
F. & B. Ch. O'Lannon Copper Penny CD, winner of the triple crown.

DARLING, MRS. MARION T., San Jose, Cal.
Ch. Blayneywood Country Squire (Ch. Draherin Irish Chieftain-Ch. Kinvarra Shiela) represents a double cross to Ch. Tyronne Farm Malone II. Widely shown by Larry Downey, Squire has a very impressive record of 10 Best in Show, 40 Best Sporting Group and 61 Best of Breed awards.

DAVID, HERMAN H., Cleveland, O.
Dog writing, field trials and bibliography represent only a part of Herm's activities in the dog game. He often recalls with fond memories his first Irish Setter, Seamus Red Tuxedo CD, which won first place in the Open Gun Dog Stake at the ISC of Indiana trials in 1950. Next came The Dude, a son of the famous F. Ch. Askew's Carolina Lady. He placed in a dozen field trial stakes and sired 7 field trial winners, including F. Ch. Fyn and Cooper's Tennessee Riley. Later Herm bought Sulhamstead Nat D'Or.

DAVIS, CURTIS E. & RUTH (McGowan), Belmont, Cal.
Ruth has owned Irish Setters since 1934. Her Queen of Ardkeen's Molly O was the dam of Ch. McGowan's Dugan, sire of Ch. McGowan's Miss Mahoney; and she in turn produced Ch. McGowan's Michael. There are other champions, too, but this lineage serves to show that the strain has continued in the family for several generations.

Ch. Wautoma S861909 (Ch. Carrvale's Terry Terhune-End O'Maine Claret).

Ch. Redman A861910 (Ch. Carrvale's Terry Terhune-End O'Maine Claret).

DAVIS, RALPH & ANN, Malibu, Cal.
Ch. Red Arrow Stardust CDX and Ch. Butcher Boy.

DEAN, HARRY (Ardee), Saskatoon, Sask.
See field trial chapter.

DELANO, MISS LAURA F. (Knocknagree), Rhinebeck, N.Y.
Miss Delano who has long been a breeder and judge expressed
her sentiments concerning the Irish Setter in an address to the
Irish Setter Club of America in 1952: "Perfection is our goal for
the Irish Setter, be it yours or your neighbor's. For me the
tears of joy that have come to my eyes each time the great dogs
have come under my sight and hands cannot be exceeded by
any other joy. We must never let the attainment of this perfection discourage us and it will not, if we stick to what is top."
For Knocknagree setters see previous chapter.

DOWNS, JOHN L. & RUTH (Charles River), Sudbury, Mass.
Ch. Red sails of Salmagundi (Beorcham Blazes-Beocham
Radiant), brought to America by Percy Roberts for Justin W.
Griess, was transferred to John Downs and later to Mrs. Allan
A. Ryan. Red Sails sired a dozen litters, including 7 champions. As his bloodlines differed from the American strains,
they served as a distinct outcross. He contributed great quality
to his progeny, especially sound rears, impressive style and exceptional spirit. Particularly good was the Red Sails-Wamsutta
Susie Q combination that produced the Charles River champions: Color Sergeant, Blazing Beauty and All Afire. In 1946
when Downs moved to Oregon, he sold Sarge to the Corys in
Chicago; and on his return to the East he again continued his
own strain, later represented by Ch. Charles River Streamliner.

DREW, GERTRUDE W. (Wildair), Toronto, Ont.
Fourteen or more Canadian Irish Setter champions have been
owned by Mrs. Drew since 1940, including Sweet Sentiment of
Wildair, Ace Flyer of Aragon and Wildair Sweet Sixteen.

EARL, JOE A. & L. JETT (Jo-Ett), Bonner Springs, Kans.
Among the Jo-Ett champions are three by Ch. Shamrock
Flamingo ex. Shamrock Heather: Reta, Rudolph and Bell Star
O'Bonner.

125

Ch. End O'Maine Red Cloud S898416 (Ch. Carrvale's Terry Terhune-End O'Maine Claret).

Ch. End O'Maine Lady Amherst S861908 (Ch. Carrvale's Terry Terhune-End O'Maine Claret).

Ch. End O'Maine Morning Bird S861911 (Ch. Carrvale's Terry Terhune-End O'Maine Claret).

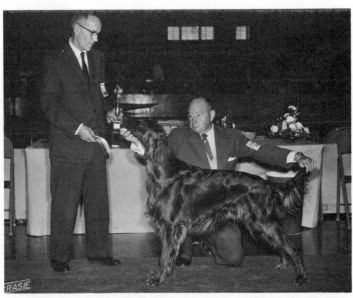

Ch. End O'Maine Reddy-Go S989837 (Ch. Yorkhill's Achilles-Ch. End O'Maine Morning Bird).

Ch. End O'Maine Royal Anne S250219 (Ch. Pinebrook Hi-Hat-Ch. End O'Maine Refrain).

Ch. End O'Maine Encore S751759 (Ch. Laurel Ridge Star Rocket-Ch. Mid-Oak Rose of Sharon).

EBERHARDT, MICHAEL & PHILLIP, Milwaukee, Wis.
These brothers own D. Ch. Titian Duke CD and F. Ch. Seamus of Greenfields.

EKEY, FAUNT L. & HELEN (Kopper Key), Spencerport, N.Y.
Kopper Key Hennessy is the best known of the Ekeys' 8 field trial winners.

ELDREDGE, E. IRVING & MRS. (Tirvelda), The Plains, Va.
See previous chapter.

EMORY J. BROOKS & DODIE (Phantom Brook), Ridgefield, Conn.
One of their first brood bitches was Ch. Bullet Hole's Clare, a granddaughter of Ch. Milson O'Boy. Bred to Ch. Tyronne Farm Malone II, she produced Ch. Phantom Brook's Molly Malone, dam of Can. & Am. Ch. Phantom Brooks Burgundy CDX and the granddam of Ber. & Am. Ch. Phantom Brook's Brian Boru. These two setters acquired an impressive string of show awards and they sired several Dix-Mac and Tercor champions.

FORD, CHARLES P. & SHIRLEY (Blayneywood), Belleville, Mich.
Pat's Irish Folly CD was shown by the Fords in 1956. His dam, Peggy Primrose, mated to Ch. Tyronne Farm Malone II, produced Ch. Kinvarra Malone and Ch. Kinvarra Shiela. Then Shiela bred to Ch. Draherin Irish Chieftain, also sired by Malone II, produced the stylish Ch. Blayneywood Country Squire which thus represents a double cross to Malone II. Both Squire and Ch. Kinvarra Malone are well balanced, beautiful Irish Setters with excellent show records. The latter sired Ch. Ivor Glen Cardinal Valiant and two Tirvelda champions.

FOSTER, ROBERT G. & RUTH B., Sparta, N.J.
Ch. Rusthills Bounce of Sharon.

FOX, KELLY (Kilkara), Huntington, N.Y.
Kelly's first Irish Setter, Ch. Kinvarra Lord Raglan CD, went from the Novice Class to Winners Dog at the last Morris & Essex Show in 1957. He also owned Ch. Kinvarra Flicker, Ch. Kilkara Redwing and others.

Ch. End O'Maine Pat Hand SA128196
(Ch. Conifer's Lance-Ch. End O'Maine Flyaway).

Ch. Dix-Mac Mignola SA51676
(Ch. End O'Maine Lord Bourbon-Ch. End O'Maine Lady Amherst).

130

FRASER, JAMES R. & MARY (Cu-Machree), St. Paul, Minn.
See previous chapter.

FRISCH, ROBERT D. & DOROTHY (Molly Coddled), Milwaukee, Wis.
Ch. Molly Coddled Misty CD is a likely candidate for the triple crown. Molly Coddled Mayhem, M. Maened, M. Megapod and M. Murphey's GGD are field-trial winners.

FRITZ, DR. WILLIAM J., Carleton, Mich.
Am. & Can. Ch. Michael Bryan Duke of Sussex (Ch. Thenderin Bryan Tristan-Ch. Merrilynn of Glenfield), usually handled by Horace Hollands, has the fine show record of 11 Best in Show, 40 Best in Group and 70 Best of Breed awards. Twice he placed in the Group at Westminster and once at the International. Bryan sired 11 or more champions, six in one litter from Ch. Tirvelda Nutbrown Sherry.

FRYDRYCH, JOSEPH B. & MARGARET (Argo Lane), Warren, Mich.
Joe got his first Irish Setter as a birthday present in 1943. Next came Can. Ch. Jiggs Dandy of Galway (Can CDX & Am CD). In addition to being a professional handler, Joe is a noted obedience trainer and instructor. At least a dozen Argo Lane setters have obtained obedience titles. In 1953, the Frydrychs obtained Am. & Can. Ch. Esquire of Maple Ridge (Ch. Thenderin Brian Tristan-Crosshaven Lea of Maple Ridge), which won 1 Best in Show, 15 Best Sporting Group and 95 Best of Breed awards in his long career on the bench. Squire loves to win and has become so accustomed to his consistent winning in the show ring that immediately after the judging he will head for the platform to receive the honors. He has received several annual trophies offered by the parent breed club. However; it is as the sire of 31 champions that Squire is especially renowned. Among them are Ch. Argo Lane Lad of Ulster, Ch. Argo Lane's Rixans Squire, Can. & Am. Ch. Argo Lane's Tippity Wicket, the famous litter of six champions ex B & F. Ch. Red Arrow Show Girl UDT, and others. Furthermore, there are many illustrious grandchildren. In fact, much of the high quality of Irish Setters in the Detroit Area should be credited him. Strong, sound, short bodied, beautifully coated dogs

131

Ch. Tyronne Farm Shangay S679044
(Ch. Tyronne Farm Shanahan-Gay Lady of Wildwood).

Ch. Tyronne Farm Gloribee SA123208
(Ch. End O'Maine Red Cloud-Tyronne Farm Victoria).

with wonderful dispositions have been produced. There will never be another Squire.

FUNK, JACK L. & ANN (Flaming Beauty), Chicago, Ill.
Both Jack and Ann show dogs professionally and have finished several hundred champions. The former has had a lifelong interest in Irish Setters, starting when he was 11 years old. Since 1939, when he acquired Ginger The Flaming Beauty, there have been many Flaming Beauty champions, including Patrick, Sally, Duchess and Michael. The most famous of all of them is Am. & Can. Ch. Headliner the Flaming Beauty (Ch. Thenderin Brian Tristan-Ch. Larrie of Tidewater), which topped all sporting dogs in 1962 show wins. He was retired from the ring in 1963, with 9 Best in Show, 56 Best in Group and 103 Best of Breed awards. Several of his progeny have become champions. Jack also bred Am. & Can. Ch. Tamara of Last Chance which figures in the pedigrees of Ch. Patrick of Tidewater, Am. & Can. Ch. Conine's King of the Reds and three Muckamoor champions.

GALLAGHER, C. H. & PATRICIA (Gala Glen), Melbourne, Fla.
Ch. Sunny Acre Top O' the Mark and Ch. Harmony Lane Sandpiper.

GALLUS, GEORGE S. & LILLIAN (Glenfield), Detroit, Mich.
Their first Irish Setter, acquired in 1920, was a trained retriever for duck hunting; and it was not until considerably later that they bred Irish Setters. Can. & Am. Ch. Merrilynn of Glenfield represented Ch. Kleiglight of Aragon and Kinvarra bloodlines. When she was mated to Ch. Thenderin Brian Tristan, two noted champions resulted: Michael Bryan Duke of Sussex and Merri's Rita of Glenfield. It is of interest that these two littermates appeared in the Shakesperian play "A Midsummer Nights Dream" at Detroit's Cass Theatre in 1960. George's latest champion is Ch. Electra of Glenfield.

GARDNER, WARD & MRS. (Crosshaven), Walla Walla, Wash.
See previous chapter.

Ch. Tyronne Farm Shenandoah
SA143963 (Ch. End O'Maine Red Cloud-
Ch. Tyronne Farm Sharon).

Ch. Runwild Kathleen Ni'Houlihan
S666550 (Ch. Sergeant Red Sails of
Devon-Ch. Runwild Sturdy Nancy).

134

GAVIN, JANE A. (Gavingarth), Decatur, Ga.
Ch. Gavingarth's Bonnie Heather is sired by Tarawil's Sequoia, a member of the famous litter of 7 champions by Ch. Carrvale's Terry Terhune ex End O'Maine Claret. Ch. Sagaquarius Racing Rita is sired by Ch. Tarawil's Geronimo, a brother to Sequoia.

GEBHART, ARTHUR J. & JESSIE, St. Paul, Minn.
Ch. Cherry Point Chukar Draherin Lord Kendrick.

GERBO, MARKO & DONNA (Mardonte), Ypsilanti, Mich.
Ch. Rogue's Darragh.

GIVAN, GEORGE & MARY, Detroit, Mich.
Ch. Argo Lane Brian Adair CD, Ch. Argo Lane Torpedo CD and Ch. Argo Lane Mike O'Rourke.

GLASSFORD, THOMAS A. & SANDRA (Tuxedo), Galena, O.
Tom, a professional handler, owns Ch. Tuxedo's Sugar and Spice, dam of the noted show dog, Ch. Tuxedo's Duffy of Mos'n Acre. Tom's father, George, bred Ch. Tuxedo's Royal Trooper which took breed honors at Westminster in 1960.

GLYNN, FRANK A. & POLLY (Of the Lodge), Waukesha, Wis.
The field trial winner, Lady of the Lodge, earned the UD title in a whirlwind campaign in 3 trials in 9 days, scoring more than 190 points on each occasion. Shela of the Lodge and Darby of the Lodge are field trial winners.

GOLDEN, WILLIAM R. & LAURETTA P., Pacific Palisades, Cal.
Muldoon of Haleridge obtained his CD in 1957 and his UD a year later. Next came the refined Ch. Webline Mi-Golden Flame CD (Ch. Innisfail Color Scheme-Ch. Knightscroft Erin McCuhl). Both Flame and Erin are beautiful type Irish Setters. In May 1963, Flame whelped the "Golden" litter with the musical names, sired by Ch. Thenderin Chaparal Cayenne. Four from the litter obtained the CD title: Symphony, Crescendo, Lyric and Jubilee. Ch. Webline Golden Jubilee CD, handled by Walt Shellenbarger, is one of the top Western sporting dogs of 1965.

Ch. Thenderin Brian Tristan S226483
(Ch. End O'Maine Luckalone-Ch. Kinvarra Portia).

Ch. Cu-Machree Tim S630082
(Ch. Thenderin Brian Tristan-Ch. Tattersall Tenaj).

GONSOR, RAYMOND J. & VALERIE (Varagon), Granada Hills, Cal.

Ch. Innisfail Best Regards CDX was their well bred, prepotent foundation bitch. She produced Ch. Maveric of Varagon and Ch. Ballyheige in a litter by Ch. Rhu Shane of Haleridge. Then she had 3 prominent champions sired by Ch. Innisfail Color Scheme: Flash Back, Legend and Enchantment of Varagon. Enchantment, indeed enchanting, won 19 Best Opposite Sex awards in 1964. Mated to Am. & Can. Ch. Michael Bryan Duke of Sussex, she produced Ch. Donamar Bold Echo of Varagon.

GOUDGE, HENRY, JOHN & CATHERINE (End O'Lane), Hammond, Ind.

Am. & Can. Ch. Sir Kevin of End O'Lane, sire of 6 champions, was extensively shown in the Mid-West and Canada. Kevin and Ch. Gaye Deborah of End O'Lane, both of Sunny Acre stock, produced many of the End O'Lane dogs of the last decade, including the following champions: E. Afterall, E. Coquette and E. Reward.

GRINDELL, GEORGE L. & DOLL (Gaelic Farm), Romulus, Mich.

From Ch. Sunset Emerald CD came 3 champions sired by Ch. Esquire of Maple Ridge: Ch. Donett's Copper Penny, Ch. Argo Lane Cuchulain and Ch. Argo Lane Gaelic Charm.

HADDOCK, DWIGHT & MARGARET (D Mar), Norfolk, Neb.

The Haddocks raised 2 litters by Taylor's Whirlaway Pat ex D Mar's Dixie. They also own Kinvarra Kathleen.

HALE, JAMES W. & EVELYN (Haleridge), Malibu, Cal.

Marksman's Shamus, long the "Grand Old Man" of Haleridge, sired 3 bench champions: Rhu Shane, Joy and Sean of Haleridge. Among his numerous obedience titled progeny are: Muldoon, Sullivan, Brannigan, Maureen, Darien, Amber and others. The Hales bred 60 "Little Reds" over a ten-months period for sequences in Walt Disney's "Big Red" movie. In the whelping scene the part of Molly was played by the Haleridge Irish Setter, Princess Cenna.

HAMMON, ELLEN, Manhattan Beach, Cal.

Ch. Thenderin Maximillian, first known as Pee Wee the bottle baby, was later noted for his excellent head and true Irish ex-

Ch. Conifer's Lance S958845
(Ch. Red Rogue of Maple Ridge-Conifer's Princess Ace).

Ch. Argo Lane Lad of Ulster S984169
(Ch. Esquire of Maple Ridge-Argo Lane's Gem of Ellair).

Ch. Argo Lane Squire's Dandy Cadet SA262676
(Ch. Esquire of Maple Ridge-Ch. Argo Lane's Tippity Wicket).

(left) Ch. Michael Brian Duke of Sussex S778836;
Ch. Merri's Rita of Glenfield S805485.

139

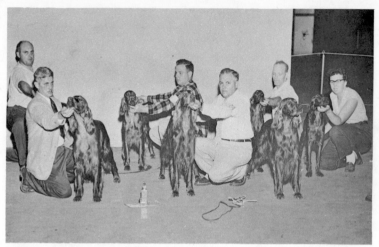

(left) Ch. Esquire of Maple Ridge, Shaun of Farmington, Ch. Thenderin Brian Tristan, Ch. Rogue's Darragh, Ch. Red Rogue of Maple Ridge, Ch. Sunny Holiday of Valmar.

(left) Yankee Doodle Dandi CD, SA160954; Ch. Argo Lane Bracelette CD, S984171; Clark's Independent Duchess CD, SA161459.

140

pression. Ch. Thenderin Kiss, Ch. Thenderin Bittersweet and Thenderin Eastwind spent their retirement years at the Hammon home.

HANLEY, MAY H. (Shawnlea), Rehoboth, Mass.
See previous chapter.

HARDIN, VIRGINIA (Runwild), Northbrook, Ill.
Virginia handles dogs professionally. Among her first Irish Setters were Verbu Christopher Oogh UD, and his half sister Ch. Runwild Alannah CD. Prominent in the early Fifties at Midwestern shows was Ch. Runwild Fin McCoul, a son of Ch. Charles River Color Sergeant. Ch. Runwild Fiona, which finished her championship at the early age of 11 months and 20 days, is the dam of 4 Runwild "F" champions by Ch. Carrvale's Terry Terhune: Finnagain, Failinis, Finnola the Fay and Fitzgerald. Not only is this litter well known in the show ring (Finnigan has 4 Best in Show awards), but also in field trials. Finnola placed in at least 7 stakes and Ginnagain in three. The latter sired the two Milwaukee champions: Ch. Mahogany's Socair Buacaill CD and Ch. Molly Coddled Misty. Fiona and Misty are also field trial winners. At Runwild emphasis is placed on the dual type Irish Setter. Among the dozen or more Runwild champions was Ch. Runwild Kathleen Ni'Houlihan, a beautiful setter with typical Irish expression owned by Marjory M. Billow.

HARRIS, THORNE D. & MYRA (Glendee), New Orleans, La.
Glendee has Ch. Tyronne Farm Midnight Flash CD, Ch. Tyronne Farm Midday Flame CD (both sired by Ch. Wautoma), Ch. Tyronne Farm Gloribee and Ch. Tyronne Farm Rex.

HARTMANN, ERICH H. & ELSIE, Lincoln, Neb.
Erich has shown dogs professionally for 15 years and Elsie has taught obedience training. Their foundation brood matron, Ch. Shamrock Hit Parade, is the dam of 3 champions sired by Ch. Wautoma.

HASINGER, DAVID J. & JANE (Valli Hi), Philadelphia, Pa.
See field trial chapter.

141

Ch. King Size S173090 (Major Red Flag-Lady Red Velvet).

Ch. Dorwayne's Kandi Shannon SA148595
(D.Ch. Titian Duke-Dorwayne's Kristi Shannon).

142

HEATH, DOROTHY P. (Heathcrest), Wauwatosa, Wis.

Dorothy, who is one of the founders of the ISC of Milwaukee in 1949, owns Heathcrest's Mahogany Dream.

HEIST, LAWRENCE M. & ELEANOR (Red Arrow), Fontana, Cal.

The Heists started about 1951 with Irish Setters of Waterford bloodlines from the Marted Kennels of Colonel Rand. Through the years they have participated in obedience, field, bench and professional handling activities. They have trained no less than 19 Red Arrow, Marted and O'Shaughnesy obedience titlists. The ultimate in obedience was achieved with the famous Am. & Mex. Ch. Red Aye Scraps, Am. & Mex. UD, the star in Walt Disney's Technicolor motion picture, "Big Red." The special additional training of Scraps for the role was accomplished by Bill Koehler, who found that his apt and intelligent pupil possessed the ideal physical attributes, the wide range of emotional attitudes and the marvelous personality necessary for the part. For his superb and versatile performance in the movie, Scraps received the "Patsy Award," given each year to the best animal actor in the movies. Big Red's stand-in was Ch. Red Arrow Smooth Sailing. Another famous setter was D. Ch. Red Arrow Show Girl, UDT & Mex. PC, noted for her own unique titles and for her 8 Red Arrow champion progeny, all of which had obedience degrees. Four of them were also Canadian champions, and 6 of them were in one litter sired by Can. & Am. Ch. Esquire of Maple Ridge: Smart Guy, Solid Gold, Son of A Gun, Sportsman's Guide, Show Guardian Rufus and So Go (a Best-in-Show dog). Ten Red Arrow dogs are field trial winners. Show Girl placed in 20 or more stakes. Dirty Bird and Smooth Sailing have been prominent in California trials.

HELM, NICHOLAS C. & MARY BETH (Yorkhill), St. Paul, Minn.

It might be said that Mary Beth grew up with Irish Setters, as her father, Dr. Thomas J. Gehan, kept them in the Thirties. Her field, obedience, bench and brood bitch for 12 years was Ch. Yorkhill's Red Rhapsody CDX (Ch. Kleiglight of Aragon-Ch. Claire Girl of Knocknagree II). "Ginger" was the dam of Ch. Yorkhill's Top Gallant and Ch. Yorkhill's Achilles. The latter was the sire of 3 End O'Maine champions and the grandsire of Ch. Yorkhill's County Kerry II CD.

Ch. Verbu Maureen SA99416 (Knockross' O'Boy-Ch. Caldene Maura).

Ch. McCoy's Squire of Verbu SA87204 (Knockross' O'Boy-Ch. Caldene Maura).

144

HENKE, ROBERT L. & ELAINE (Flaming Sunset), Manchester, Mo.

Henke's Flaming Sunset, whelped in 1953, and Ch. Even Direct of Aragon were foundation stock for the Henke breeding program. From these two setters came Ch. Flaming Sunset's Princess Gay, which produced 2 champions sired by Ch. Headliner The Flaming Beauty. The Henkes also have Ch. Treasure Trove's Raybar (Ch. Conifer's Lance-End O'Maine Claret).

HEYDE, MARTHA, San Francisco, Cal.

Ch. Shiralee Audacious Annabel CD, and Ch. Allirish Minstrel Boy.

HOBBS, H. VON & DOROTHY DELL (Merry-Dell), Gary, Ind.

'Tis said that the Hobbs' kennel prefix was derived from the names of the daughter and the wife, and that the hyphen was Von. Their first setter was Fleetwood Farm Sedan De Ville, one of a litter whelped in a Cadillac automobile. Her sister Am. & Can. Ch. Fleetwood Farm Coupe De Ville is the dam of Am. Can. & Ber. Ch. Merry-Dell's Autumn Glory. The theme song of this triple champion is, "Come look me over;" and indeed she is a beautiful setter. Widely shown, she was the top winning Irish Setter bitch of 1963 and 1964. Glory and her dam won the Irish Setter brace class at the International in 1963, and the Best in Show Brace award at Corn Belt Kennel Club the same year. Glory whelped a nice litter of 10 puppies by Ch. Headliner The Flaming Beauty in 1964. Another Hobbs setter was Ch. Draherin Irish Chieftain, a son of Ch. Tyronne Farm Malone II. Other Merry-Dell champions are Copper Chief, Bronze CD and Daring Damsel.

HOFMEISTER, LOUISE M., Oak Park, Ill.

Ch. Abbeyleix Shane an Sionnach.

HOLLANDS, HORACE S. & MELBA, Port Huron, Mich.

Horace has had setters since he was 7 years of age. Among the many fine dogs he has handled in the show ring, the Irish Setter Can. & Am. Ch. Michael Bryan Duke of Sussex stands out prominently. When Bryan sired the well known litter of 6 champions from Ch. Tirvelda Nutbrown Sherry in 1962, the

Western Irish Setter Club at *Big Red* Movie Premier, Chicago Theatre, 1962.

Ch. Verbu Missy Oogh CDX, S855732 at *Big Red* Movie Premier, Chicago, 1962.

Hollands family obtained Ch. Tirvelda Michael Bryan and Ch. Tirvelda Michele.

HOLVENSTOT, CLYDE E. & LUZ (Westwind), Flanders, N.J.
Luz's first Irish Setter, obtained in 1942, was Knightscroft Magic CD, a daughter of Ch. Milson O'Boy II. Luz has been showing, breeding and handling ever since. Being especially interested in obedience training, she has finished 6 or more Westwind Scarlet CD titlists. Among the Westwind Scarlet bench champions are: Kismet, Star Kist and Applause. Then there is also the well bred Ch. Knockross' Sally (Knockross' O'Boy-Ch. Knockross' Shiela).

HOMUTH, ELMER E. & JANE (Elmho), Fond du Lac, Wis.
Elmer has owned Ch. End O'Maine Burnie Burn, Ch. End O'Maine Twinkle Toes, Ch. Blush of End O'Maine, Ch. Redman and the field trial winners Weatherwise and Elmho Paddy O'Ardee.

HONSBERGER, KENNETH & JEAN (Kenten), Streetsville, Ont.
Can. Ch. Prince Rory of Kenten CD, and Can. Ch. Toni of Kenten.

HUIZENGA, JAKE D. & SALLY (Oxton), Salinas, Cal.
Jake has owned Irish Setters for more than 40 years, including Ch. Oxton Rex CDX, Ch. Oxton's Irish Perfection CDX, F. Ch. Oxton's Shosaph, F. Ch. Oxton's Shosaphine and other field trial winners.

HURD, HAROLD & JOANNE (Apache Acres), Utica, Mich.
The Hurds, who are especially interested in field and obedience work, own Ch. Argo Lane Bracelette CD and the field trial winners, Yankee Doodle Dandi CD, Ward Wilcharbo CD, and Apacheacre Drumbeat Salli.

HURST, DONALD J. & MARY (Donamar), Tujunga, Cal.
Ch. Donamar Bold Echo of Varagon and Holly's Hapenny of Varagon CD.

HYLAND, ROBERT C. & JEANNETTE M., Omaha, Neb.
Jeannette owns Ch. Shamrock Happy Clancy and her father, Daniel Murphy, owns Ch. Shamrock Firstmate.

147

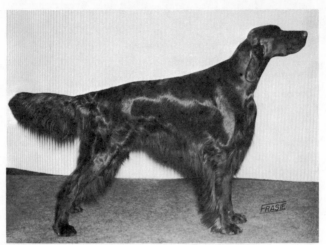

Ch. Red Dawn of Sunny Acre A913935
(Ch. Highlight of Denhaven-Debutants Daughter).

Ch. Gaye of Sunny Acre S265047
(Ch. Red Dawn of Sunny Acre-Ch. Lindy's Scarlet Lady).

IACOBUCCI, LOUIS (Celou), Providence, R.I.

About 1953, Louis obtained a Shawnlea bitch which he bred to a Charles River dog to obtain Celou's Sheena MacRory, his foundation brood bitch. It is from her that 6 Celou MacRory champions descend: Lex, Alvin, Kallyanne, Irish Prince, Tracey and Rory II. Ch. Conifer's Lance and Ch. Michael Bryan Duke of Sussex figure in some of the pedigrees.

JENNINGS, JOSEPH W. & AUDREY (Titianstar), Mahwah, N.J.

Ch. Titian Intrepid.

JENNINGS, PETER S. & CYNTHIA (Hearthstone), Danbury, Conn.

Hearthstone, the name of the family home in Danbury, was registered as a kennel prefix in 1925 by Peter's father, the late Richard D. Jennings, a prominent judge of sporting dogs. Peter purchased Ch. Gay Holly O'Dandy CD in 1957, bred her to Ch. Kinvarro Wansdyke and thereby obtained Ch. Hearthstone's High Hopes. The Jennings' program of line breeding now has its sixth generation.

JEROME, ROY R. & NEDRA (Innisfail), Sepulveda, Cal.

Innisfail to many Irish Setter breeders refers to the famous litter of 3 champions by Ch. Seaforth's Dark Rex ex Thenderin Champagne, which contained Innisfail Color Scheme CD, I. Encore and I. Mona Lisa. The Jeromes own Ch. Glen Erin's Pride of Innisfail, Ch. Margevan Madcap of Innisfail and several of their offspring.

JOHNSTON, PERCY L. & MARIE, Redwood City, Cal.

Ch. Crusader Paddy Malone.

JONES, CHARLES S. & ELEANOR, Dayton, O.

Ch. Cavalier of Maple Ridge, and Ch. Shawen's Cavalier.

KHATOONIAN, HARRY & IRENE, Reno, Nev.

This is the Irene Castle Phillips who developed the famous Phillips system for rating bench show dogs. She has not owned Irish Setters since her former husband, James H. Phillips, passed away in 1960; but in the previous 20 years, the Hagginwood Kennels at Del Paso Heights often had as many as 40 setters. It was during this period that Irene faithfully reported

149

Ch. Merry-Dell's Copper Chief SA105597
(Ch. Fergus O'Farrell-Fleetwood Farm Sedan De Villa).

(front) Ch. Merry-Dell's Autumn Glory S962881;
Ch. Fleetwood Farm Coupe De Ville S871249.

Ch. Even Direct of Aragon S418954
(Ch. Knightscroft Danny-O'Boy-Ch. Noreen of Aragon).

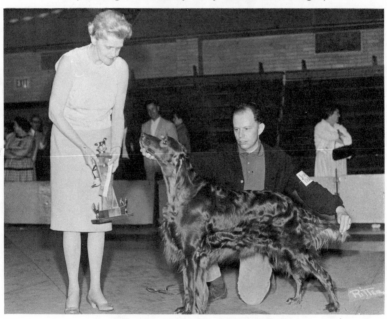

Ch. Flaming Sunset's Princess Gay S858766
(Ch. Even Direct of Aragon-Henke's Flaming Sunset).

151

Ch. Sir Kevin of End O'Lane S720333
(Sir Gaye of End O'Lane-Colleen of End O'Lane).

Ch. Fannie Red Star of Kentucky S341117
(Ch. Red Star of Hollywood Hills-Sharoc Play Girl).

152

in her classic Irish Setter breed columns of the dog magazines. Best known of the Hagginwood setters were Ch. Coppercoat of the Hills (Mike) and Ch. Lady Kathleen O'Hagginwood. Mike, which won Best in Show at Stockton in 1947, was field trained by Lee Baldock; and Kathleen was the dam of 6 bench champions. Also of note were Ch. Coppercoat's Sleepy Time Gal, Ch. Bem's Superflame, Ch. Hagginwood's Eamon CD, Ch. H. Real McCoy CDX and Ch. H. Umber Sheen CD.

KEGEL, ROBERT A. & LAREEN (White Birch), La Crescent, Minn.
Ch. Merry-Dell's Copper Chief and Ch. Merry-Dell's Daring Damsel.

KELLEHER, BEATRICE, Los Angeles, Cal.
Ch. Webline Rio Hondo.

KELSEY, MARK & JANET (Killagay), Yorba Linda, Cal.
When Janet was 11 years of age she got her first Irish Setter and trained it to do 47 tricks. Next she acquired Bridgets Sunset, which when mated to Ch. Weblyn Limelite, produced Ch. Killagay's Kelsey CD and Ch. Kilagay's Karrie CD. These 2 setters are the parents of Ch. Killagay-Aaron's Party Boy owned by Constance K. Dixon. The Kelseys are especially interested in obedience and field trials.

KESSLER, KENNETH E. (Selborune), Riverside, Ill.
Ch. Kleiglight's Image of Aragon II, Ch. Selbourne Hushy and Ch. Selbourne Tessie's Love.

KILMER, ROBERT L. & RUBY (K-Ru), Brookville, O.
Ch. K-C's Clan-See of K-Ru, Ch. Big Shot's Rusty of K-Ru and Ch. Colleen of K-Ru.

KINNAMON, HOWARD F., M. D., Easton, Md.
Ch. Knockross' Red Patti.

KLAPPER, IVAN & LENORE (Banshee), Gardiner, N.Y.
The Banshee Kennels, established in 1947, have Knightscroft and Red Barn bloodlines. The beautifully headed Ch. Knightscroft Lady Vogue CD brightened the Veterans' and the Brood Bitch Classes in her later years and proved that Irish Setters

Ch. Muckamoor's Marty McCuhl SA127455 (Muckamoor's Michael McGuire-Ch. Weblyn Masterpiece).

Ch. Jo-Ett's Rudolph O'Bonner SA166173 (Ch. Shamrock Flamingo-Ch. Shamrock Heather).

154

have a long show life. She was the dam of Ch. Banshee Sharpshooter and Ch. Banshee Rebel Brigadier CD, and the granddam of Ch. Banshee Bushwhacker.

KLINCK, HAROLD A. (Orchard Farm), Oldcastle, Ont.
Can. & Am. Ch. Danny of Orchard Farm, and Can. & Am. Ch. Lucky of Orchard Farm.

KLUSSMAN, WILLIAM & PAT, Whittier, Cal.
The Klussmans own Ch. Webline Sir Mark, a double cross to Ch. Innisfail Color Scheme CD, and Ch. Webline Zamara, one of the famous "Z" litter of 6 champions sired by Color Scheme ex Am. & Mex. Ch. Thenderin Valentine CD & PC.

KNIGHT, JOSEPH P. & HENRIETTA (Knightscroft), New York, N.Y.
See previous chapter.

KNOLL, D. J. & B. (Bayknoll), Edmonton, Alta.
Can. Ch. Glen Erin's Red Velvet and 5 Bayknoll Canadian champions.

KOONTS, NIAL A. & MARIE (Rusthills), Louisville, O.
Nial, who is a professional handler, has owned many Irish Setter champions, among which were: Ch. General Beauregard, Ch. Aragon's Rustic Rover, Ch. Argo Lane's Countess of Cork, Ch. Mid-Oak Rose of Sharon, Ch. Rusthills Irish Serenade, Ch. Rusthills Irish Duke CD and others. Ch. General Beauregard (Ch. Tyronne Farm Malone II-Knockross' Fern), a consistent winner at shows, sired 8 champions.

KRAUSS, GEORGE A. & MARION, Milwaukee, Wis.
Ch. Tarawil's Geronimo and the field-trial winners Mahogany Sputnik and Comet's Katuri o' Colburn Acres.

LANE, JOHN A. & MYRTLE (Wildwood), Muskego, Wis.
Ch. Tyronne Farm Shangay, Ch. Tyronne Farm Lady Lee and Tabelina of Wildwood.

LAWRENCE, JUDITH V. (Juvilair), Berkeley, Cal.
Ch. Juvilair Queen of the Night.

Ch. Taradell's Bright Future SA169369
(Ch. Gay Michael of Sunny Acre-Ch. Tara's Theme).

Ch. Harmony Lane's Gone South SA90033
(Ch. Erin of Ellair-Sunset Flair).

156

LAW, WILLIAM M. & ARLENE (Oakshire), Berkley, Mich.
Ch. Jim O'Reilly of Oakshire and Ch. Argo Lane's Vin Rouge.

LEWIS, ERNEST J. & VIRGINIA (County Clare), Pacific Palisades, Cal.
Several years ago the Lewises set out to help the Irish Setter and their results have been successful on the bench and in the field. They owned the great Ch. Innisfail Color Scheme CD, the prepotent sire of 25 champions, which had a tremendous influence on the breed in California. The County Clare bench champions trace back to Ch. Tyronne Farm Shanahan and Ch. Tyronne Farm Malone. Other Lewis dogs under the professional guidance of Stanley Head have made significant contributions to the status of the Irish Setter in field trials. He trained and campaigned AKC F. Ch. Oxton's Shosaphine, National Red Setter Shooting Dog Ch. Mighty Fawn, National Red Setter Shooting Dog Ch. County Clare's Shandy and others. Fawn was chosen as a member of the 1965 Irish Setter *Sports Afield* Pointing Dog Team.

LUGONJA, SAM A., Los Altos Hills, Cal.
Ch. Treasure Trove's Pirate Pearl CD.

LYNCH, RONALD S. & MARJORIE (Glen Erin), Richland, Wash.
Ch. Glen Erin's Dan O'Boy, Ch. G. E. Jolly Jester, Ch. G. E. Pride of Innisfail, Ch. Bright Accent's Erin and others.

MARTIN, HAYDEN H. & LOIS (Sunny Acre), Gary, Ind.
The Martins have had Irish Setters for more than 20 years. Ch. Lindy's Scarlet Lady and Debutante Daughter, representing Aragon and Denhaven bloodlines, were 2 of their early brood matrons. The 2 dozen Sunny Acre champions include: Red Dawn, Red King, Rebel, Gaye Michael, Sir Jeffrey, Lady Beth and Gaye (all of Sunny Acre). Sweet Gaye was perhaps the favorite, not only because she was outstanding in conformation but also because she was intelligent and 'understanding. She went Best in Show twice and usually placed high in the Group. Red Dawn had four Best-in-Show awards. Sunny Acre dogs were important to the breeding programs of Mid-Oak, Hotze, End O'Lane and many other kennels. In 1961, "Doc" Martin retired from the handling profession to become a dog show judge.

Ch. Sunny Acre Top o'the Mark SA187185
(Sunny Acre's Mahogany Caper-Ch. Hotze's Red Rose).

Ch. Harmony Lane Sandpiper SA115147
(Ch. Conifer's Lance-Ch. Argo Lane's Fancy Dancer).

MAURER, KEN A. & DOROTHY (Kendor), Manitou Springs, Colo.
Ch. Kendor's King of Red Mountain, and Ch. Tarashan's Brian of Kendor.

McATEER, JOHN C. & PAULA (Redlog), Bermuda.
Can. & Am. Ch. Red Star of Hollywood Hills CDX, Ch. Redlog Strawberry Blonde, CDX, Ber. Ch. Red Barn Apache and others.

McCORMACK, ELDON H. (Eldomac), Yakima, Wash.
Ch. Cherry Point Brask II, Ch. Eldomac Senarc Rhu and others.

McCOY, WALTER, Evanston, Ill.
Ch. McCoy's Squire of Verbu.

McCUNE, MARY & CAPERS, IDA (Dix-Mac), Coraopolis, Pa.
The Montour Farm Kennels of the late Mary McCune and the late Ida M. Capers showed many prominent Irish Setters in the period from 1948 to 1961. Among these show dogs were: Ch. Patrick Sarsfield, Ch. Dix-Mac Saintfield CD, Can. Am. Ch. Tadg of Tercor, Can. & Am. Ch. Phantom Brook's Burgundy CDX, Ch. Brazen Bridget of Englewood, Ch. Dix-Mac Mignola, etc.

McIVOR, EDGAR W. & ROBERTA (Ivor Glen), Plymouth, Mich.
In addition to D. Ch. Tyrone's Mahogany Mike CDX, F. Ch. Ivor Glen Devilera and other field trial winners, the McIvors owned bench champions: Lady La Rouge, Ivor Glen Bidse, Argo Lane's Golden Skylarker, D'Arcey's Kim-O-Mike and Ivor Glen Cardinal Valiant. See field trial chapter.

McVICKER, GEORGE & CORINNE, Sonoma, Cal.
Ch. Easy's Moonyean Claire and Shardmore Main Attraction.

MEIER, RAYMOND W. & MILDRED, Sandstone, Minn.
Ch. Kinney's Modie, Ch. Biram's Highland Hondo and Ch. Tirvelda Neerb's Paddy.

MERIAM, R. S. & DOROTHY (Merimont), South Lincoln, Mass.
Professor Meriam, now retired, held the Wilson Chair of Business Policy at Harvard University. The Meriams' best known

Ch. Gavingarth's Bonnie Heather SA154716 (Tarawil's Sequoya-Gunner's Daughter of O'Killala).

Ch. Shannon's Shawn of Erin SA159829 (Ch. Draherin Irish Regardless-Ch. Knockross' Ruby).

setter was Ch. Cu-Machree Tim (Ch. Thenderin Brian Tristan-Ch. Tattersall Tenaj).

METZLER, CLINTON D. & IRENE, Vallejo, Cal.
Ch. Shardmore's Autumn Echo CD and Pat's Centurion Flame CD.

MILLER, ARLENE D. (Kalibank), Eatontown, N.J.
Ch. Kalibank's King of Eatontown.

MONROE, JOHN H. & SANDRA (Threejay), Canoga Park, Cal.
Ch. Threejay's Caravan Commander.

MOREHEN, C. W. & MRS. (Conifer), Highland Creek, Ont.
Am. & Can. Ch. Conifer's Guarda Siochana and several other Conifer champions.

MORONEY, JEAN W. & PHYLLIS (Lismoro), Castro Valley, Cal.
Ch. End O'Maine Lord Bourbon, and Ch. Glendee's Duke of Wicklow.

MORRISON, EARL L. & JOAN (Sunnymoor), Gross Pointe, Mich.
Ch. Sunnymoor Red Rhapsody and the other field trial winners Kilkenny of Sunnymoor, Sunnymoor Miss Red Boh and Echo of Three Oaks.

MURPHY, WALTER B. & JULIA (Beauhart), College Park, Ga.
Ch. Sunny Acres Sweet Helen and Ch. Killane Duffy.

MYERS, LUCY JANE (Draherin), Duluth, Minn.
Lucy obtained her first Irish Setter, My Rusty Boy CD, as a birthday present in 1948. Next came her beautiful foundation brood bitch, Am. & Can. Ch. Thenderin Elixir CD, the dam of 8 champions in 6 litters. Ch. Draherin Irish Regardless, Ch. D. Irish Chieftain, Ch. D. Centurion, Ch. D. Coronado, Am. & Can. Ch. D. Mahogany Gaye and Ch. D. Echo of Elixir are prominent in present day pedigrees. Draherin Kennels have raised more than 40 litters and have housed a wide variety of bloodlines, such as Red Sails Pride of Devon, Patrick Red Jacket, Ch. Cu-Machree Tim, Ch. Kinvarra Hartsbourne Flurry, Red Barn Dorian, Ch. Tyronne Farm Malone II, Ch. Yorkhill's County Kerry II, Shannon's Erin and others. Can. & Am. Ch. Draherin Auburn Artistry by Ch. Innisfail

Ch. Red Aye Scraps S844773
(Marted O'Shaughnesy-Lady Sheila O'Shangabragh).

Ch. Shardmore's Autumn Echo SA143268
(Ch. Shardmore Autumn Sheen-Watson's Mary Monahan).

Ch. Shardmore Autumn Sheen S832058
(Ch. Patrick of Ide-Raferty's Kathleen Magee).

Ch. Red Arrow Smooth Sailing S864355
(D.Ch. Tyrone's Mahogany Mike-D.Ch. Red Arrow Show Girl).

163

Ch. Baker's Buck-Ette S997283 (Ch. Draherin Centurion-Baker's Penelope).

Ch. Cherry Point Ambush SA195704 (Ch. Cherry Point Chukar-Cherry Point Corey).

164

Color Scheme CD is one of the recent stud dogs. In addition to her extensive experience as a breeder and exhibitor of Irish Setters, Lucy is also interested in the breed from the standpoint of judging, obedience tests and field trials. She owns Lady's Colleen, a daughter of F. Ch. Askew's Carolina Lady and the dam of at least a dozen field trial winners. There are 7 Draherin field trial winners, including 2 that were sired by F. Ch. Ike Jack Kendrick. Two of the high points of Lucy's career were when she won the Children's Handling Class at the International show with 22 in competition, and when her Ch. Draherin Echo of Elixir went Best in Show from the classes at the 1960 Duluth show.

NELSON, ALLAN C. & DORA, Upland, Cal.
Ch. Red Arrow So Go CDX.

NELSON, MARY E. (Glockomorro), Elmhurst, Ill.
Ch. Glockomorro's Old Gold, the field trial winner Glockomorro Duke of Westdale and several obedience titlists.

NEVILLE, WILLIAM B. & MARION (Red Barn), Blauvelt, N.Y.
One of the largest Irish Setter kennels in the United States is Red Barn, established in the Forties. Their foundation stock was Knightscroft, Boxley and other strains. Ch. Knightscroft Primrose, a double cross to Ch. Milson O'Boy II, produced Ch. Red Barn Rosabelle UDT, the dam of three Enilen champions and obedience titlists. In 1952, the Nevilles obtained Ch. Kendare Red Dawn, which became the sire of 13 Boxley, Maple Ridge and Red Barn champions. Prominent among them was Ch. Boxley Holly Anne renowned as the dam of the noted 1953 Red Barn litter of 5 champions by Can. & Am. Ch. Red Star of Hollywood Hills CDX: Red Barn Red Stardust, Royal Charm, Royal Holly, Royal Talisman and Redstar Talent Scout. Talisman sired 7 champions, including Ch. Red Barn Talleyrand, Ch. Phantom Brook's Brian Boru and others. There is a long list of Red Barn bench-show and obedience-trial winners which have contributed much to the development of the Irish Setter in America.

NEWHALL, WELROSE L. (Knockross), Coraopolis, Pa.
See previous chapter.

Ch. Rhu Shane of Haleridge S856974
(Marksman's Shamus-Princess Patt O'Lori).

(left) Ch. Maveric of Varagon S955172; Ch. Ballyheige of Haleridge S955165;
Ch. Rhu Shane of Haleridge S856974.

166

NICKERSON, WALTER E. & MADELINE, Chatham, N.J.
Ch. Tirvelda Rick O'Shea.

NILSEN, ATHOS & JOYCE (Thenderin), Venice, Cal.
See previous chapter.

NITZ, HAROLD J. & ALIDA (Har-Nel), Grand Rapids, Mich.
The litter brothers, Ch. Indian Copper of Har-Nel CD and Autumn Rusty of Har-Nel, are field trial winners.

NORCROSS, ARTHUR E. & ALICE, Milwaukee, Wis.
Ch. Mahogany's Socair Buacaill CD and Mahogany Sue CDX.

OAKS, HARRY A. & NORMA (Oak-Eire), Acworth, Ga.
Ch. Red Barn Fancy and Ch. Red Barn Martha W.

OLIVO, HELEN A., Brooklyn, N.Y.
Ch. Garden State Reno's Blaze has an excellent bench show record, including some Group awards in Puerto Rico.

OPP, KENNETH F. & SHIRLEY (Kenshire), Garden City, Mich.
Ch. Argo Lane's Lady Dawn of Erin CD, Argo Lane's Gallant Lad CDX (Can. CD), Ch. Argo Lane Star of Dawn, Ch. Argo Lane Peg O' My Heart and Old Orchard CD.

OVERMAN, DORIS (Autumaura), Los Angeles, Cal.
Ch. Autumn Aura Blazing Tim.

PAHY, DANIEL L. & MARION (Kerry), Blairstown, N.J.
Ch. McGovern's Rusty O'Rourke and the field trial winners Kerry's Mavourneen O'Talisman and McGovern's Kerry O'Red.

PALMER, THOMAS J. & NORMA, Torrance, Cal.
Ch. Weblyn Westerner CDX, Am .& Mex. Ch. Webline Winning Way CD (& Mex. PC), Webline Xclamation Mark CD and Webline Triumph CD.

PALUSZYNSKI, LEROY & MARCY, Wind Lake, Wis.
F. Ch. Lady Bronze.

PARMENTER, GENE & PHYLLIS J. (Citadel), Omaha, Neb.
Ch. Tyronne Farm Shenandoah CD, the first Companion Dog in Nebraska, is known to his friends as "That Wild Irishman." He has that gay, happy-go-lucky spirit so characteristic of the

167

Ch. Legend of Varagon SA67238 (Ch. Innisfail Color Scheme-Ch. Innisfail Best Regards).

Ch. Flash Back of Varagon SA76263 (Ch. Innisfail Color Scheme-Ch. Innisfail Best Regards).

breed. According to his owner he has more fun than any other dog in history. For instance, in obedience trials on the command to jump Shen has been known to leap all the hurdles in the ring (some twice) and then to look around for more. In retrieving he dives, skids, seizes the dumbbell and makes a grand sweep around the ring showing it to all the spectators before delivering it to his handler.

PARSONS, RAY S. & BARBARA (Raybar), Orange, Cal.
Ch. Sporting Acres Get Set, and Ch. Treasure Trove's Raybar.

PELISSIER, JOHN L. & HARRIOT, Stirling, N.J.
Both Pelissiers are professional handlers. They owned Ch. Pelissier's Kimson Parade CD, and Ch. Redstar Miss Gay, and they bred several Garden State champions.

PELLEGRINI, RUTH A. (Flarelane), Seattle, Wash.
Am. & Can. Ch. Flarelane Irish Boy, Ch. Flarelane Red Rogue CD, and Ch. Rocket Flare O'Storm CD.

PHANEUF, BERNARD G. & JEANNETTE (Beau Rouge), Hollywood, Cal.
Marted Gypsy, Cormac of Beau Rouge and Gydd of Beau Rouge.

PHILLIPS, A. L. & FRANCES (Mos'n Acre), Lock Haven, Pa.
Ch. Tuxedo's Duffy of Mos'n Acre.

PIERCE, MICHAEL E. (Mid-Oak), Lansing, Mich.
Ch. Mid-Oak Aragon Flash, Ch. Mid-Oak Rose of Sharon and Ch. Mid-Oak Wyckham of Orange.

PIPER, WAYNE A. & DOROTHY (Dorwayne), Hartland, Wis.
Ch. Dorwayne's Kristi Shannon CDX and several obedience titlists.

POOL, GEORGE F. & NORMA (Flann), Longview, Tex.
Ch. Wharfwood's Valentine and Ch. Flann's Sir Boss.

PORTER, MRS. CHEEVER, New York, N.Y.
In addition to the superb Irish Setters Ch. Milson O'Boy, Ch. Rosecroft Premier and Ch. St. Cloud's Fermanagh III described in previous chapters, several others have been shown under Mrs. Porter's colors, including Ch. Shawnlea's Fanfare, Ch.

Ch. Enchantment of Varagon SA69657 (Ch. Innisfail Color Scheme-Ch. Innisfail Best Regards).

Ch. Donamar Bold Echo of Varagon SA192360 (Ch. Michael Bryan Duke of Sussex-Ch. Enchantment of Aragon.

Kinvarra Malone, Ch. Wautoma, Ch. Tyronne Farm Rex and Ch. Cherry Point Brask. Brask's marvelous show record is 8 Best in Show, 51 Best Sporting Group and 145 Best of Breed awards. He holds the all time record for the most Irish Setter breed awards and also the most breed wins per year—64 in 1964. He was handled by Jane Kamp. In the overall panorama of Irish Setters through many years, these gorgeous dogs of Mrs. Porter's are commemorated in history as outstanding representatives of the breed. Shown widely and often in group competition against other top sporting dogs, they have kept the Irish Setter in the limelight.

PRESCOTT, LEONA & DERBY, LUCILLE (Tirnanog), Sheridan, Ore.

In addition to several Tirnanog champions and obedience titlists, these kennels had Ch. Ri Daragh Gorgeous Georgaine CD, Ch. Muckamoor's Merry Malarky CD and the well known field trial winner Tir Na N Og Merrymike Larkey.

RAY, ROBERT H. & CONSTANCE (Corray), Roseville, Mich.

Ch. Duchess Derrycaine of Valmar CD, and Kelton of Hartsbourne Hei-Lo CD, both field-trial winners.

REA, JOSEPH L. & NATALIE A., Harper Woods, Mich.

Ch. Argo Lane Squires Dandy Cadet.

REESE, C. R. & SALLY (Candia), Hopkins, Minn.

Tyronne Farm Flame, Ch. Draherin Echo's Guy and Draherin Echo's Hope.

REINDL, JOHN P. & BARBARA (Oakhills), Morton Grove, Ill.

Ch. Treasure Trove's Incendiary CD.

REYNOLDS, WAYNE & BARNES, THOMAS (Barrewyne), Sellersville, Pa.

Ch. Knightscroft Rene and Ch. Barrewyne Brian Redmond.

RINN, ROBERT L. & DORIS (O'Rinn), Fayetteville, Ga.

Ch. Tirvelda Val O'Rinn and Ch. Tirvelda Penny O'Rinn.

RIVETT, BEV, Georgetown, Ont.

Can. & Am. Ch. Conifer's Guarda-Siochana and Can. Ch. Conifer's Prince O'Shannon.

171

Ch. Innisfail Color Scheme S557130
(Ch. Seaforth's Dark Rex-Thenderin Champagne).

(left) Ch. Weblyn Limelite S824640; Ch. Weblyn Luminous Lass S824642.

ROYSTON, JOHN F. & MURIEL (Killane), Meadowvale, Ont.

Am. & Can. Ch. Argo Lane's Rising Star, Am. & Can. Ch. Killane Rogue, Ch. Killane Duffy, Can. Ch. Ellair Velvet Token and 6 or more other Killane Canadian champions have been owned by the Roystons. It is pointed out that of the 400 Canadian Irish Setter champions, approximately one quarter of them are also American champions, which indicates the close relationship between the two countries in dog affairs.

RUMBAUGH, HUGH M. & VIRGINIA (Fleetwood Farm), Bath, Ohio.

Among 8 Fleetwood Farm champions are Peg o' My Heart, Sixty Special, Noreen and Coupe De Ville. The Rumbaughs used Ch. Thenderin Brian Tristan, Ch. Gay Guy of Aragon, Ch. Kleiglight's Red Tuxedo and others in their breeding program.

SCHOEN, LEE M. & MARJORIE (Kinvarra), Darien, Conn.

See previous chapter.

SCHWEITZER, EMILY L. (Verbu), Dundee, Ill.

Some of the numerous activities of the Verbu setters are related in a previous chapter, but there is an additional item of special interest. When Walt Disney's "Big Red" movie premiered at the Chicago Theatre, the Western Irish Setter Club was invited to stage a display of their Irishmen on State Street in front of the theatre. Among the dogs that performed for the crowd was Ch. Verbu Missy Oogh CDX, a veteran of bench, field and obedience activities. Not only did she take the hurdle in the obedience routine, but she pointed a real, live pheasant in a simulated bird field right in the middle of Chicago's heavy, noisy traffic.

SIMA, CARL S. (County Doromar), Northbrook, Ill.

Ch. County Doromar's T. F. Special and Ch. County Doromar's Aileen.

SLICK, JOSEPH G. & MARILYN, Mineral Ridge, Ohio.

Am., Can. & Ber. Ch. Shannon's Shawn of Erin.

SMITH, FREDERICK D. & DOLORES, Oaklawn, Ill.

Ch. Lady Bridget XII CD and Sergeant Red Sails of Devon II.

(left) Ch. Webline Sir Mark SA228763;
Webline Sensation SA216494; Webline Senator SA263363.

Ch. Knightscroft Troubadour S339811
(Ch. Knightscroft Fermanagh-Knightscroft Cynthia).

Ch. Killagays Karrie SA34318 (Ch. Weblyn Limelite-Bridgets Sunset).

Weblyn "L" Litter by Ch. Innisfail Color Scheme ex Ch. Thenderin Heigh-Ho.

175

(left) Ch. Enilen Michael Terrence UDT; Ch. Enilen Ginger Snap
UDT; Ch. Red Barn Rosabelle UDT.

Ch. Webline Zephyr SA33304 (Ch. Innisfail Color Scheme-Ch.
Thenderin Valentine).

SMITH, HOWARD C. & BARBARA (Wamlay), Avon, Conn.
Am. & Can. Ch. Wamlay's Colonel, Ch. Wamlay's High Fidelity, Ch. Waterford Coolan of Oak Grove and Ch. Thenderin Kismet.

SMITH, RICHARD E. & ANNE (Harmony Lane), Roswell, Ga.
Anne is the daughter of Dr. Arthur W. Erkfitz, one of the founders of the Irish Setter Club of Michigan. She has had Irish Setters since childhood, some of the well known ones being Shelley of Sunny Acre, Argo Lane's Gem of Ellair, Am. & Can. Ch. Erin of Ellair CD, Can. Ch. Killane Gayla of Ellair, Can. Ch. Ellair Velvet Token and Ellair Red Thane CD & Can. CD. Dick, who is a professional handler of dogs, obtained the outstanding brood bitch Ch. Argo Lane's Fancy Dancer CD from Joe Frydrych. Bred to Ch. Conifer's Lance, Dancer produced Ch. Harmony Lane Sandpiper. Then there are Ch. Harmony Lane's Gone South, Ch. Harmony Lane Comanche and others.

SMITH, THEODORE H. (Town and Country), Elmhurst, Ill.
Ch. King Size.

SPALDING, LT. COL. MALCOLM C. & Mrs. (Woodfield), Fairfield, Conn.
In the early Fifties the Spaldings obtained Ch. Kinvarra Dandy Boy, a son of Ch. Kinvarra Bootsie, and Thenderin Queen o' Hearts, a daughter of Ch. Seaforth's Dark Rex. From these 2 setters came a 1957 litter containing 3 champions: Gay Holly O'Dandy, Irish Imp·O'Dandy and Irish Kate O'Dandy. Later Woodfield and Hearthstone dogs trace back to these bloodlines. Kate won Best in Show at Denver in 1960.

SPEAR, JACK A. & EVELYN (Tyronne Farm), Tipton, Ia.
See previous chapter.

SPILIOS, WILLIAM P. (Tarawil), Palatine, Ill.
Ch. Carrvale's Billy Boy, Ch. Carrvale's Terry Terhune and Ch. Tarawil's Geronimo.

SPILLER, VIRGINIA (Tattersall), Scott Field, Belleville, Ill.
Virginia is a civilian employee of the Air Force. The best known Tattersall litter by Ch. Tyronne Farm Clancy ex Ch.

177

Ch. Copper Coat's Prince Jeff A556267
(Ch. Copper Coat of Crosshaven-Becca Jane).

Ch. Coppercoat of the Hills A787100 (Ch. Copper Coat's Prince Jeff-Serena).

Tattersall Tenaj contained 3 champions: Amber, Clanceen and Tweed. The 2 last named dogs were also Bermuda champions.

STILES, DAVID F. & JOAN (Commodore), Bartlett, Ill.
Ch. Tyronne Farm Patricia.

STINES, BUCK & LA VERNE (County Cork), San Francisco, Cal.
See field trial chapter.

STOLL, DR. SELMA, Canoga Park, Cal.
Ch. Flash Back of Varagon (Ch. Innisfair Color Scheme CD-Ch. Innisfail Best Regards CDX) won Best in Show at Santa Barbara in 1964 with 2106 dogs in competition.

STUMPF, WOLFRAM C. & FRIEDA (Marflow), Painesville, O.
Wolfram started in 1931 with Swampland Sally, his pride and joy, his early hunting companion. Bred to a son of Ch. Tyrone Terry, Sally had an unusual litter of 13 males. Wolfram has enjoyed the individual personalities of his various Irishmen, among which are Marflow Susan, Ch. Marflow Red Defender and Sulhamstead Nell D'Or. He became interested in field trials in 1951, and now judges both field trials and conformation. "Show dogs that hunt" is his slogan and a dual champion is his ambition.

SVETLIK, LOUISE (Modder Rhu), Brunswick, Ohio.
Ch. Tyronne Farm Shamus.

SWANSON, DR. RAYMOND B. & CAROL (Galruadh), St. Paul, Minn.
Brookwillow's Memento CDX, Ch. Yorkhill's Top Gallant and End O'Maine Sumac.

SWARTZ, MERRITT M. & DORIS (Laurel Ridge), Canton, Mass.
In 1951, Ch. Honors Even Rakish Jane had an Independence Day litter which contained the famous Am. & Can. Ch. Laurel Ridge Star Rocket, Bombshell and Firecracker. Other Laurel Ridge champions are Paddy O'Shea, Doll-Baby and Digaluppins. Both Rocket and Paddy have very impressive bench show records.

TAYLOR, RONALD R. & RENEE (Kamron), Reseda, Cal.
The Taylors' first Irish Setter, Manorvue Magnificent, was ob-

Ch. Crosshaven O'Hollywood Hills A822762 (Ch. Rufus of Hollywood Hills-Ch. Faig-a-Baile of Crosshaven).

Ch. Margevan's Young McCabe S277116 (Ch. End O'Maine McCabe-Ch. Kleiglight's Echo of Red Dawn).

tained from Dr. A. C. Foster in 1944. They own Am. & Mex. Ch. Legend of Varagon UDT & Mex. PCE and 2 other obedience titlists.

TEEGARDEN, WALTER T., Littleton, Colo.
Ch. Red Arrow Show Guardian Rufus CD, Ch. Kinvarra Flicker and Ch. Kilkara Redwing.

TERRY, JACK H. & JEAN (Treasure Trove), Naperville, Ill.
Crown Gold of Treasure Trove CDX was one of Terry's first obedience title winners. They raised a number of bench champions from End O'Maine Claret and from Ch. Kinvarra Mary Eileen CD, Best of Breed at Morris & Essex in 1957. Ch. Treasure Trove's Pirate Pearl CD, owned by Sam Lugonja, has been shown extensively on the West Coast.

THOMPSON, WILLIAM C. & HELEN (Red Hills), Minneapolis, Minn.
Bill has owned Irish Setters for more than 40 years, raised an occasional litter and shot over his own dogs.

THOMSEN, DR. FREDERICK H. & PENNY, Lakewood, Cal.
It is said that Ch. Webline Zephyr gave birth to 2 puppies of the "S" litter of 8 in a station wagon while travelling in the middle lane during rush hour traffic on Lakewood Freeway on the way to the veterinarian. Ch. Webline Sir Mark, Sensation, Sindy CD, Senator and Shamrock were in this litter, sired by Ch. Weblyn Mystic Mark and representing a double cross to Ch. Innisfail Color Scheme CD.

THRASHER, MAURICE M. & RUTH (Baldpate), Boxford, Mass.
The Thrashers bred 3 Baldpate champions and owned the field trial winner, Sharoc's Colleen of Baldpate.

TOBIN, THOMAS N. & JEANNE, Garden Grove, Cal.
The late Ch. Webline Zircon produced 10 puppies of the "Q" litter by Am. & Can. Ch. Cherry Point Brask in September 1963. The Tobins also own Ch. Weblyn Scarlet Saber.

VALIQUETTE, MYRON E. & ROSEMARY (Valmar), Flat Rock, Mich.
Tulla O'Dea CD and Ch. Sunny Holiday of Valmar are the

Ch. Caldene Mickey Mischief A696696
(Ch. Milson O'Boy II-Jordan Farm
Molly).

Ch. Thenderin Maximillian SA46415
(Thenderin Wind-Warrior-Dorkin Cloud).

foundation brood bitches from which the 5 Valmar champions descended. Ch. Cherokee Chief of Valmar and Ch. Valmar's Robin Rocket are best known. Myron Valiquette died in 1964.

WAGNER, RONALD V. & BEV, St. Paul, Minn.
Ch. End O'Maine Bandana.

WALKER, L. DALE & IRENE (O'Lannon), Menomonee Falls, Wis.
In addition to the O'Lannon field-trial setters previously mentioned, 10 or more obedience titlists and a number of bench champions have been campaigned by the Walkers, including Ch. Shanty Kate, D. Ch. Titian Duke, Ch. Mahogany's Grand-Slam Flirt and others.

WALLIS, B. BAIRD (Brenwood), Deerfield, Ill.
Ch. Hotze's Red Rose, a great brood matron and the dam of 11 champions, had a litter which contained 4 champions: Brenwood's Rhythm, B. Starfire, B. Red Knight and B. Kingpin. Rose is also the dam of the Sunny Acre champions: Sir Jeffrey, Lady Beth and Top o' the Mark.

WALSH, LESLIE A. B. & HELEN (Waterford), Monrovia, Cal.
A dozen or more Waterford champions have been prominent through the years since 1930, including W. Bronze Monarch, Comet, Red Pat, Margaret Ruth, Sally, Coolan and others. Helen Walsh is highly regarded as a dog show judge.

WATTS, THOMAS B., Austin, Tex.
Red Diabol's Dancing Flame.

WAY, DR. ROBERT F. & MARY (Windsor), Levittown, Pa.
Windsor Brilliant Challenge, W. Michael Son O'Kelly and Dariabar Adonia.

WEBB, CLAYTON R. & MADELINE (Webline), El Monte, Cal.
The Weblyn prefix originally used by Clayton R. Webb and Averil H. Rosslyn was later changed to Webline. In 1952, Dick Webb got Ch. Innisfail Color Scheme CD (Ch. Seaforth's Dark Rex-Thenderin Champagne) as a puppy from Roy Jerome, showed the dog and studded him until he was retired at 9 years of age. Then Pat spent his later years in comfort at the home of Ernest and Virginia Lewis. Pat's bench record is very

183

Ch. Coppercountry Brian O'Boy S595310 (Ch. Seaforth's Dark Rex-Ch. Coppercountry Trilby).

Ch. Thenderin Trailblazer SA204648 (Thenderin Chaparal Genie-Thenderin Mame of Ellandale).

impressive; he won the Irish Setter Club of Southern California specialty show 3 times and received several special awards from the parent club. But it is as the sire of 25 champions that he is most renowned. Pat stamped his get with great style, substance and beauty—long lean heads, dark mahogany coats and strong running gear. He was the prepotent sire of 10 uniform litters from different bitches. From Ch. Thenderin Heigh-Ho CDX came the "L" litter with Ch. Weblyn Limelite CD, Ch. W. Luminous Lass and others. From Ch. Knightscroft Erin McCuhl came four noted champions: W. Madrigal, Masterpiece, Mystic Mark and Mi Golden Flame. Then there was the famous "Z" litter from Am. & Mex. Ch. Thenderin Valentine CD & PC containing 6 champions: Webline Zamara, Zeason Ticket, Zephyr, Zingaro, Zircon and Zodiac. Mention should also be made on the half-brother and sister mating of Pat and Ch. Innisfail Best Regards CDX, which resulted in the noted Ch. Flash Back of Varagon, Ch. Enchantment of Varagon and Am. & Mex. Ch. Legend of Varagon UDT & PC. It seemed that every litter sired by Pat was superior and his progeny have continued to carry on. There are the younger dogs such as: Ch. Webline Golden Jubilee CD, Am. & Mex. Ch. W. Winning Way CD & PC, Ch. W. Wizard of Micapa, Ch. W. Sir Mark, Ch. W. Valorous Piper CD, Ch. W. Very Coppercountry, Ch. W. Rio Hondo and many others. On several occasions Dick Webb, who handles dogs professionally, has received "Breeder of the Year" and "Litter Breeder" awards.

WELCH, KENNETH L. & ISABEL (Ki-Engirset), Northboro, Mass.
Ch. Ki-Engirset's Thunder Sargant and Ch. K. Prince of Flame.

WETTLE, ARTHUR H. & THELMA (Oak .Lynn), Coldwater, Mich.
Ch. Joe of Oak Lynn, Ch. Oak Lynn's Min-Jo, Ch. O. L. Tammy and Ch. O. L. Tam-O-Shanter.

WHEATLEY, FRANK & KATHERINE, South Rockwood, Mich.
If ever the Wheatleys were thrilled, it was at the Chicago International show in 1961, when their Ch. Conifer's Lance scored a spectacular Best in Show win with 2479 dogs in competition. In the big ring at the final judging this magnificent son of Ch.

Ch. Sergeant O'Shaun of Oak Grove S206313
(Ch. Charles River Color Sergeant-Ch. O'Shaungabragh's Lady).

Ch. Cill Choinnigh Paganach S43036
(Ch. Copper Coat of Crosshaven-Ruxton's Nora Mavourneen).

186

Ch. Thenderin Kismet A595307
(Ch. Seaforth's Dark Rex-Ch. Memory of Devon).

Ch. Margevan's Real McCoy S277117
(Ch. End O'Maine McCabe-Ch. Kleiglight's Echo of Red Dawn).

Ch. Thenderin Endorsement SA47454 (Thenderin
Sun Swift-Ch. Thenderin Benedictine).

(left) Ch. Coppercountry Trilby S241261; Ch. Waterford's Sally A814681.

Red Rogue of Maple Ridge and Can. Ch. Conifer's Princess Ace demonstrated to all the flowing style and grace of a great setter in action. In the weeks that followed, Lance added four straight Best in Show awards (5 total) to receive the Ch. Milson O'Boy Memorial Trophy. Lance died at the height of his career in 1962, but his 12 or more champion children carry on in various parts of America. The Wheatleys also owned Lance's sire, Ch. Red Rogue of Maple Ridge, which had an excellent show record. He sired 10 champions, including Ch. Les Va Will's Peggy O'Neil, Ch. Rogue's Molley O'Malley, Ch. Rogue's Darragh, Ch. Sunny Holiday of Valmar, Ch. Brazen Bridget of Englewood and others. The dam of Molley was a setter of lovely type, Am. & Can. Ch. Wildair Visionary Hour, which the Wheatleys got from Mrs. Drew in Toronto. They also own Ch. Caldene Ailene.

WHITE, CAROLE A. (Caroleigh), Washington, D.C.
Ch. Caroleigh Red Colt.

WILSEY, MYRON C. & CLAIRE, Los Angeles, Cal.
Am. & Can. Ch. Red Arrow Son of a Gun CD and the field trial winner, Lady Claire of Ardee.

WILSON, HOLLIS & JOSEPHINE (End O'Maine), Amherst, Wis.
See previous chapter.

WILSON, DR. JAMES B. & PHYLLIS (Cherry Point), Milltown, Wis.
Jim was raised with sporting dogs as his father, also a veterinarian, kept field dogs including Irish Setters. Even when he was in college Jim owned litters by Milson Superb and Ch. Red Helmet of Glen Ryan. Later there were litters by Red Barn Brierwood, Ch. Hedgewood Big Red, Ch. Tyronne Farm Malone, and others. The Wilsons mated their Ch. End O'Maine Encore to Ch. Thenderin Brian Tristan, producing the famous Am. & Can. Ch. Cherry Point Brask, Ch. C. P. Chukar and Ch. C. P. Hun. Brask is the sire of Ch. Cherry Point Brask II and Ch. Eldomac Senarc Rhu; and Chukar sired Ch. Cherry Point Ambush. The Wilsons own Ch. End O'Maine Morning Bird, one of the 7 champions in one litter by Ch. Carrvale's Terry Terhune ex End O'Maine Claret. Being interested in field

189

Ellair Red Thane A733639 (Ch. Tyronne
Farm Tyrone-Kendare Nano Nagle).

Ch. Bem's Superflame A968065 (Ch.
Copper Coat of Crosshaven-End
O'Maine Nola).

190

as well as bench, Jim also has field-trial winners that are descended from Fld. Ch. Ike Jack Kendrick.

WINEGORD, EVERETT O. & JEAN, Columbiana, Ohio.
Am. & Can. Ch. Argo Lane's Rixans Squire and Ch. Kilmacrenan Storm Lark.

WITT, GEORGE A. & IDA (O'Wit), Tangent, Ore.
One of the Witts' early setters was Coppercoat Rita O'Hagginwood, whelped in 1947. She was the great granddam of the recent champion, Scarlet Bronwyn O'Wit, through Am. & Can. Ch. Titian Tamya O'Wit and Ch. Scarlett Caprice O'Wit. Bronwyn is a daughter of Ch. Conifer's Lance. The Witts own Ch. Rogue Casey O'Wit and others.

WIXSON, LEONE H. (Coppercountry), Tucson, Ariz.
The foundation stock of Coppercountry was Ch. Waterford's Sally, bought as a puppy from Helen Walsh in 1944. Bred to Ch. Rufus of Hollywood Hills, Sally produced Ch. Coppercountry Trilby; and she to Ch. Seaforth's Dark Rex produced Ch. C. Brian O'Boy CD. Successive generations from O'Boy resulted in Ch. Mallyree's Red Regan CD and Ch. Coppercountry Claret CD. Leone owns Ch. Thenderin Endorsement and Ch. Webline Very Coppercountry.

WOODS, CATHERINE I. (Tekene), Stanton, N.J.
Ch. Tekene Aberdeen, Ch. Tekene Elysian and Ch. Tekene Honey.

WRIGHT, ORVILLE C. & ARNETT B. (Brianwood), Cincinnati, Ohio.
When the Wrights' Shaker Wood Flame was mated to Ch. Thenderin Brian Tristan in 1953, a litter containing 3 Brianwood champions resulted: Brianwood Gaelic Girl, B. Kerry Dancer and B. Queen Mab. The Wrights also own Ch. Brianwood Red Devil and Ch. Shawen's Cavalier.

Ch. Argo Lane Star of Dawn SA50121
(Ch. Argo Lane Independence-Ch. Argo Lane's Lady Dawn of Erin).

Ch. Westwind Scarlet Kismet S945061
(Westwind Scarlet Harvest-Westwind Scarlet Matchless).

192

10

Field Trials

T HE first Irish Setter to win a scheduled field trial according to available literature was Queen owned by Charles V. Kaeding, a San Francisco sporting goods dealer. It was a match race with four starters at $50 per entry, held in Marin County, California, in 1870.

Another purely local event was run October 8, 1874, a few miles from Memphis by the Tennessee State Sportsmen's Association. In the Free-For-All Stake with an entry of ten gundogs, H. C. Pritchett's black setter, Knight, placed first and J. H. Drew's red and white setter placed fourth.

The second Memphis trial the following year was a battle between the native bird dogs and the blue-blooded imports from Europe. Imported English Setters won all three places in the Puppy Stake; but the native red and white setter Tom (Joe-Buck Sr.), owned by George W. Campbell, Spring Hill, Tennessee, won the Free-For-All Champion Stake (5 starters).

Tom was a rugged dog with plenty of pace, range and class. Campbell, who handled him, was a big fellow with a voice to fit his size. As he walked through a cornfield he would fill his pockets with ears of corn. When Tom came tearing by, George would yell and fire an ear at him. Then Tom, a hard-headed rascal, would turn on

Double Jay 514167 FDSB
(Rusty's Jinx-Willow Winds Eve).

Willow Winds Hobo 516558 FDSB
(Rusty's Jinx-Willow Winds Eve).

more speed and get as far away as possible. This was the first Irish Setter to win a Championship Stake. He was said to be an excellent shooting dog and bevy finder. Colonel Hughes of Texas paid $300 for him, a good price in those days.

During the next summer many handlers trained their dogs on the Iowa and Minnesota prairies where there was a long open season with no bag limit on the plentful prairie chickens; and then they finished their dogs on quail in the South. So, at the 1876 Memphis trials there were 33 well broken entries in the four stakes that could find and point coveys as well as work carefully on singles. The trials were run on the five-point system, which scored merits and demerits with regard to pointing, backing, pace, style, quartering and retrieving. There were few bolters or backcasters in those days, because all the dogs were trained to turn out at the end of their casts and to sweep the course before them.

At the fourth annual Tennessee trials held on General Harding's Belle Meade Estate near Nashville, the famous English Setter Gladstone won the Puppy Stake and the native red setter, Joe Jr., owned by M. C. Campbell, won the Champion Stake (20 starters).

The battle between the blue bloods and the natives was reopened in 1878, at the fifth and last Tennessee Association trials when Joe Jr. and Adam's Drake tied for first place in the Champion Stake.

Probably the culmination of the feud was the two-day match race on quail at Florence, Alabama, in December 1879, when the native red setter, Joe Jr., defeated the renowned English Setter Gladstone by a score of 61 to 52 points. Joe was a fast dog with a wonderful nose and great bird sense. Bigger than average, he travelled with a long-stretching, wolf-like gait. He was red with a little white and was registered as an Irish Setter. His sire was the noted Irish Setter Ch. Elcho and his dam was the native cross-bred Buck Jr., (Old Joe-Buck Sr.) of the Campbell strain.

It was fairly common practise in the Seventies to interbreed the native stock and the purebred imports, or to cross-breed to improve hunting qualities. There were many well known cross-breds such as Colburn's Dash (English, Irish and Gordon), Waddell's Fanny (English, Irish and Gordon), Stoddard's Mar (Irish and Gordon), Valentine's Fanny (English and Gordon) and others.

The first prairie chicken trials were held at Hampton, Iowa on September 4, 1877. Berkley and Carrie II placed second and third in the Puppy Stake. A year later the second prairie chicken event was held at Sauk Center, Minnesota, a town made famous by Sinclair Lewis' *Main Street*. The imported Irish Setter Friend carried off the premier honors in the All-Age Stake.

During the next decade Ch. Elcho's progeny (Berkley, Raleigh, Jessie, Leigh Doane, Yoube and Bruce) were prominent in the trials of the Fishers Island, Eastern and Philadelphia Clubs. Raleigh, probably the best of them, placed second in the All-Age Stake at Robins Island in 1879. Since the trials were infrequent and open to all breeds, they evidently were highly competitive. The significant thing about this period was that the Irish Setter owners ran their bench dogs in the field trials and also used them as shooting dogs.

Max Wenzel, one of the founders of the Fishers Island Club and active in promoting the red setter afield, owned Ch. Tim, Ch. Yoube and Jersey Beauty. His Ch. Chief, a field trial winner, sired six field trial dogs of about average merit. J. S. McIntosh's Biz placed in two major circuit trials in the Midwest; Victoria and imported Desmond II won several All-Age Stakes in the vicinity of Philadelphia.

But field trials were not going too well for the Irish Setter. Like other breeds he had his ups and downs. In spite of an occasional win by an exceptional red dog, the trend for him was not bright. Until about 1890, he had competed with other breeds on even terms. As the number and popularity of field trials increased, Llewellin Setters and Pointers flourished. Imported in overwhelming numbers, they were bred solely for field trial use. "100% Llewellin" was all the rage; Rip Rap and Jingo were magic names! No longer was the all-purpose shooting dog in vogue. Field trials had changed, had become a specialized activity. With dogs worked from horseback, more emphasis was placed on speed and range. An early maturing dog, fast in getaway, wide going to locate many coveys and stylish on point was required. A dog had to be bred for all these qualities, and it was not sufficient that he just possess the instinct to hunt.

Because Irish Setters had not been bred to meet these new specifications, they lost out in major circuit competition. Hoping to improve the situation the breeders imported field stock like Finglas (Fingal III-Aveline) and his litter sister, Coleraine. The former was the Absolute Winner All-Age Stake, American Field Trial Club, 1892 (21 starters). Seven of his progeny placed in trials: Fingaln,

196

Loo, Currer Maud, Donoway, Flyaway, Nugget II and Lady Finglas.

The inaugural trials of the Irish Setter Club were held at High Point, North Carolina, on November 23, 1891. There were four annual Carolina trials at which the dogs of George E. Gray, Dr. Gwilym G. Davis and E. B. Bishop predominated. Gray was a professional trainer of field dogs, Davis was long the President of the Irish Setter Club and Bishop was proprietor of the Glenmore Kennels in Kansas.

When the breed trials were held again in 1907, Bell & Chappell's Rob Rollo won the Derby and the All-Age Stakes. The following year he placed in the Club trials, as did his kennelmates, St. Cloud's Blarney and Virginia Belle. It is also of note that a bitch named Hurrah won the Derby Stake at the Western Irish Setter Club trials of 1902.

In general, the picture for the first 20 years of the twentieth century was not encouraging, for according to the records there were only 18 Irish Setter field trial placements in open stakes during that period. Five of these wins were obtained by the Law strain dogs of F. A. Johnson of Detroit, who made a sincere effort to further the cause of the red setter afield.

It was during this era that the Fremont, Nebraska, fancier, Otto Pohl assembled his Donegal Kennels of Irish Setters with a similar purpose in mind. He was making good progress toward that goal when his death occurred in 1919. He had acquired the native hunting stock of the Midwest in Ch. Drug Law, Ch. Pat-A-Belle and McKerry. From the West Coast came Ch. St. Lambert's Caltra M and Donegal's Noreen, representing the old California hunting strains. In addition there were his English imports Ch. Rheola Clanderrick, Rheola Judy, Rheola Pedro and Morty Oge. The small, dark mahogany Pedro was reputedly the best field dog among them.

McKerry (Nebraska Ranger-Lyon's Kathline) ran in the Second Series, All-Age Stake (29 starters), American Field Trial Club, Aberdeen, South Dakota in 1914. Thereafter he became a popular sire and his name appears in the pedigrees of many later field trial dogs.

An important win for the breed was in the 1918 All-America Trials at Grand Junction, when Otto Pohl's Donegal's Alizon (Ch. Drug Law-Rheola Judy) placed third in the Derby Stake. She was the granddam of Elcova's Kinkie, which with her kennelmate Modoc Bedelia, placed in open competition at several Eastern trials.

Shady Crest Shawn 568867 FDSB (F.Ch. Ike Jack Kendrick-Willow Winds Kate).

F.Ch. Ike Jack Kendrick S790833 (Ike Kendrick-F.Ch. Askew's Carolina Lady).

Kinkie was sired by Donegal's Morty Oge and Bedelia by Morty Oge's King. Both bitches were owned and handled by the well known professional trainer Elias C. Vail.

A prefix to gain considerable notoriety about this time was "Smada," which spelled backwards referred to Dr. L. C. Adams, one of the early presidents of the Dayton Pointer Club. This sportsman, who had owned Irish Setters for thirty years, obtained the Donegal dogs after Pohl died; and he raised a few litters from them, in one of which was Donegal Morty Oge II (Donegal's Morty Oge-Donegal's Noreen). Morty II sired two champions, but his real claim to fame lay in being the sire of that famous little field trial winner, Smada Byrd.

Dr. Adams was the breeder of the litter whelped in 1921, from Killarney Babe of utility stock. J. Horace Lytle of Dayton, dog writer and field trial judge, obtained Byrd as a puppy, trained her, handled her in trials and cherished her until her death in 1935. Much of her success afield might be attributed to the bond of affection and mutual understanding which existed between the little setter and her master. The pride, joy, tribulations and triumphs of a field trial man are described by Lytle in his fascinating biography of Smada Byrd, *Breaking A Bird Dog* (1924). In her busy field trial career, Byrd placed in strong open competition at eight Class B Midwestern trials, which had a total of 139 starters. She had two litters sired by King, in the first of which was Smada Byrd's King, which was advertised at stud by Lytle for a number of years.

Some excellent field trial stock has come from Ireland. A popular import was Tipperary Eamon, brought to America by G. O. Smith in 1920. Everyone had a good word to say about this dog. In a short three-year period he sired 47 litters, which included four field trial winners: Tipperary Eamon's Ghost, Tipperary's Bell, Tipperary June and Queen Alizon.

Royal A. Ferris of Dallas campaigned Ch. Bran of Boyne, Ch. Saccy Redall and the field trial winners Red Hot, Vernon's Sport and Tipperary Eamon's Ghost. Red Hot had an impressive record in five Texas All-Age Stakes; but unfortunately his pedigree was unknown.

Ben M. Curtis of Tulsa ran McKerry's Pat, McKerry Pat's Dusty and Linda Louisa in the Oil Circuit trials. He also owned Red Law's Ghost and Ch. Belle's Anniversary. Then there were others from Oklahoma: J. D. Smith with Smith's Irish Pat, Tipperary's Bell, Flymac's Kate and Ch. Drug Ray Law; Fred X. Sulzbach with Okla Bess and Okla Tynie; J. A. Puryear with Ch. Hubbard's Max and Puryear's Rheola Judy; A. A. Scott with Ch. Sally Red Jacket; and O. T. Graham with Red Flag's Peggy and Sarsfield. Dr. Lloyd Thompson had Tipperary June, McKerry's Queen, Queen of Mc-Kerry, Dennis of Boyne and Auburn Prince, all of which were trained to the gun. Dennis, a small energetic fellow that posed in the show ring like a statue, died at four years of age with a bone in his esophagus. Dr. Thompson wrote an entertaining field trial story *King of Mapledale* (1927), featuring an Irish Setter hero.

Every part of the country had its field trial advocates. In California Irish Setters were represented for a number of years by the Valley View prefix of Dr. J. C. Negley of Los Angeles. His initial stock came from Dr. R. H. Washburn of Colorado, who raised ten litters from one pair of setters, his own Major Clanderrick and Patsy Jane Law. Negley obtained Valley View Peggy from one of these matings and bred her to Duke Clanderrick, thereby making a double cross to imported Ch. Rheola Clanderrick. Thus came to be Valley View Jiggs, the prolific sire of more than 200 registered dogs from 46 bitches. The fact that one third of his puppies bore the name of "Jiggs" is an excellent example that advertising pays, for this setter was widely publicized as a producer of field dogs. Perhaps the greatest of his offspring was Ch. Valley View Pat, a bench champion as well as a field trial winner. Other progeny of note were Valley View Ruddy, Valley View Butterfly, Valley View Hogan and Valley View Dinty.

About 1932, the new field trial rules of the American Kennel Club became effective. To acquire the title of field champion, a setter had to obtain a total of ten points by winning first place at approved field trials, the number of points per stake being based on the number of starters in the stake. Under the *American Field* rules, the winner of a designated championship stake was referred to as a field trial· champion, but if the dog's performance was not considered of championship calibre, the title was withheld by the judges.

The turn of events at this period more or less classified the Irish Setter field trial dogs in to those that placed in restricted breed trials and those that won in open competition against Pointers,

English Setters and other breeds. Very few Irish Setters competed in the major circuit trials, but there was a marked increase in the number of entries in Irish Setter Stakes at the all-breed trials and the specialty club events. About this time the Western Pointer and Setter Club, Jersey Irish Setter Club, Irish Setter Club of Southern California, Irish Setter Club of New England and others held field trials.

The Irish Setter Club of America, which renewed its field trial program in 1927, had an impressive list of first place winners in the All-Age Stakes of the pre-war years: (Starting in 1934, there were two trials per year)

1927	Gibbs' Carolina Queen
1928	Ch. Elcova's Terence McSwiney
1929	Ch. Cloudburst Red
1930	Ch. Cloudburst Red
1931	Ch. Elcova's Admiration
1933	F. Ch. Elcova McTybe
1934	Sussex Millie
	F. Ch. Tipperary McKerry
1935	F. Ch. Elcova McTybe
	F. Ch. Elcova McTybe
1936	F. Ch. Tipperary McKerry
	F. Ch. Tipperary McKerry
1937	Ruxton's Rhu Brenda
	F. Ch. Clodagh McTybe of the Cloisters
1938	Brian McTybe of the Cloisters
	F. Ch. Clodagh McTybe of the Cloisters
1939	F. Ch. Uncle Ned R
	Skyline Ephraim
1940	F. Ch. Uncle Ned R
	F. Ch. Shaun McTybe of the Cloisters
1941	Brownie
	F. Ch. Shaun McTybe of the Cloisters
1942	Boots of Arlington
	Brownie

F. Ch. Elcova McTybe (Ch. Elcova's Terence McSwiney-Modoc Bedelia), the first Irish Setter field champion under the new American Kennel Club rules, sired seven field trial winners: F. Ch. Shaun

Taylor's Whirlaway Pat SA338559 (F.Ch. Ike Jack Kendrick-Willow Winds Kate).

Likely's Mr. Casey 553743 FDSB (Colonel Red of Coronado Hites-Winnie).

McTybe of the Cloisters, F. Ch. Clodagh, Brian, Dail, Dick, Tyron (all of the Cloisters) and McTybe's McSwiney. Mac's career afield was somewhat restricted because he had heart worms; but in spite of this handicap he had a good record. Another Berolzheimer dog, Rufus McTybe O'Cloisters (Brian McTybe of the Cloisters-McSwiney's Style), placed in about a dozen Open Shooting Dog Stakes. He was best known as being the Runner-up in the 1950 National Amateur Pheasant Championship.

A consistent winner at a score of Eastern trials in open competition over a ten-year period was J. H. Graham's Duke IX of Canadian breeding. Among the noted Hibernian color-bearers from Massachusetts was Sally of Kildare, owned by Patrick W. Hehir, who also had Polly of Kildare, Lassie of Kildare and Bright Eyes O'Kildare.

H. A. Simms' F. Ch. Tipperary McKerry (Skyline Valley's Red-Betsy McKerry) had more than a dozen field trial wins, most of which were in open competition with other breeds. Another field Irish Setter of similar bloodlines was Skyline Ephraim (Skyline Tex-Princess McKerry's Pat), owned by the noted Pennsylvania judge, Thomas M. Marshall. Charles M. Coale's Lehigh Pat, a grandson of Rheola Pedro and Donegal's Morty Oge II, was a favorite of Pennsylvania sportsmen. Then there was F. Ch. Uncle Ned R (Chamois R-R. Belle), owned by Alvin R. Bush. Among his contemporaries were Padriag Reddleman, Wheeler's Rusty, Niall of Aileach, Paul's Andy and Judge Red Pal of Oakdene. Jack Spear's Tyrone Farm Lady placed in several Open All-Age Stakes at Missouri Valley trials. Other winners from his kennels included Tyronne Farm Collette, Malone, O'Flare, Red Robin and Monahan. On the West Coast, Mason's Bridget O'Flynn was a well known field trial Irish Setter.

The Sulhamstead Kennels of Mrs. Florence Nagle of England, which bred so many splendid field trial setters from 1925 to 1965, were represented in American trials of the pre-war period by Sulhamstead Beppo D'Or and Sulhamstead Trace D'Or, both imported by Ernest D. Levering.

S. L. Taylor, Mount Sterling, Kentucky, owned a prepotent sire of good field stock called Joffre Rookwood (Appreciation Joffre-Walters' Fay), an honest-to-goodness bird dog, big going, with brains and bird sense. He would rapidly cover a 40-acre field and

(front) Valli Hi Town 677657 FDSB; Valli Hi Country 677656 FDSB.

Vanita's Wild Gael 724190 FDSB (Mr. O'Leary-Tara O'Shadycrest).

snap decisively into a stylish point on locating quail. His owner posted "a $1000 wager against any Irishman his age as a shooting dog in the field"—and no one ever challenged it. Joffre was solid red, compact in build and about 24 inches at the shoulder. Although he himself was never entered in field trials, he was the sire of eight field trial winners. His progeny must have numbered several hundred, for most American-bred shooting dogs of the Fifties had him as an ancestor. In fact later on, Taylor sold numerous puppies sired by Joffre's great grandson Rookwood's Field Master and out of Trace D'Or's Belle, a daughter of Sulhamstead Trace D'Or.

There were certain breeders in various parts of the country who bred and sold Irish Setters shooting dogs without much regard to their bench qualifications. These persons, recognizing the fundamental importance of intensity, style and staunchness on point in a gun dog, used only certain hunting strains. The blood of McKerry, Morty Oge, Rheola Clanderrick, Tipperary Eamon, Raneagown, Smada Byrd, Rufus McTybe O'Cloisters, Chieftain Law, Joffre Rookwood and many others seemed to carry the instinct to point and to retrieve naturally from land and water; also Jordan Farm Abe was considered a good dog to have in any pedigree.

Among those breeders of field stock were W. J. Thayer, Bergen, N.Y. with Skyline Tobias; Mrs. Beatrice Everett, Atkinson, Neb. with Everett's Irish Skipper; Les Blackwell, Sacramento, Calif. with Sulhamstead Major D'Or; E. A. Smith, Clover, S. C. with Tipperary Smada King; Bill Duncan, Weston, Mo. with Boyne's Carolina Pat; J. E. Hill, Ward, Ark. with Hill's Rambling Red; Earl Bond, Albert Lea, Minn. with Kentucky Bill, etc.

In the early Fifties a group of sportsmen was organized under the banner of the National Red Setter Field Trial Club for the purpose of promoting the Irish Setter afield. Among the members were A. E. Church, A. E. Bortz, R. C. Baynard, Herm David, W. E. LeGrande, J. G. Cassidy, J. T. Clifton, John Van Alst, Charles Winter, T. P. Ward, Robert & James Finn, D. L. Martin and others. They held semi-annual field trials for the red dog alternately in Delaware and Ohio, the first event being on April 13, 1952.

Winners of the Open Shooting Dog Stakes in the early trials included Cedar Bluff Paddy, High Point Captain McKerry and Tippy Tipperary McKerry.

(left) Can.D.Ch. Elmcroft Mahogany Sue 182455 CKC; Can.Ch. Red Echo of Ardee 187503 CKC; Red Lady of Ardee 191875 CKC.

Lady Billy of Ardee 216575 CKC (Can.Ch. Red Echo of Ardee-Can.D.Ch. Elmcroft Mahogany Sue).

The first National Red Setter Open Shooting Dog Championship Stake, run on October 17, 1953, was won by Askew's Carolina Lady (Kentucky Bill-Poker Faced Alice), although the title was withheld. In spite of the fact that Lady failed to obtain the championship crown on this occasion, she gave many fine performances in her long career, and later was awarded the title of AKC field champion. She won at least 28 stakes, most of them in open competition, defeating more than 300 dogs.

Her forte was not only in winning at trials—she did that in between litters—but it was as the great producing dam of 15 field trial winners and the granddam of many more. She had six litters by Ike Kendrick, Ike Jack Kendrick, Willow Winds Duke and Willow Winds Hobo.

Lady, a key bitch in the Willow Winds breeding program of Ned LeGrande, was bred by Earl Bond, Albert Lea, Minnesota, from a mating that was repeated six times. Her sire was from the Rookwood Kennels of S. L. Taylor in Kentucky and her dam represented Minnesota and Western Illinois hunting stock. She had the ability to convey to her offspring that quality of exceptional style on point for which she was famous. It is said that she even stamped her progeny with a few white hairs on the chin as though they were her trademark.

The most noted of her sons was F. Ch. Ike Jack Kendrick, the winningest Irish Setter in field trials, having placed in 66 stakes. He never was started in the Puppy and Derby Stakes; most of his wins were obtained in Open Shooting Dog Stakes.

"Happy Jack," as he was called, was a plucky, little, perfectly trained shooting dog that possessed great heart and a most appealing personality. Afield he was conscientious and thorough, exhibiting unusual endurance and stamina. Like his dam, he pointed and backed with high style. Appearancewise, he was a small, compact, dark red setter, strong in loin and hard as nails.

At least 30 bitches were mated to Jack, some of which had several litters sired by him. The records of his 40 or more field trial winning get are evidence of his great worth to the breed. Among these get are such well known ones as F. Ch. Windyridge Tammy, Shooting Dog Ch. Lady's Queen, Shadycrest Shawn, Taylor's Whirlaway Pat, Moffat's Apache Bill, Thorleen and others with impressive field trial wins. The progeny by Jack out of F. Ch. Askew's Carolina

Lady, Lady's Colleen and Willow Winds Kate, seemed to be especially successful at the trials. It is fortunate that several of Jack's sons have carried on as producing sires, including in addition to those named previously, Bruns Red Ike, Draherin Lord Kendrick, Phil's Red Ike, Mike's Jack Dandy, Cherry Point Nickjack, Lady's Last Son, etc.

Besides Lady and Jack, LeGrande owned Willow Winds Smada and Citation Lass of Ardee as foundation stock in his Willow Winds Kennels at Douglassville, Pennsylvania. Then with the infusion of early American hunting strains, represented by Royal Red Patrick of Erin and that old campaigner Rusty's Jinx, he began his breeding program. About 1955, he imported for outcross purposes Sulhamstead Norse D'Or (Shane) from Mrs. Florence Nagle of England; and found afterward that some of the same Sulhamstead blood occurred in the background of his F. Ch. Askew's Carolina Lady.

With the cooperation of the National Red Setter Club and other sportsmen in various sections of the country, the LeGrande setters and their progeny became popular field trial dogs. In the thirteen years following 1952, these dogs placed in more than 500 recognized field trials by actual count.

What a far reaching accomplishment this is! The Irish Setter is indeed a worthy competitor to be reckoned with in the field trial game. Such prefixes are prominent as Tweedhall, Byrdfield, Highpoint, Davant, Springwillow, Gaythorn, Windyhill, Windyridge, Kopper Key, Murcrest, Barton Creek, Magnolia Run, Schnets, Shady Crest, Autumn Hills, Coopers, Turkey Talk, Erin, Valli Hi, Marflow, County Clare, Draherin, Cherry Point and many more.

While space does not permit an account of every dog, mention should be made of some of them. Particularly impressive are the numerous wins of Shooting Dog Champion Willow Winds Hobo and Willow Winds Cathy in Puppy and Derby Stakes at open competition trials. The fact that Hobo lost the sight of one eye due to spear grass while training on the Canadian prairies did not seem to handicap his performance afield.

The Dude (Willow Winds Duke-F. Ch. Askew's Carolina Lady), owned by Herm David, sired seven field trial winners, including F. Ch. Fyn. Others of note include Mr. Mack Triplett, Mr. Finnigan, Mr. O'Malley and Mr. Mulligan. Mr. O'Leary (Willow Winds

Hobo-F. Ch. Askew's Carolina Lady), a Shooting Dog Champion owned by F. C. Bean, Athens, Ohio, turned in many a consistent field trial performance over a ten-year period. As a sire he stamps his progeny not only with field ability but also with short coupled loin and high tail placement.

Another Shooting Dog Champion, Autumn Hills Duke (Mr. O'Leary-Redfield Ginger), owned by the late Frederick A. Kremer of Minneapolis, has a long list of field trial wins, mostly in open competition. He received the *Sports Afield* All American Award three times. Fred, who owned Irish Setters since 1936, was dedicated to the progress of the red setter afield. After his death in 1964, his wife Ruth continued the Autumn Hills Kennels.

Ralph C. (Rusty) Baynard's Double Jay (Rusty's Jinx-Willow Winds Eve) won the Shooting Dog Championship twice, in 1955 and again in 1957. This fast, wide-going dog was trained in open country on native quail. He was the prepotent sire of at least a dozen field trial winners, including Son of Double Jay, Valli Jay Hi and several of the G. Wood Smith Windyhill dogs. Baynard also owned Rusty's Jinx, which placed in ten stakes.

The Valli Hi setters of David and Jane Hasinger of Philadelphia have been prominent in trials for many years. Their F. Ch. Valli Hi Lacey well deserved her title, having at least 20 field trial placements. Valli Jay Hi also assembled a good record. When these two dogs were mated, two field trial winners resulted, Rhapsody owned by Paul Whiteman and Tax Free by Thomas McCahill. Then when the Hasingers bred their Ike's Lady Pride (F. Ch. Ike Jack Kendrick-F. Ch. Askew's Carolina Lady) to F. Ch. Sulhamstead Norse D'Or, four Valli Hi field trial setters of great merit were produced: Counselor, Country, Esquire and Town.

F. Ch. Sulhamstead Norse D'Or placed in 41 stakes, mostly in open competition. He was runner-up in the 1959 Middle Atlantic States Regional Shooting Dog Classic (31 starters) and he won the April 1962 National Red Setter Championship Stake (title withheld). This popular stud dog is credited with siring no less than 21 field trial winners, including the Valli Hi foursome, two from F. Ch. Miller's Bonnie Loo, four from McGovern's Kerry O'Red, three from Betty J. Schneider's Rustic Lady III and two from John Lane's The Babe. His get inherited his good looks and his strong running style afield.

F.Ch. Lady Bronze S947981 (F.Ch. Mahogany Friction II-Brown Sugar).

D.Ch. Titian Duke S850878 (Mahogany Tim II-King Size Scarlet Lady).

One of Shane's sons is the field trial winner, Schnet's Little Red, owned by Retired Marine Lt.-Col. Edward L. Schnettler, St. Cloud, Minnesota. Ed has had Irish Setters since the 1930's; and the Schnet prefix appears in the names of many well known dogs, such as Schnet's Hellfire, S. Rufus of Havelock, S. Timuquana Jackie, S. Beau, S. Joe C, S. Tara, S. Darky and others. More than a score of field trial winners have come from his kennels, representing the bloodlines of Rufus McTybe O'Cloisters, Wheeler's Red Boy, Willow Winds Hobo, Ike Jack Kendrick and Mr. O'Leary.

About 1960, James R. and Lil Lewis, Georgetown, Kentucky, acquired The Golden Doll (Schnet's Hellfire-Bridey Murphy) and her half-brother, Mighty Red Man, from B. C. Cotton. They also obtained Erin's Sally (Mr. O'Leary-F. Ch. Pride of Millis) from J. G. Cassidy. From this stock a number of field trial winners have been produced, including Mighty Fawn, Diamond, Golden Hoss Colt, Mighty Gale and others.

Mighty Fawn, purchased by Ernest J. Lewis of Los Angeles in 1962, won the Midwestern Red Setter Open Shooting Dog Championship title in October 1964, under the guidance of the noted West Coast professional trainer, Stanley Head. He has trained and handled other E. J. Lewis setters, including F. Ch. Oxton's Shosaphine, County Clare's McCool and County Clare's Shandy (Mr. O'Leary-F. Ch. Windyridge Tammy). Shandy won the Midwestern Red Setter Open Championship title in October 1965.

Shooting Dog Champion Mr. O'Leary with over 40 field trial placements and F. Ch. Windyridge Tammy with more than 45 are owned by Fred C. Bean, who also has Moffat's Apache Bill and Windyridge Vixen. W. S. Cooper's best known setters are Cooper's Hollyberry Scarlet and Cooper's Tennessee Riley. D. E. Bruns has Bruns Red Ike and Bruns Rusty Hobo. Daniel and Marion Pahy have Kerry's Kevin O'Red and Kerry's Kathleen O'Red. Thomas and Marge Moffat own Moffat's Red Flame, M. Red Mickey and M. Red Jack.

In the trials of the Santa Caligon Irish Setter Club at Kansas City, there are such well known red setters as Likely's Mr. Casey (T. J. Likely), Shady Crest Shawn (D. L. Johnson), Taylor's Whirlaway Pat (H. J. Taylor), Patty of Mission (Wiley Jewel), Tara O'Shadycrest and Vanita's Wild Gael (Dr. & Mrs. J. S. Van Wye).

The Irish Setter Club of Minnesota has held 18 field trials since

211

1956. Some of the winners are: Son O'Double Jay, Lady's Last Son, Wilson's Red Dot (D. W. Wilson), Sarnia Red (R. L. Swanson), Cherry Point Nickjack (Dr. J. B. Wilson), Shooting Dog Ch. Autumn Hills Duke (F. A. Kremer), Draherin Lord Kendrick (L. J. Myers), Double Jet (W. Johnson), Peet's Rusty Maverick (D. S. Peet) and Ric O'Double Jay (A. W. Anderson).

In summarizing the activities of the National Red Setter Club it is desirable to list those setters which have been awarded field trial championships.

National Red Setter Club Open Shooting Dog Champions

DATE	IRISH SETTER	FDSB #	SIRE	DAM
10–30–55	Double Jay	(d) 514167	(Rusty's Jinx—Willow Winds Eve)	
11–17–56	Willow Winds Hobo	(d) 516558	(Rusty's Jinx—Willow Winds Eve)	
4–13–57	Double Jay	(d) 514167	(Rusty's Jinx—Willow Winds Eve)	
11– 7–58	Lady's Queen	(b) 558165	(Ike Jack Kendrick—Lady's Colleen	
4–13–63	Autumn Hills Duke	(d) 579956	(Mr. O'Leary—Redfield Ginger)	
4–11–64	Mr. O'Leary	(d) 543749	(Willow Winds Hobo—Askew's Carolina Lady)	
10–17–64	Mighty Fawn	(b) 648590	(Mighty Red Man—Erin's Sally)	
10–16–65	County Clare's Shandy	(d) 673198	(Mr. O'leary—Windyridge Tammy)	

The Irish Setter made great progress also in field trials conducted under American Kennel Club rules and held by specialty clubs in various sections of the country. At these events thirty one Irish Setters have won the title of AKC Field Champion. Four of them have been awarded both bench and field championships. The first one to become a dual champion was B. & F. Ch. Tyrone's Mahogany Mike CDX, bred and owned by "Mr. Field Trial Himself" Edgar W. McIvor, Plymouth, Michigan. During the period from 1952 to 1960, Mike placed in two dozen stakes against strong competition in Michigan, Indiana, Ohio, Delaware and New England. He sired four bench champions and at least 23 field trial winners, including F. Ch. Miller's Bonnie Loo, F. Ch. Ivor Glen Devilera, Ivor Glen's Red Hellion, Ch. Red Arrow Smooth Sailing and others. Because of his likable personality, Mike was greatly missed by all when he died in June 1965 at the age of fourteen years.

Another famous dual champion died in 1965, B. & F. Ch. Red Arrow Show Girl UDT, which won the top titles in field, obedience

212

and bench, plus a Mexican PC degree (comparable to CD). Owned by Lawrence and Eleanor Heist, Fontana, California, she was whelped in 1953. Although she placed in twenty field trial stakes, she was best known as being the dam of eight bench champions, all obedience trial winners. Two of them were sired by D. Ch. Tyrone's Mahogany Mike and the other six were in a litter by Am. & Can. Ch. Esquire of Maple Ridge. Four of the latter litter also won Canadian championships: Red Arrow Solid Gold, Smart Guy, Sportsman's Guide and Son of a Gun.

AKC Irish Setter Field Champions

1-1-66

Askew's Carolina Lady (b) S-744906
    (Kentucky Bill—Poker Faced Alice)
Clodagh McTybe of the Cloisters (b) A-58519
    (Elcova McTybe—Queen of Style)
Countess Suzanne II (b) SA-146451
    (Sulhamstead Norse D'Or—Rustic Lady III)
*County Cork's Red Knight UD (d) S-963747
    (Greenhill's County Cork Count—Green Hill's Countess Colleen)
Elcova McTybe (d) 861800
    (Elcova's Terence McSwiney—Modoc Bedelia)
Emerald Isle Angel (b) SA-129638
    (Sulhamstead Norse D'Or—The Babe)
Fyn (d) S-864998 (The Dude—Lee Mac)
Ike Jack Kendrick (d) S-790833
    (Ike Kendrick—Askew's Carolina Lady)
Ivor Glen Devilera (b) S-767874
    (Tyrone's Mahogany Mike—Ivor Glen's Red Hellion)
Jackson Brook Angler's Rusty (d) 501054 FDSB
    (Boy Angler—Puddy O'Boyne)
Lady Bronze (b) S-947981
    (Mahogany Friction II—Brown Sugar)
Mahogany Friction II CDX (d) S-791628
    (Mahogany Tim II—King Size Scarlet Lady)
Miller's Bonnie Loo (b) S-812666
    (Tyrone's Mahogany Mike—Lady La Rouge)
Miller's Tiger Lily (b) SA-122339
    (Sulhamstead Norse D'Or—Miller's Bonnie Loo)
O'Lannon Copper Penny CD (b) SA-79827
    (Mahogany Friction II—Shanty Kate III)
Oxton's Shosaph (d) S-230817
    (Oxton's Irish Perfection—Oxton's Imp O'Erin)
Oxton's Shosaphine (b) S-969039
    (Oxton's Shosaph—Tir Na N Og Merrymike Larkey)
Pride of Erin IV (b) S-511832
    (Rufus McTybe O'Cloisters—Rockwood Sally)
*Dual Champion

213

(left) Ch. Runwild Finnola the Fay SA72688; Ch. Runwild Fiona S942236; Molly Coddled Mayhem SA48633; Ch. Runwild Finnagain SA72690.

Ch. Runwild Finnola the Fay SA72688 (Ch. Carrvale's Terry Terhune-Ch. Runwild Fiona).

*Red Arrow Show Girl UDT (b) S-595678
  (Hollywood Hills O'Shaughnesy—Marted Annie Rooney)
Seamus of Green Fields (d) SA-6245
  (Guinea Gold of Aragon—Shanty Kate III)
Sharon IV (b) S-320518
  (Red Star of Hollywood Hills—Red Shadow)
Shaun McTybe of the Cloisters (d) A-58520
  (Elcova McTybe—Queen of Style)
Sulhamstead Norse D'Or (d) SA-55526
  (Sulhamstead Montebellos Norseman—Sulhamstead Banco D'Or)
Tam of Ballarrel CD (d) SA-74823
  (Carrvale's Commodore—Duchess Gore of Ballarrell)
Tipperary McKerry (d) 828668
  (Burns' Valley's Red—Betsy McKerry)
*Titian Duke CD (d) S-850878
  (Mahogany Tim II—King Size Scarlet Lady)
*Tyrone's Mahogany Mike CDX (d) S-452547
  (Lord Tyrone Trent—McIvor's Kathleen)
Uncle Ned R (d) A-216064
  (Chamois R—R. Belle)
Valli Hi Lacey (b) 551851 FDSB
  (Tyrone Red Laddie II—Little Red Lady)
Van's Cindy (b) 528761 FDSB
  (Rusty's Jinx—Willow Winds Smada)
Windyridge Tammy (b) 580789 FDSB
  (Ike Jack Kendrick—Van's Cindy)
*Dual Champion

The third Irish Setter winner of the triple crown, B. & F. Ch. Titian Duke CD, owned by Michael Eberhardt, was bred by Mrs. Irene M. Walker of Milwaukee. Duke is one of five Wisconsin field champions having the prepotent Mahogany Tim II either as a sire or as a grandsire: Lady Bronze, Mahogany Friction II, O'Lannon Copper Penny, Seamus of Green Fields and Titian Duke. Tim II was by Ch. Charles River Color Sergeant ex Small Change, which came from a long line of experienced Midwestern shooting dogs such as Jahudi, Terry of Hurst, Jamerook and Judy V, which in turn trace back to Joffre Rookwood, Valley View Jiggs and F. Ch. Elcova McTybe.

The Walkers' O'Lannon Kennels started in the Forties with a bitch called Lady Left Over. Through the years since then they have produced dual type Irish Setters, some of which were also successful in obedience trials. Among twenty or more dogs bearing the Mahogany prefix in field trials, the following are probably the best known: F. Ch. Mahogany Friction II, Ch. Mahogany's Grand-Slam

Flirt, M. Mr. Duffy, M. Red Stone, M. Sue, M. Sweet Briar and M. Titian Jingo.

B. & F. Ch. County Cork's Red Knight UD, owned by Buck and LaVerne Stines, San Francisco, is the fourth Irish Setter to win titles in field, obedience and bench competition. His bloodlines, which trace back to old California hunting stock, are different than those of any other field champion. Red has placed in no less than 18 field trial stakes, most of which were at the Irish Setter Club of the Pacific trials.

This club, which was organized in 1945, held its first field trials in 1949. During the years since then there have been some outstanding field dogs: F. Ch. Oxton's Shosaph (J. D. Huizenga), Ch. Patrick of Ide (R. R. Mann), Red Spark's Titian Rose (W. J. Cunningham), Duke of Dublin IV (W. L. White), Irish Jig (J. Splendid), La-Honda's Danny Boy (D. H. Smith), Ch. Easy's Moonyean Claire (G. McVickers), Fancy Dan (E. Westervelt), Sprig's Rusty (M. A. Scaduto), Shosaph's Irish Perfection (C. E. Kilgore), Buck Acres Prince Ballyroan (D. F. Buck), Ch. Shardmore's Autumn Echo (C. D. Metzler), Hunter's Lady Tizzalia (R. L. Blair) and others.

The Irish Setter Club of Southern California had its inception in 1926, when W. R. Williamson and R. Knost made the initial plans while exercising their red setters at the corner of Sixth and Rampart Streets in Los Angeles. The first specialty show of the club was held in 1932, and the first field trial in 1939. Mrs. O. L. Bailey's Miss Shamus Killarney won the "Green" Dog Stake among 15 starters. Trials were discontinued during the war. During the last decade the following setters have been prominent in the field trials: B. & F. Ch. Red Arrow Show Girl (E. Heist), Red Arrow Dirty Bird, Red Arrow Shotgun Sally (L. Heist), Tir Na N Og Merrymike Larkey (J. D. Huizenga), F. Ch. Oxton's Shosaphine, County Clare's Mc-Cool, County Clare's Shandy (E. J. Lewis), Enilen Titian Tyronne (H. & J. Bayless), Thenderin Luimneach Siege (S. & K. Byrne), Killagay's Welkin Warrior (G. S. Hiscox) and Lady Claire of Ardee (M. C. Wilsey).

A specialty club that is extremely active in field activities is the Irish Setter Club of Michigan, which started in 1952. Emphasizing the dual type Irish Setter, the members enter their bench dogs in the field trials and each autumn they shoot over their own setters. The best known field trial winners in this area include the McIvor dogs mentioned previously, Ch. Robin O'Dea (F. Tetreau), Timothy Shawn O'Dea, Aaragon's Kilarney Klipper (C. B. T. Benton), Kelton of Hartsbourne Hei-Lo, Duchess of Derrycaine (R. H. Ray), F. Ch. Miller's Bonnie Loo, F. Ch. Miller's Tiger Lily (Dr. P. T. Miller), Kilkenny of Sunnymoor (E. L. Morrison), Yankee Doodle Dandi (H. Hurd), Lady Katie of Greenleaf (J. C. Campbell), Donovan's Red Erin O'Mally (J. L. Turcott), Bird Comet of ˙Ardee (G. L. Colburn), McNamara's Shanty Shannon (P. F. McNamara) and others.

The Irish Setter Club of Milwaukee, which is also interested in the dual-type Irish Setter, held its first licensed field trial in October 1955. Its members are responsible for seven AKC field champions—the five progeny of Mahogany Tim II mentioned previously and two daughters of F. Ch. Sulhamstead Norse D'Or: F. Ch. Countess Suzanne II (W. M. Wong) and F. Ch. Emerald Isle Angel (G. O. Ingraham). Other Wisconsin field trial winners are: Walkers' Mahogany dogs previously listed, Michael of Burnham (A. L. Wilson), Elmho Paddy O'Ardee (E. E. Homuth), Shadilane Lady (J. P. Malick), Lady of the Lodge (F. Glynn), Molly Coddled Mayhem, M. Misty (R. D. Frisch, Tabelina of Wildwood (J. A. Lane), Ch. Muckamoor's Marty Magee (E. A. Buck), Glockomorro Duke of Westdale (L. Geyer), Rustic Charm Puetzer (B. J. Schneider), Mahogany's C. J. Duchess (J. W. Urban), F. Ch. O'Lannon Copper Penny (S & E Dansin), F. Ch. Tam of Ballarrell (C. F. Ballard), Comet's Katuri O'Colburn Acres (G. A. Krauss), Hi View Lady Cindy (J. N. Kanauz) and others.

Among the noted field trial winners of the Western Irish Setter Club in the Chicago area were: Ch. Verbu Shawn Oogh, V. Meath Oogh, Ch. V. Missy Oogh, V. Midgie Oogh, V. Eileen Oogh and Ch. V. Maureen (E. Schweitzer), Ch. Runwild Fiona, Ch. R. Finnagain, Ch. R. Finnola the Fay (V. Hardin), Ch. Brenwood's Kingpin (B. B. Wallis) and Ch. Tara's Theme (R. J. Bridell).

The Irish Setter Club of Indiana held field trials from 1948 to 1959. Representatives from these events include: Byrdfield Kate, B. Zet (D. L. Martin), Patrick King Ranger (E. L. Cude), Rufus Killarney O'Kerry (A. W. Kipp), and Bruns Rusty Hobo (D. E. Bruns).

Mary Svetlik and Wolfram C. Stumpf are charter members of the Irish Setter Club of Ohio, which started in 1947. Through the years the club has sponsored both bench and field events. Some of best

Ch. Runwild Finnagain SA72690
(Ch. Carrvale's Terry Terhune-Ch. Runwild Fiona).

Mighty Fawn 648590 FDSB (Mighty Red Man-Erin's Sally).

known Ohio dogs at the trials were: Seamus Red Tuxedo, Sulhamstead Nat D'Or, The Dude (H. David), Thor, Thorleen (T. Stronski), F. Ch. Fyn (F. Nielsen), Marflow Susan, Sulhamstead Nell D'Or (W. C. Stumpf), F. Ch. Windyridge Tammy, Shooting Dog Champion Mr. O'Leary (F. C. Bean) and many others.

The Irish Setter Club of Western New York held its first field trial in September 1961, at which the Kopper Key setters of F. L. Ekey and the McGovern dogs of D. L. Pahy placed. Kopper Key Henessey, a son of F. Ch. Fyn, has at least 15 placements. Other dogs in these New York trials include: Willowview Gamester, W. Flame, W. Easter Sunday (all of Ardee breeding and owned by H. C. Little), Murcrest Mollie Mischief (L. C. Crum), Love's Liz (G. Love), Brandy's Darlin' Dinty (L. McAfee) and Kerrykeel's April Folly (F. J. Bingham).

One of the oldest specialty clubs aside from the parent club, is the Irish Setter Club of New England, founded in 1928. It has held specialty shows since 1930 and field trials since 1937. Some of its more prominent field trial winners were: Highpoint Captain McKerry, H. Fleet, H. Flame (A. E. Church), Rookwood Sally (M. Cavanaugh), Red Velvet's Duke, Playgirl's Holiday Lass (R. & J. Finn), F. Ch. Pride of Erin IV (J. G. Cassidy), F. Ch. Sharon IV (T. P. Ward), F. Ch. Jackson Brook Angler's Rusty (F. H. White), Cloister's Wendy McTybe (Mrs. A. E. Berol), Pride's Red Rambler (T. P. Grant), Ch. Kinvarra Bootsie (Kinvarra Kennels), Shayne of Erin (G. Payson), Erin's Red Duke (J. Mandell) and others.

The Eastern Irish Setter Association, the Southeastern Red Setter Club, the Irish Setter Club of Missouri and other organizations have held field trials for the breed.

This chapter would not be complete without a word about Harry Dean (Ardee Kennels), Saskatoon, who has done so much since 1934 to support the cause of the Irish Setter in field trials. He has owned or bred more than 25 Canadian Irish Setter champions, including the five dual champions of the breed in Canada: (Canadian Kennel Club numbers)

Ardee's Irish Ace 450130
    (D.Ch. Moanruad Ambassador—Ch. Bird Dixie of Ardee)
Elmcroft Mahogany Sue 182455
    (Ch. Sugaun of Shaunavon—Ch. Elmcroft Molly)
Glenderry's Amber Prince 420234
    (Ch. Monarch of the Vale—Ch. Ardee's Shooting Star)

Lady Amber of Ardee 248428
    (Ch. Red Echo of Ardee—Kenogami Queen of Ardee)
Moanruad Ambassador 396714
    (F. Ch. Admiral of Rye—F. Ch. New Square Red Lassie)

Some of his other well known dogs were: Ch. Bird Dixie of Ardee, Ch. Elmcroft Red Ace, Ch. Lady Gadeland of Ardee, Ch. Red Ace of Ardee III and Ch. Red Echo of Ardee. He imported Ch. End O'Maine Billboard from the United States and F. & B. Ch. Moanruad Ambassador from Ireland. The latter, of select hunting stock with 8 field trial champions in his immediate pedigree, is the prepotent sire of 7 Canadian champions and several field trial winners. In the United States he is represented by F. Ch. Bird Comet of Ardee, Willowview Gamester, Lady Claire of Ardee and others.

Harry Dean, who is a field trial judge, has raised, trained and sold hundreds of Irish Setters all over the world, as far away as Turkey and Brazil. He has travelled widely to acquire good breeding stock. His objective is a moderate-sized, well balanced, dark mahogany setter with high intelligence, keen bird sense and friendly disposition.

11

Irish Setter
Breed Standard

(*Courtesy of the Irish Setter Club of America*)

General Appearance—The Irish Setter is an active, aristocratic bird-dog, rich red in color, substantial yet elegant in build. Standing over two feet tall at the shoulder, the dog has a straight, fine, glossy coat, longer on ears, chest, tail, and back of legs. Afield he is a swift-moving hunter; at home, a sweet-natured, trainable companion. His is a rollicking personality.

Head—Long and lean, its length at least double the width between the ears. The brow is raised, showing a distinct stop midway between the tip of nose and the well-defined occiput (rear point of skull). Thus the nearly level line from occiput to brow is set a little above, and parallel to, the straight and equal line from eye to nose. The skull is oval when viewed from above or front; very slightly domed when viewed in profile. Beauty of head is emphasized by delicate chiseling along the muzzle, around and below the eyes, and along the cheeks. Muzzle moderately deep, nostrils wide, jaws of nearly equal length. Upper lips fairly

Correct type

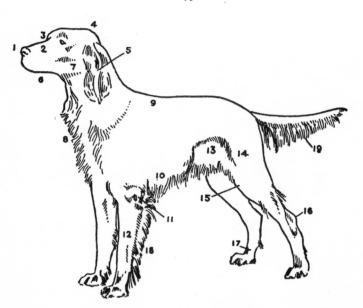

1. Nose	6. Flews	11. Elbow	16. Hock joint
2. Muzzle (Foreface)	7. Cheek	12. Forearm	17. Pastern
3. Stop	8. Chest	13. Loin	18. Feathering
4. Occipital bone	9. Withers	14. Thigh	19. Stern
5. Ear	10. Brisket	15. Stifle	

1. Snipey muzzle, large eye.
2. Lack of stop, pendulous flews.
3. Good side view.
4. Undershot jaw.
5. Wide skull, high ears.
6. Good front view.

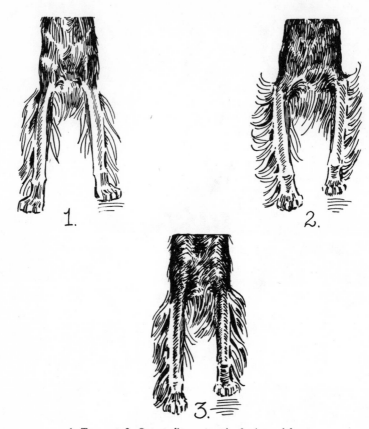

1. Toes out. 2. Out at elbows, toes in. 3. A good front.

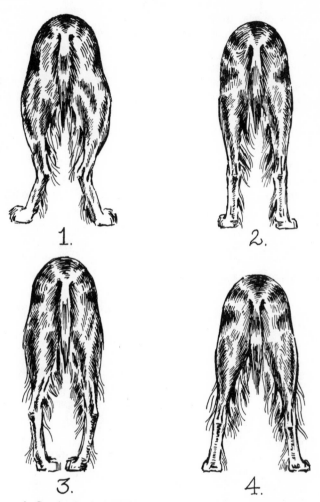

1. Cow hocks. 2. Straight hocks. 3. Bow legs. 4. Good hocks.

square but not pendulous, the underline of the jaws being almost parallel with the top line of the muzzle. The teeth meet in a scissors bite in which the upper incisors fit closely over the lower, or they may meet evenly.

Nose—Black or chocolate.

Eyes—Somewhat almond-shaped, of medium size, placed rather well apart; neither deep-set nor bulging. Color, dark to medium brown. Expression soft yet alert.

Ears—Set well back and low, not above level of eye. Leather thin, hanging in a neat fold close to the head, and nearly long enough to reach the nose.

Neck—Moderately long, strong but not thick, and slightly arched; free from throatiness, and fitting smoothly into the shoulders.

Body—Sufficiently long to permit a straight and free stride. Shoulder blades long, wide, sloping well back, fairly close together at the top, and joined in front to long upper arms angled to bring the elbows slightly rearward along the brisket. Chest deep, reaching approximately to the elbows; rather narrow in front. Ribs well sprung. Loins of moderate length, muscular and slightly arched. Top line of body from withers to tail slopes slightly downward without sharp drop at the croup. Hindquarters should be wide and powerful with broad, well-developed thighs.

Legs and Feet—All legs sturdy, with plenty of bone, and strong, nearly straight pastern. Feet rather small, very firm, toes arched and close. Forelegs straight and sinewy, the elbows moving freely. Hind legs long and muscular from hip to hock, short and nearly perpendicular from hock to ground; well angulated at stifle and hock joints, which, like the elbows, incline neither in nor out.

Tail—Strong at root, tapering to a fine point, about long enough to reach the hock. Carriage straight or curving slightly upward, nearly level with the back.

Coat—Short and fine on head, forelegs, and tips of ears; on all other parts, of moderate length and flat. Feathering long and silky on ears; on back of forelegs and thighs long and fine, with a pleasing fringe of hair on belly and brisket extending onto the chest. Feet well feathered between the toes. Fringe on tail moderately long and tapering. All coat and feathering as straight and free as possible from curl or wave.

Color—Mahogany or rich chestnut red, with no trace of black. A

226

small amount of white on chest, throat, or toes, or a narrow centered streak on skull, is not to be penalized.

Size—There is no disqualification as to size. The make and fit of all parts and their over-all balance in the animal are rated more important. Twenty-seven inches at the withers with a show weight of about 70 pounds is considered ideal for a dog; the bitch 25 inches, 60 pounds. Variance beyond an inch up or down to be discouraged.

Gait—At the trot the gait is big, very lively, graceful and efficient. The head is held high. The hindquarters drive smoothly and with great power. The forelegs reach well ahead as if to pull in the ground, without giving the appearance of a hackney gait. The dog runs as he stands: straight. Seen from the front or rear, the forelegs, as well as the hind legs below the hock joint, move perpendicularly to the ground, with some tendency towards a single track as speed increases. But a crossing or weaving of the legs, front or back, is objectionable.

Balance—At his best the lines of the Irish Setter so satisfy in over-all balance that artists have termed him the most beautiful of all dogs. The correct specimen always exhibits balance whether standing or in motion. Each part of the dog flows and fits smoothly into its neighboring parts without calling attention to itself.

12

Interpretation of
the Standard

THE Irish Setter breed standard has been approved by both the American Kennel Club and the Irish Setter Club of America; and it has also been accepted by the majority of breeders and judges. Evolved from earlier standards and past experiences, it represents the consensus of opinion among many who are concerned with the development of the breed. Of course, there will always be some differences of opinion as to the relative importance of certain points in the standard, which in turn make dog show awards unpredictable.

The ideal Irish Setter has been described by various authors in their books, and it is of interest to note the viewpoints of Charles H. Lane, Charles Mason, Dr. J. H. Walsh, Vero Shaw, Corn. Schilbred and Mrs. M. Ingle Bepler.

The purpose of this chapter is to present a comprehensive explanation of the standard and to interpret some of the finer points of the breed.

At the outset it is freely admitted that each owner thinks his own Irish Setter is the perfect one! Be that as it may, there are some

228

fanciers who are not kennel blind. It is always a good policy to see as many Irish Setters as possible and to form a true mental picture of the ideal dog. Photographs of Ch. Milson O'Boy and of Ch. Higgins' Red Pat have been used to illustrate the breed standard in publications of the American Kennel Club.

General—That Irish Setters have changed through the years is apparent from a review of the illustrations in this book, comparing the famous old dogs of the past with the modern setters. There has been a definite advance in the development of the red dog just as there has been improvement in agricultural livestock.

One purpose of breeding has been to establish individual breed characteristics like a prominent occipital bone, short forearm, high tail placement, accentuated top line and elegant head carriage. It can no longer be said that the various setter breeds look alike except for color, because they differ in head, muzzle, quarters and many other ways.

That there is far more uniformity in Irish Setter type than formerly is shown by the fact that some modern litters contain four or five champions that are as alike as peas in a pod. Furthermore, there has been marked improvement in over-all balance, a point which the standard particularly emphasizes.

Disposition—Perhaps no physical quality or breed characteristic contributes as much toward the general impression created by a dog as does his disposition. A dog can exhibit an outstanding personality in the home, kennel, field or show ring which often credits him far above his physical merit. Consequently, breeders should give attention to disposition, individuality and character, variously described as showmanship, intelligence, responsiveness and faithfulness. Likewise a good doer and a good eater is important; and nobody wants a gunshy dog or a tense, nervous one.

The Irish Setter is said by some writers to be bull-headed and stubborn, an accusation entirely unsupported by quantitative evidence. Individual dogs differ in temperament just as people do; but of course, it is possible now and then to find an Irish Setter that is too independent. One of the most unique and at the same time fitting descriptions of this breed is the "devil-may-care Irishman."

Three different types of heads.

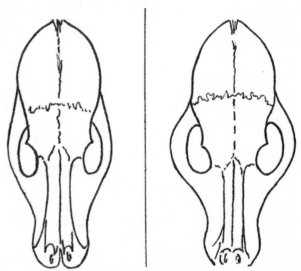

Coarse head due to round cheek bones:
(left) flat cheek bones (right) round cheek bones.

230

Balance—Over-all balance combined with a lovely head, beautiful coat and brilliant color contributes to a favorable general impression and to a certain pleasure in beholding a glorious animal. From a utilitarian viewpoint also, a dog that is built right will be equipped to use his strength to the best mechanical advantage. The relative proportions of the various parts of the setter must be conducive to his use afield as well as pleasing to the eye.

Each part of the dog serves a definite purpose and there should be coordination, balance and symmetry between these parts. Harmony of the whole is preferable to outstanding good qualities marred by numerous defects. Sometimes there seems to be a lack of balance with size; the smaller the dog the closer to perfection it appears to be and the less its faults seem, while in a larger animal the faults are magnified much as in the enlargement of a photograph which reveals details readily overlooked in a small print.

The Irish Setter in the past has been a rather long-bodied dog, which characteristic is often accompanied by a slack loin. One of the best balanced setters, according to the opinion of many, had height at the withers equal to his body length. The general contour of the dog emanates from bone structure and angulation rather than from flesh and tissue development. Occasionally faulty bone structure is concealed by a layer of fat.

The relative size of the head and the body is important. Some strains produce a small head in proportion to the body, not necessarily short or square or snipy, but insufficient to balance the rest of the dog. Another common fault is the lack of harmony between the front and the rear quarters of the animal—the two parts do not seem to belong to the same setter.

Size—Although the breed standard has no size disqualification, it specifies an ideal height at the withers of 27 inches and a show weight of 70 pounds for a male (25 inches and 60 pounds for a bitch). A height tolerance of plus or minus one inch serves to discourage extreme dimensions.

There are insufficient data in the literature to show statistically the average increase in size of the Irish Setter through the years; however, the following table indicates the trend:

DATE WHELPED	IRISH SETTER	HEIGHT AT SHOULDER, INCHES	WEIGHT POUNDS
1868	Plunket	22	40
1874	Ch. Elcho	24	56
1924	Ch. Higgins' Red Pat	27	68
1932	Ch. Kinvarra Son of Red Coat	27	70
1941	Ch. Kendare Red Duke	30	80

One reason for this increase in size may be that the smaller dogs seem to be overshadowed in the show ring by the bigger specimens. The breeders' problem has been to maintain size without coarseness and ruggedness without clumsiness.

Head—While too much emphasis is sometimes given to the head, even to the point of obscuring other more important features of the dog, nevertheless the head deserves due consideration for its conveys character, type, expression and personality; and a nicely molded, well proportioned, clean-cut head is much to be prized. The head of a setter is a parallel development, in which both the skull (cranium) and the foreface (muzzle) are bounded by parallel planes. It should be long and deep rather than broad. A desirable length of head is from 10 to 11 inches, about equally divided at the stop into a skull and a muzzle.

Skull—The skull should be long, narrow, rounded at the top, and as wide at the base as at the brows. The top-skull when viewed from the front should be well domed without any suggestion of square corners at the top. A slight furrow or median line between the eyes, sufficiently pronounced to eliminate that plain-faced look, contributes to a pleasing expression by accenting brow elevation. The earlier Irish Setters did not show this triangular elevation above the eyes, which probably could be attributed to the Boyne strain, especially through Ch. Higgins' Red Coat. One of the distinguishing characteristics of the breed is a fully developed and defined occipital bone. There should be a distinct indentation about three-quarters of an inch below the occipital bone, where the back of the head joins the arch of the neck.

Cheeks—The cheeks should be flat without bulge or that fault referred to as broken-cheeked, which is inherited and not caused by chewing bones as some persons erroneously believe. The shape of the cheek bones is very important in that it determines the thickness of the head and also the proportions of the head. Should round cheek bones project outward excessively, the head will appear massive and coarse; whereas if flat cheek bones lie close to the skull, the head will appear long and lean proportionately. The depth of cheek should be in pleasing proportion to the depth of muzzle. Wedginess is undesirable.

Stop—The foreface under the eyes should be cleanly chiselled with no fullness. The forehead is raised distinctly at the brows to form a clearly defined, medium stop.

Eyes—The stop and the eye relationship is important. A line drawn through the inner and the outer corners of the eyes should be horizontal. The eyes should not be placed on the edge of the skull nor too wide apart; but preferably with less than $2\frac{1}{2}$ inches between the inner corners. They should not be round and staring like the early day engravings of dogs, nor should they be protruding, deepset or sunken. Their outlook should be straight forward, although a setter eye can be seen in profile. A small almond-shaped eye is desirable, in fact an Irish Setter eye is somewhat small in proportion to the head as compared to many other breeds.

The color of the iris should be of uniform shade whether light or dark; preferably rich dark brown to harmonize with the coat, nails and eye rims. An otherwise good dog ought not to be penalized too heavily for a light eye, because it is in no way detrimental to the utility of the dog; but a washed-out, gooseberry eye is far from pleasing. A very black eye lacks expression. Eyes have been known to darken with age.

Eyelids should be close fitting, of thin texture and of a brown shade to match the lips and nose. An eye with a loosely fitting lower lid tends to expose the haw which can be easily irritated by weed seeds or other foreign matter encountered in the field. Strongly developed haws ruin the appearance.

The intelligent, fearless and yet kindly expression of the Irish Setter is due in a large part to the eyes. A belligerent or antagonistic expression is not to be desired; and a beady, terrier-like eye is likewise to be avoided.

Ears—The ears should be of moderate size, pendulous, set low and well back so that they hang as if in narrow folds close to the neck with their front edges close to the cheeks. When the ears

Streamlined body

Barrel-shaped body

234

are drawn forward they do not extend beyond the nose, usually only to within one-half inch thereof. Generally about 6 inches long and wider at the skull than at the tip, they are not hound-like in texture or set, nor too thick. They should be well covered with straight, fine hair—not just wool—and have a guard coat extending at least an inch below the ear leather. The tips, which are half oval-shaped (not half diamond-shaped), should have a short velvety coat. A setter ear is not as proportionately long and heavily fringed as that of a spaniel. A wide, flat ear is usually accompanied by a large ear box. The line of attachment of the ear to the head should not be long.

Muzzle—"Like a brick on edge" is a good description of the fore-face, which should be the same width at the tip of the nose as at the eyes, and its top and bottom lines should be parallel. Roman nosed, downfaced and dishfaced types are bad. A moderate depth of muzzle is desirable. The end of the muzzle should be neither snipy or pointed—its squareness is fundamentally due to the width of the bone between the lower teeth and the chin. Substance in the foreface is from bone rather than from lip thickness. The jaws should be of equal length, long and strong; and the arch of the jawbone should not be cramped as it has an influence on the placement of the teeth.

The lips, which should completely cover the lower extremity of the jawbone, should be tight and of fine leather. For a pleasing appearance the mouth should be small and not cut too far back. An excess of lip and of mouth corners look bad. There should be a long cheek, finished foreface and plenty of distance from the corner of the mouth to the hinge of the jaw.

The whiskers are red. In the old days the color of the lips, nose and palate was supposed to be black; but ordinarily the nose is dark mahogany. At certain periods bitches' noses become lighter, almost a flesh shade. A very full, large nose with not too large nostrils is desirable. Its fleshy part is wide across, well blown and filled. The nostril should be moist and have a certain mobility about it, indicating perhaps a well developed sense of smell. A sharp squareness in profile at the very tip of the nose finishes off the head nicely; whereas in contrast, a heavy muzzle rounding off into a small, pinched nose detracts from the appearance of the head.

235

Teeth—Either a scissors bite or a level mouth is permitted by the standard. Both undershot and overshot mouths are faults which usually are apparent from the appearance of the muzzle even without a detailed examination of the teeth.

The normal setter mouth has 42 teeth, including 12 incisors, 4 canines or tusks and 26 molars (12 in the top jaw and 14 in the lower jaw), which vary considerably in form. The tusks should be clean and well developed with the lower ones fitting closely ahead of and against the uppers. The teeth, which should have regular and proper placement in the jaws, should not be cramped, crooked or diseased.

Body—The general impression is that the Irish Setter is long bodied, but upon closer analysis it is evident that he is well coupled and devoid of that looseness of loin and that houndish appearance of the waist which is invariably found in the coursing breeds.

When viewed in profile the torso of the ideal setter should possess top line, bottom line and front line intersecting each other to form a triangle. The height at the withers should be sufficiently more than at the hips to provide a pleasing slope to the top line, which should not be marred by a sag behind the shoulder points, sway in the back, roach in the loin or too abrupt slant of the hip bones.

The bottom line should show a pronounced let-down of brisket which ought to carry through between the forelegs and avoid any semblance to a terrier. The dog does not appear wasp-waisted if his loin is deep as well as broad, short and slightly arched. Long back ribs contribute to a good bottom line, but short ones present a tucked up appearance. Some setters have barrel-shaped bodies with a shallow brisket. When viewed from above such a dog usually reveals excessive spring of rib but almost no indentation ahead of and behind the ribs.

The front line from the chin to the toes viewed in profile should be smooth and unbroken by rough protruding shoulders. This is a most critical test for correct shoulder angulation. The same test applied to a side view of the rear quarters will differentiate those dogs that have drive from those that do not. The latter carry their rear legs too far underneath their bodies.

Chest—The chest should be deep like the keel of a ship, carrying through between the forelegs. From the front it appears narrow with just about enough room for the palm of the hand between the forelegs. When a dog is sitting, his chest seems wide.

There are two types of setters based on the shape of the chest, one with a deep streamlined brisket and the other barrel-round. Arguments have been many as to the relative lung capacities of the two types. It is the consensus of opinion that the barrel-shaped body has less capacity because of increased fat and tissue inside of the bone structure of the chest.

Experience has shown that certain points of conformation seem to accompany the barrel body, such as short upright shoulder blades, straight stifles, square head, short neck, round feet, heavy tail and rough coat. By way of contrast, the deep chested dog usually approaches closer to the standard in fine points.

Shoulders—One of the most important points of a dog's physical makeup is the shoulder assembly, the relative proportions of the blades, upper arms and lower arms and the angles at which the bones meet (called angulation). If the angulation of the front quarters is correct, then that of the rear quarters is usually satisfactory. Long, sloping shoulder blades with good layback result in a long neck, short back and smooth gait; while short upright blades produce a short neck, long back and choppy stride. The blades should be broad, flat, finely textured, close together at the withers and well finished, i.e. not rising above the line of the back. Shoulder muscles should be smooth and hard rather than bunchy and flabby. Some setters add excessive and bullish weight over the shoulders with age.

Neck—Hasn't it been said that the neck can either make or break the appearance of a dog? One need only picture a short thick neck with head set directly on upright shoulder blades to realize how true this is. The neck should be nicely arched, lean and deep rather than wide. It should gracefully blend into the shoulders and come well down onto the chest with no pronounced line of anatomical division—it should flow into the body with no "horse-collar" effect. There is a marked rise of neck from the withers to the back-skull, a pleasing arch at the crest and no suggestion of ewe-neck. Throatiness is undesirable; but a certain fullness at

237

Shallow chest, upright shoulder blades, roach back, straight stifles and long tail.

Three types of shoulders. Center—long sloping shoulder blades; left—average; right—rough shoulders.

238

the throat is not to be confused with it. At times when a dog is at ease, he may relax the throat muscles and permit the gullet to sag.

Loin—A strong, firm, slightly arched and well developed loin of moderate dimensions is desirable. Depth as well as width is wanted. The flank should be fairly short. A roach back and loose couplings are to be condemned.

Hips—The hips should be wide, muscular and slightly sloping to the root of the tail. The tendency is to breed for higher tail placement so that the top line appears unbroken over the croup. Instead of being rounded out and well covered with flesh, the hip bones of some strains stand out prominently, referred to as "ragged hips."

Running Gear—Although a setter's running gear is of great importance, other desirable qualities should not be sacrificed entirely for it. A true moving specimen without correct body type is not necessarily to be preferred to one of proper breed type but having minor faults of legs or feet. Many an alley dog is sound. The question of type versus soundness could be answered by a reasonable evaluation of the relative importance of faults. For breeding purposes a dog that is both sound and of correct breed type is desired.

Legs—It has been said that the Irish Setter is higher on the leg than his English and Gordon cousins. Be that as it may, the setter derives his height upwards from the elbow rather than in length of forearm, which should be relatively short—less than half the height. The forearm should be straight, not bowed, of good substance, flat boned, streamlined like an aeroplane strut and oval in cross section. Desirable also is a long upper arm joined to a long, sloping shoulder blade with an angle of 90 degrees.

An item of no small concern to the setter breeder is reasonably sloping pasterns to absorb shock in the field and to allow sudden turning and stopping without knuckling over.

The hindlegs, which should have wide, thick, muscular thighs and well developed lower thighs, are long from hip to hock and short from hock to foot, with moderate bend in stifle and hock. Hocks should be wide, flat and inclined neither in nor out.

Joints—In the breed standards for horses, joints are considered important, yet few dog standards even mention them. The elbows and the hock joints should be broad and strong; and they should extend over considerable length of leg so as to furnish good attachment and placement of muscles and tendons for efficient leverage. The elbows should be well let down, free from the brisket and neither pinched nor loose. Free action of all joints is essential if a dog is to move properly at all speeds.

Feet—The feet, which should turn neither in nor out, should be compact with deep tough pads and tight arched toes. Round cat feet as well as elongated hare feet are found on Irish Setters. The feet should not be thin, flabby and flat. Open or splayed feet are a constant aggravation to a field dog that must run, turn and stop on stubble, rocks or rough ground. Sore feet have cut short many an otherwise pleasant shooting trip. It is true that considerable protection is afforded the toes by the short thick growth of hair between them. In winter close tight feet do not ball up with wet snow as readily as splayed feet; and they are also more resistant to icy conditions. Deep heel cushions are desirable. The strong red-brown nails should arch to touch the ground.

Gait—Perhaps the main contributing factor to tireless motion afield is the proper relative proportion and angulation in the bone assembly of the running gear. A long sloping shoulder blade and correct turn of stifle are conducive to a smooth flowing stride in which the foot, when viewed from the side, seems to move in the pattern of an elongated elipse. This results in a swinging, enduring trot with little lost motion, whereby the rear foot may overstep the front footprint by 6 to 10 inches.

In contrast an upright blade and straight stifle can cause a restricted stilted gait where the foot appears to travel in a circle, cutting back with wasted action just before it strikes the ground. Such a handicap in the field usually means that the dog tires quickly and gallops rather than trots.

A dog with excessive width of chest is inclined to move with a rolling action as seen in the Bulldog, especially true if the dog is out at the elbows. An Irish Setter carries his weight over his legs instead of hanging between them. Out at elbows is usually accompanied by toeing in, a fault that seldom can be corrected.

Too narrow a front with pinched elbows and toeing out results in a lack of freedom and a paddling gait. The nails fail to function so as to grip the ground and furnish traction. In puppies, toeing out generally corrects itself with proper exercise.

240

The drive power of a setter, which has its source in the muscles of the loin and the rear quarters, can be developed by exercise afield. One of the first places where an old dog starts to fail is a weakening and fading of the muscle on the outside of the rear legs. Lack of drive is also apparent in the dog that carries his rear legs too far under his body.

Slow motion movie film reveals the different gaits in a most convincing manner.

Tail—Early day breed standards stated that the Irish Setter tail should be "set on rather low"; but later breeders have selected for higher tail placement in horizontal line with the back. Important for equilibrium and appearance the tail should be in balance with the rest of the dog. It is scimitar-like, gradually tapering to a point in bone formation as well as in feathering. There have been extremely short tails, 14 inches in length and missing the hock by 2 inches, which were heavy at the root with abrupt taper and bushy furnishings. Such occur on setters with curly body coats. Much to be preferred is a somewhat longer tail, fine in bone, adorned with straight flat furnishings and accompanied by a smooth coat of proper texture. Cocked, gay, hooked or curly flags, which are difficult to breed out of a strain, are undesirable.

The action of the tail indicates the dog's activity at the moment. When he is traveling afield it appears to serve as a rudder. On winding birds it stiffly beats his hindlegs, an indication that he is on game. When the dog is in repose, the very tip of his tail may wiggle a sleepy but expressive greeting to his master nearby.

Constant whipping of the tail when the dog is working combined with the effects of burrs and briars, sometimes pitifully depletes the feathering; and a sore and bleeding appendage may result. However, it is surprising how much protection the hair on the tail provides.

Coat—The coat should be of moderate length, flat, straight and as free as possible from wave or curl. On the head, front of legs and tip of ears it should be short and fine. Certain strains seem to carry profuse coats and others short ones; and it is not unusual to find both types represented in the same litter.

Feathering—Flat, straight, silky feathering on the upper portion of

241

Husky hindquarters.

Refined hindquarters.

242

the ears, back of legs, belly, chest and tail is desirable. It usually is a little lighter in shade than the body coat.

Color—The color should be rich golden chestnut or magnificent mahogany red with no trace whatever of black. It should be brilliant. Henry Blake Knox described it as "deep pure blood red resembling port wine." It seems that most fanciers prefer the dark red shades. Sometimes the shade is uniform for the entire length of each hair, but often the undercoat is slightly lighter. Although the solid color is preferable, a little white on the face, neck, breast or toes in accordance with the standard is not objectionable.

Ch. Cardinal Flaming Rocket UD, S461527 (Ch. Knights-croft Irish Lancer-Ch. Lady Kathleen O'Hagginwood).

13

Irish Setter Club
of America

THE guiding spirit for Irish Setter affairs in the
United States for over three-quarters of a century has been the
Irish Setter Club of America (ISCA), officially founded in 1891.
It is fitting to devote a chapter to some of the numerous activities
of this important club and to the many dedicated members who
have conscientiously given their time, energy and resources in the
best interests of the breed. To do justice to this notable subject in
limited space is difficult, and perhaps a chronological history of
the club might be the best approach.

The first gathering of breeders and owners for the purpose of
forming a club to sponsor, improve and popularize the Irish Setter
was held at the Westminster show in February 1891. The meeting
was called to order by William Dunphy. Dr. N. Rowe was chosen to
be chairman, and then William H. Child was elected president of
the new group that was to draw up its constitution and by-laws, as
well as plan its future activities.

Major James M. Taylor, in his *Records & Standards of Dogs in*

America (1892), lists the following officers, executive committee and charter members of the Irish Setter Club of America:

Irish Setter Club of America

Officers

William H. Child, *President*
Dr. N. Rowe, *Vice-President*
Dr. Gwilym G. Davis, *Secretary & Treasurer*

Executive Committee

Max Wenzel	F. L. Cheney
C. T. Thompson	E. B. Bishop
F. H. Perry	

Members

Anderson, H. B., Glen View, N.J.
Beale, E. M., Lewisburgh, Pa.
Bishop, E. B., Coffeyville, Kan.
Blossom, J. B., Morrisania, N.Y.
Cheney, F. L., Pittsfield, Mass.
Child, William H., Philadelphia, Pa.
Clements, B. L., New York, N.Y.
Contoit, Louis, West Farms, N.Y.
Davis, Dr. G. G., Philadelphia, Pa.
Dunphy, William, Peekskill, N.Y.
Flynn, Michael, Jr., Bristol, R.I.
Jarvis, Dr. W., Claremont, N.H.

Leach, George T., High Point, N.C.
Mannioers, J. J., Pittsburgh, Pa.
Perry, Frank H., Des Moines, Ia.
Rowe, Dr. N., Chicago, Ill.
Rothrock, Boyd D., Williamsport, Pa.
Scanlon, John J., Fall River, Mass.
Thompson, Charles T., Philadelphia, Pa.
Washington, W. L., Pittsburgh, Pa.
Wenzel, Max, Hoboken, N.J.

From this relatively small beginning came the large specialty club of today, with its 500 or more members from 44 states and several foreign countries. Among those who performed yeoman service for the club in its earlier days were, William H. Child, also the third president of the American Kennel Club; Dr. N. Rowe, editor of *The American Field*; Max Wenzel, a prominent advocate of the working setter; Dr. William Jarvis, dean of the breeders of his time; Charles T. Thompson, known for his Rockwood Kennels; and others. On the executive committee, the East was represented by F. L. Cheney and Michael Flynn, and the West by E. B. Bishop and Frank H. Perry. James B. Blossom was primarily a Gordon Setter breeder.

A year or so after the organization of the club, W. Lanier Washington (Kildare Kennels) became president. When personal business pressures compelled him to resign about 1895, Dr. Gwilym G. Davis succeeded to the presidency and held that office until he died in June 1918. Dr. Davis, described as "a lovable and high-minded gentleman from Philadelphia," was a strong supporter of field dogs and field trials.

One of the charter purposes of the Irish Setter Club of America has been "to promote the breeding of pure red setters and to develop and to bring to perfection their natural high qualities for field use." The first field trial sponsored by the club, held at High Point, N.C. on November 23, 1891, had 24 starters in two stakes. Cash prizes amounting to $350 were donated by the club. The trial was a pronounced success, and additional trials were run in 1892, 1893 and 1895. Then the interest in field trials for Irish Setters seemed to wane until they were revived by the club in 1907 and 1908 at Barber Junction, N.C.

The governing body for dog affairs in the United States is the American Kennel Club (AKC), founded in 1894. Its "active members" are all-breed and specialty dog clubs in this country. For a while in its earlier years there were also "associate members," those individuals especially interested in the breeding and showing of pure-bred dogs. However, in 1906, they became "associate subscribers," and in 1923 they were dropped entirely. Since then the AKC has consisted only of member clubs, which now number 369. It is significant that throughout the history of the AKC, the ISCA has been the only Irish Setter member club, and as such it is recognized as the national representative of the breed.

Among the first ISCA delegates to the AKC was G. H. Thomson, who held that post for several years. Indeed, the club has been fortunate in having dedicated delegates, some of whom had long tenures of office: R. Walter Creuzbaur (1910–1922), William Cary Duncan (1925–1945) and John C. Neff (1945–1965).

One of the functions of each AKC member specialty club is to formulate, supervise and control its own breed standard. One of the first official acts of the new ISCA in 1891 was to adopt the "Standard and Points of Judging the Red Irish Setter" that had been in effect since July 1886. Even this early standard emphasized such breed characteristics as a long lean head, well-defined occipital protuber-

247

ance, deep chest, etc. Although there were slight revisions of this standard in 1895, 1908 and 1919, in general it was quite satisfactory over a long period. It contained a "Standard of Points" which established arbitrary ratings for 11 parts of the ideal Irish Setter:

Head	10	Hind legs	10
Eyes	5	Tail	8
Ears	5	Coat & feather	8
Neck	5	Tail	8
Body	15	Size, style, general	
Shoulders, forelegs & feet	12	appearance	14
		Total	100

The latest revision of the Irish Setter Standard, which became effective June 14, 1960, no longer contains a scale of points. The new standard is the result of more than four years of intensive study by the executive committee of the ISCA, which in the course of its thorough consideration canvassed the entire Irish Setter fancy for its opinions. The superlative style and appearance of today's Irishmen testify to an excellent specification.

During the era of four-day dog shows, VHC awards, Backus dog crates and Spratt's dog cakes, Louis Contoit was Secretary of the ISCA (1904–1912). R. Walter Creuzbaur succeeded him (1913–1917). The first ISCA Specialty Show, scheduled for May 12, 1917 at Broomhall, Pa., had to be cancelled. During the period from 1918 to 1920, Joseph S. Wall (Lismore Kennels) was president of the club, Mrs. Helen M. Talbot (Muskerry Kennels), secretary and Warren Delano (St. Val Kennels), treasurer.

At the 1918 annual meeting an unusually handsome three-inch bronze ISCA medal, executed by the renowned sculptress Mrs. Laura Gardin Fraser, was revealed to the club for the first time with the request that the donor's name be withheld. Later, upon the death of Mr. Delano on September 10, 1920, the members learned that he had not only donated the medal but designed it as well. One side of it bears the statement, "To Encourage Breeding and Develop and Perfect Nature's Contribution to a Noble Race," while around the border are the shamrocks of Ireland and the words, "Affection, Courage, Beauty and Intelligence." On the other side of the medal appear in bas-relief one of the St. Val setters and the Harp of Peace from the Flag of Ireland. For approximately half a

Special bronze medal of the Irish Setter Club of America, designed by Warren Delano, 1918.

William H. Child, first president of the ISCA.

century the club has awarded these attractive medals to members whose dogs qualify by winning certain awards at bench shows and field trials. Fortunate is he who receives one!

The 1918 meeting was also of interest in that Charles Esselstyn, publicity chairman, reported that 36 stories about the Irish Setter had been printed during the previous year. Then, too, at the meeting an unusual gift was presented to the club by Thomas M. Hilliard, manager of the Waldorf-Astoria Hotel. It was the original mounted head of the famous Irish Setter, English Champion Palmerston. In the 1870's, the white blaze on Palmerston's forehead had started the rage for the so-called "Palmerston snip," a blaze, which was more than a line, starting down on the foreface and widening as it extended back between the eyes.

The twenties was a period of change and advancement for the ISCA, as it conducted a campaign to promote the breed and to encourage breeders to improve their stock. Generous money prizes were offered at bench shows and field trials, and by 1926, the club was flourishing, with more than 200 members. It thus became one of the most active and progressive organizations in the dog fancy.

Among the novel ideas introduced by the ISCA in 1927 was the "dinner meeting" of the Board of Directors, which not only brought together a large representation of members but also created much enthusiasm. At the initial dinner meeting, the directors made plans for the first annual Specialty Show and Field Day to be held August 26, 1927. The scheduled event proved to be an informal, congenial get-together at McKeon's Grove, Albany, N.Y., for admirers of the Irish Setter. Keen interest, friendly rivalry and a fine fraternal spirit persisted.

The second annual Specialty Show and Field Day, held at the Milson Kennels of Sidney H. Sonn, Harrison, N.Y. on October 6, 1928, was a "barking success" according to Bill Duncan. A novelty at this show was a prize cup for each exhibitor who had not previously shown an Irish Setter.

The third and the fourth annual Specialty Shows followed in succession on the estate of Miss Elizabeth Stillman, Cornwall, N.Y. The fifth Specialty was held in conjunction with the Storm King Kennel Club All-Breed Show. Then came six specialties associated with the spectacular Morris and Essex Shows (1932–1937) and many more with Westchester Kennel Club. The ISCA promoted large entries to encourage the breeding and showing of pure-bred setters, and the shows proved of inestimable value in establishing and preserving correct breed type.

As the years went by and interest in dog shows increased, local breed clubs were organized in various parts of the country. Being the oldest Irish Setter specialty club and the only AKC member representing the breed, plus having a long background of experience, the ISCA was given added responsibilities by the AKC. Because of its position between the AKC and the subsidiary local Irish Setter clubs, the ISCA is known as the Parent Club (the active guardian of the breed), and as such it has certain administrative duties. Its functions now include supervisory consent for local Irish Setter clubs to hold specialty shows, obedience trials and field trials. Dates, judges and other requirements must be approved by the ISCA. The club has long required that its specialty judges must have judged previously at "point shows" a minimum of three times, the first time at least three years prior to the proposed specialty show. Licensed handlers of long experience may also judge specialty shows.

In 1931, the AKC revised its field trial regulations. The first championship points under the new rules were awarded to Ch. Elcova's Admiration, and the first Irish Setter to win the newly created AKC field championship title was Field Ch. Elcova McTybe. During the decade prior to World War II, the semi-annual ISCA field trials with their attractive prizes stimulated great interest in working setters. The Elcho Prize of $500, offered by two members of the club, was one of the most sought-after field trial awards.

In 1940, Michael J. Flynn, the last of the charter members of the ISCA, was elected an Honorary Life Member of the club.

During the War many dogs of the larger breeds were enrolled in the K-9 Corps of Dogs for Defense. In general the pointing breeds were barred from the Corps because of their persistent pointing instinct, for it was next to impossible to train it out. Wartime field trials and bench shows were almost at a standstill, partly because of the lack of gasoline for transportation. Extensive breeding operations also declined due to the scarcity of meat and of kennel help, but there was no marked loss of premium bloodlines, as in Europe.

During those trying times, the ISCA continued to function under the efficient guidance of John C. Neff, secretary (1937–1939), president (1940–1946), delegate (1946–1964), AKC executive secretary (1947–1951) and executive vice-president (1951–1964). In 1951 he was voted "Dogdom's Man of the Year," thereby receiving the "Fido" award. John Neff's devotion to sport, his unusual executive ability and his wide business experience in dog affairs have contributed greatly toward making the ISCA the efficient organization that it is today.

One project he started in 1945 was the *Memo to Members,* a newsletter prepared after each executive committee meeting to inform all members about the club's activities. This publication is still functioning well and, of course, has grown tremendously in number of pages and coverage during the past 20 years. It now includes Committee Reports, President's Column, Minutes of Meetings, Parade of Champions, Litter Box, Consents to Clubs, Trophy Awards, Club Officers' and Members' Roster, Directory of Irish Setter Winners in Bench, Obedience and Field, and other special articles. The responsibility for *Memo to Members* now seems to rest on the shoulders of President Ivan Klapper and his able assistants, who are continuing this fine publication.

The first Irish Setter Futurity in this country was held by the Eastern Irish Setter Association in 1938. Since then the ISCA and local Irish Setter clubs have held many futurities in conjunction with specialty shows and all-breed clubs. Sometimes they are divided into junior and senior classes. They offer rewarding cash prizes and stimulate interest in breeding better stock. In the early days there was no place to which a breeder could turn for reliable information on breeding Irish Setters, but with the advent of futurities and specialty clubs, that problem no longer exists.

The list of local Irish Setter specialty clubs has been growing: two in 1927, 14 in 1946, 17 in 1959 and at least 20 in 1967. Among them are the Irish Setter Clubs of Arizona, Colorado, Georgia, Greater St. Louis, Michigan, Milwaukee, Minnesota, Nebraska, New England, Ohio, Pacific, Southern California, Texas, Western New York, and the Western Irish Setter Club, Eastern Irish Setter Association, Potomac Irish Setter Club and Hoosier Irish Setter Club. Still in the early stages of development are the Irish Setter Clubs of the Northwest, Long Island, Florida, Louisiana and Lake Shore. These organizations, with a total membership of more than 1,000, comprise

252

the backbone of the Irish Setter fancy. They reciprocate with entries and trophies at each others' fixtures, lend films, exchange newsletters and maintain puppy sales registers. Some schedule classes on how to exhibit dogs and on how to train them. Under the supervision of the parent club they hold sanctioned and licensed shows and trials, both independently and in conjunction with all-breed clubs.

About 1953, at the suggestion of Lee Schoen, a novel bench show idea, the "Hidden Identity Match," was initiated, whereby every entry was exhibited by an experienced person other than his owner and was selected by lottery. The purpose was to demonstrate to the newcomer to the breed that his dog could compete on equal terms with the others.

Another device for helping local clubs to understand each other better and for passing along ideas was the *Combined Bulletins,* assembled and distributed to members once or twice a year by the ISCA from 1954 to 1963. Each local club contributed 250 copies of a single issue of its own newsletter toward this bulletin.

Before 1947, the ISCA had held its specialty shows and field trials mainly in the East, but when membership from other parts of the country increased, the system of regional events hosted by the local clubs was inaugurated. Accordingly, the United States was divided into four regions: East (I), Midwest (II), South (III), and West (IV). The first regional specialty show was held June 7, 1947, at the Ladies Dog Club Show with the Irish Setter Club of New England as host. Since then it has been the aim of the parent club to hold annual regional specialty shows in each district so that all can participate in the functions of the parent club. Sometimes obedience trials are included. The events have been most satisfactory, perhaps because better prizes, larger entries and wider representation have resulted.

The numerous outdoor ISCA regional specialty shows are popular, frequently having more than 100 entries. Of special mention is the indoor regional Combined Setter Specialty Show held annually in New York preceding the Westminster Kennel Club Show. The English Setter Association of America, the Gordon Setter Club of America and the Irish Setter Club of America (host club: Eastern Irish Setter Association) combine forces to stage this event, which was first held in 1960. According to *The New York Times,* "It has

253

developed into one of the outstanding show features of the East." Dr. W. A. Casper served as chairman of the Combined Setter Specialty from its inception through 1967. The Westminster weekend in New York is a busy one for Irish Setter fanciers. In addition to two bench shows, there are the ISCA annual meeting and the annual trophy luncheon. This three-day occasion offers an unusual opportunity to renew past acquaintances and to make new ones.

Regional field trials have been very successful. The first Region #II trial of the parent club, held at Joliet, Illinois on October 24, 1965, was hosted jointly by the Western Irish Setter Club and the Irish Setter Club of Milwaukee. Competition was keen for the 21 Irish Setters in the Open Gun Dog Stake. Included among the starters were three field champions, four show champions, one dual champion and several obedience titlists. One of the judges, Wolfram C. Stumpf, who has shot over Irish Setters for more than 30 years, remarked,

I'm sure more events of this kind can help us in our search for good-looking Irish that hunt. I found in this trial that the quality of the dogs' work and the conformation of the entire group was a vast improvement over what we had ten years ago. Fifteen years back, invariably, the winners at field trials could not have placed in bench shows; and very few bench dogs could hunt well enough to win at trials. Now most Irish Setter breeders are proud of their dogs' looks as well as their hunting ability.

At the Region #I field trial of the parent club, hosted by the Eastern Irish Setter Association and run at Bevans, N.J. on October 16, 1966, there were five field champions among the 21 Irish Setters in the Open Gun Dog Stake.

The definite improvement in the working ability of the redcoats during the last five years has also been noticed by those who have followed the AKC trials of a dozen or more local specialty clubs in various parts of the country operating under the supervision of the ISCA. There have been more than 150 of these trials during the past 20 years; the prominent winners at these trials and their owners are mentioned in the field trial chapter of this book.

An important factor in the progress of ISCA has been publicity. With the January 1926 issue of *The American Kennel Gazette,* a column was made available to member breed clubs for their monthly news items, entitled "Where Fanciers Gather." This policy, which has been continued in *Pure-Bred Dogs,* has kept the public

Premium List

FIRST COMBINED SETTER SPECIALTY SHOW

UNBENCHED

ENGLISH SETTER ASSOCIATION OF AMERICA, INC.

(MEMBER AMERICAN KENNEL CLUB)

GORDON SETTER CLUB OF AMERICA

(MEMBER AMERICAN KENNEL CLUB)

IRISH SETTER CLUB OF AMERICA, INC.

(MEMBER AMERICAN KENNEL CLUB)

(HOST CLUB: EASTERN IRISH SETTER ASSOCIATION)

CHELSEA SCHOOL
9th Avenue & 26th Street
NEW YORK, N. Y.

SUNDAY, FEBRUARY 7, 1960

(Day before Westminster Kennel Club Show)

The popular indoor Regional Specialty Show of the ISCA, held annually in New York preceding the Westminster Kennel Club Show.

informed about the various activities of the specialty clubs. The first breed correspondent for the ISCA was William Cary Duncan, who served in that capacity until 1945. His writings were constructive and interesting, seasoned now and then with his characteristic humor. After 1945 Lee Schoen furnished most interesting material for the next six years, and since then local specialty clubs, the Executive Committee members and various fanciers have supplied the monthly column with a great variety of text. There have been articles concerning the breed standard, trimming dogs, local clubs, bloodlines, obedience, junior showmanship, field trials, futurities, dermatology, bloat, hip dysplasia, trophies, nutrition, advertising, cowlicks, English shows, Australian setters and many other topics.

The ISCA tried three times (in 1931, 1935 and 1941) to publish a quarterly bulletin, *Irish Setter Club of America News,* but it was not a continuing venture. At various times the parent club has distributed literature on subjects pertaining to the breed, such as *Irish Setters as Pets,* by Evelyn Miller and *How to Raise and Train an Irish Setter,* by Robert Gannon.

About 1957, James Bayless, publicity chairman, started an annual file of newspaper and advertising clippings pertaining to the Irish Setter, which has developed into a big yearbook of no small historical importance. He was also instrumental in publishing under ISCA copyright a very attractive brochure, *The Irish Setter* (1960), to promote the breed for field, obedience, bench and as a companion. This pamphlet contains 21 black-and-white photographs of Irish Setters, with a text written by five authors.

In 1966, the ISCA published *Irish Setter Champions and Obedience Title Winners,* by W. C. Thompson, the first international list of Irish Setter titlists, consisting of more than 3,000 items. The following year the club distributed hundreds of copies of *The Fight Against Bloat,* a compendium of reports on acute gastric dilation compiled by president Ivan Klapper and issued as a supplement to *Memo To Members.* The club was also instrumental in publishing an article on the same subject in *Pure-Bred Dogs* (January 1967), by Charlotte S. Woodruff. This distress, which afflicts Irish Setters, Bloodhounds, Great Danes, German Shepherds and some other breeds, is usually fatal. Then, too, the club has contributed generously to research foundations investigating bloat, hip dysplasia and other canine troubles.

For many years the widespread use of Irish Setters in advertising has been a positive approach to popularizing the breed. Could it be that the appealing beauty and the magnetic personality of the redcoat have made him a salesman *par excellence?* His brilliant color portraits have promoted a variety of products from red setter boots to station wagons. For example, just to mention a few of these Irish showmen, Ch. Rufus of Hollywood Hills advertised photographic film, Ch. Erin's Beau Brummell adorned many beer billboards, Marksman's Shamus was seen on canned dog food labels and Rufus McTybe O'Cloisters stood "on point" on tire calendars. Also appearing on calendars were Dual Ch. Red Arrow Show Girl (UDT), Ch. Red Arrow Smooth Sailing (UDT), Ch. End O'Maine Patridge and Dawn's Tally O'Dare with her 15 puppies. Color plates of Ch. Milson O'Boy II and Joyce's Duke were in two national magazines. Representing the breed in television commercials were Ch. Guinea Gold of Aragon (CD), Ch. Coppercountry Brian O'Boy (CD), Red Barn Sweetheart and many others.

Irish Setters have played featured roles and also bit parts in both television and in motion pictures, probably because of their ready response to obedience training. Arthur E. Clemons once said, "It seems to me that we have in the Irish Setter an eager and willing worker and a well-mannered dog that catches the eye of the spectator." One of these Irish actors Ch. Red Barn Rosabelle (UDT), appeared in the motion picture, "Wild in the Country." But perhaps the greatest publicity for the breed was the motion picture "Big Red," adapted from the James Kjelgaard novel of the same name. The dog star was the handsome and versatile Ch. Red Aye Scraps (UD), and his stand-in was his kennelmate, Ch. Red Arrow Smooth Sailing (UDT), both owned by Lawrence and Eleanor Heist. The part of Molly in the whelping scene was played by Princess Cenna, owned by James and Evelyn Hale. Public response to this picture has been tremendous.

There are many more examples of advertising with Irish Setters, but the dogs mentioned here serve to illustrate what has been accomplished in the field of publicity. Much of the progress has been stimulated directly or indirectly by the ISCA.

Contributing factors toward the promotion of the Irish Setter through the years have been the annual prizes offered by the ISCA and its members. They bear the names of prominent individuals, top-winning setters and outstanding kennels, and they are given in a variety of categories. Competition for the trophies and medals is keen, and at the annual luncheon when the presentations are made, interest runs high. In order to show the nature of these prizes, the 1966 trophies and their donors are listed:

Champion Certificate—ISCA
Champion Trophy—Alan and Helen Cusick
Golden Leash Award—ISCA
Field Trial Winners Trophy—ISCA
Field & Show (Kilkara) Trophy—Mr. Kelly Fox
Dual Dog (County Clare) Trophy—Mr. E. J. Lewis
Best in Show (Ch. Milson O'Boy Memorial) Trophy—Mrs. Cheever Porter
Sporting Group (Ch. St. Cloud's Fermanagh III Memorial) Trophy—Mrs. Cheever Porter
Sporting Group Breeder Exhibitor (Fleetwood Farms) Trophy—Mr. and Mrs. H. M. Rumbaugh
Best of Breed Exhibitor (Phantom Brook) Trophy—Mr. and Mrs. J. Brooks Emory, Jr.
Best of Breed (Belfield) Trophy—Miss Helen Naylor
Best Bitch (Ch. Tirvelda Malva Memorial) Trophy—Mr. and Mrs. E. Irving Eldredge
Best of Opposite Sex (Knocknagree) Trophy—Miss Laura F. Delano
Best Sire (Kinvarra) Trophy—Mr. Lee M. Schoen
Best Matron (Webline) Trophy—Mr. and Mrs. C. R. Webb
Best of Winners (Wolfscroft) Trophy—Dr. and Mrs. W. A. Casper
Winners, Bred by Exhibitor Trophy—Mr. John C. Neff
Amateur Owner (Hearthstone) Trophy—Mr. and Mrs. Peter S. Jennings
Winners Dog Trophy—Mr. James R. Fraser
Winners Bitch (Laurel Ridge) Trophy—Mrs. Merritt M. Swartz
Reserve Winners Dog (Erinway) Trophy—Dr. Robert F. Way
Reserve Winners Bitch (O'Dandy) Trophy—Col. and Mrs. M. C. Spalding
Open Class Trophy—Mr. Richard H. Adams
American Bred Class (Redlog) Trophy—Mr. and Mrs. Lester Gatchell
Most Blue Ribbons Trophy—Mrs. Charles Crawford
Breeder Exhibitor (Ch. Red Star Memorial) Trophy—Mrs. John C. McAteer
Breeder's (Banshee) Trophy—Mr. and Mrs. Ivan Klapper
Litter Breeder (Knockross) Trophy—Mr. W. L. Newhall
New Members (Haleridge) Trophy—Mr. and Mrs. James W. Hale
Obedience (Glencho Ruddy Oogh) Trophy—Miss Emily Schweitzer
Obedience Trophy—Mr. and Mrs. Herbert Swift
Obedience (Ch. Van Ayl Dennis Jerold, UDT, Memorial) Trophy—Mrs. J. W. and M. Bayless
Obedience (Onesquethaw) Trophy—Mr. and Mrs. A. E. Clemons
Bronze Club Medal—ISCA

One cannot hope to mention every officer of the ISCA since 1891, but one of those deserving special recognition is Miss Laura F.

I.S.C.A. Officers, 1891–1967

President

1891–1892	William H. Child
1893–1894	W. L. Washington
1895–1918	Dr. G. G. Davis
1919–1920	Joseph S. Wall
1921–1922	Dr. C. A. Gale
1923–1927	Dr. J. D. DeRonde
1928–1929	Walter Arnold
1930	Mrs. E. A. Sturdee
1931–1933	W. Cary Duncan
1934–1935	Walter C. Ellis
1936–1937	John A. Cuneo
1938	Walter C. Ellis
1939	Dr. G. S. Currier
1940–1946	John C. Neff
1947–1949	J. P. Knight, Jr.
1950–1952	Lee M. Schoen
1953–1960	L. O. Gatchell
1961–1967	Ivan Klapper

1st Vice-President

1891	Dr. N. Rowe
1913–1914	H. S Ladew
1918	Joseph S. Wall
1920	C. Esselstyn
1921	Dr. B. C. Russell
1922–1923	D. J. White
1924	Dr. J. C. Negley
1925–1926	L. C. Fauble
1927	F. X. Sulzbach
1928–1932	Ben M. Curtis
1933–1935	Louis H. Starkey
1936–1951	Laura F. Delano
1952	Dr. G. S. Currier
1953	J. P. Knight, Jr.
1954–1959	Richard H. Adams
1960	Ivan Klapper
1961–1962	Mrs. Wm. B. Cook
1963–1967	W. L. Newhall

2nd Vice-President

1920	Dr. C. A. Gale
1921–1922	Dr. J. D. DeRonde
1923	A. E. Bieser, Jr.
1924–1926	F. X. Sulzbach
1927	G. V. Ireland
1928–1929	Mrs. E. A. Sturdee
1930	Percy C. Stoddart
1931–1932	Louis H. Starkey
1933–1939	E. D. Levering
1940–1949	E. M. Berolzheimer
1950	Jack A. Spear
1951–1952	Richard H. Adams
1953	Jack A. Spear
1954–1965	Laura F. Delano
1966–1967	Louis Iacobucci

Secretary

1891	Dr. G. G. Davis
1900–1903	G. H. Thomson
1904–1913	Louis Contoit
1914–1917	R. W. Creuzbaur
1918–1920	Helen M. Talbot
1921	Joseph S. Wall
1922	A. E. Bieser, Jr.
1923	Julian T. Bishop
1924–1927	A. L. Browne
1928–1930	Miss D. R. Porter
1931	Wm. R. Lubben
1932–1934	Miss D. R. Porter
1935–1936	James Beaton
1937–1939	John C. Neff
1940–1941	R. H. Matthiessen
1942–1944	Archer E. Church
1945–1948	Mary O'Farrell
1949–1956	M. B. Neville
1957–1959	Mrs. Wm. B. Cook
1960–1962	Mrs. M. M. Swartz
1963–1965	Mrs. Wm. B. Cook
1966–1967	Mrs. M. C. Spalding

Treasurer

1891	Dr. G. G. Davis
1913–1914	J. B. Blossom
1918–1920	Warren Delano
1921	R. W. Creuzbaur
1922–1927	B. A. Howes
1928–1930	Dr. J. D. DeRonde
1931	Miss D. R. Porter
1932	Wm. R. Lubben
1933–1935	E. M. Berolzheimer
1936–1937	Dr. G. S. Currier
1938–1939	David O. Ross
1940–1944	Richard H. Adams
1945–1947	Archer E. Church
1948–1950	Richard H. Adams
1951–1952	L. O. Gatchell
1953–1955	Edmund Brittan
1956–1957	H. M. Rumbaugh
1958–1963	May H. Hanley
1964–1967	Peter S. Jennings

Delegate to AKC

1900–1903	G. H. Thomson
1904–1906	J. J. Donahue
1907–1909	L. M. D. McGuire
1910–1922	R. W. Creuzbaur
1923–1924	F. W. Sherman
1925–1945	Wm. Cary Duncan
1946–1964	John C. Neff
1965–1966	J. P. Knight, Jr.
1967	E. I. Eldredge

Corresponding Secretary

1964–1965	Mrs. M. C. Spalding
1966–1967	Mrs. W. C. Brooks, Jr.

Delano, who served as vice-president from 1936 to 1951, and from 1954 to 1965. Her sincere advice and staunch support have helped to keep the club on an even keel. Credit should also be given to Joseph P. Knight, Jr., Lee M. Schoen, Lester O. Gatchell, Ivan Klapper, Mrs. Marion B. Neville, Richard H. Adams, Mrs. William Bolton Cook, W. L. Newhall, Louis Iacobucci, Mrs. Merritt M. Swartz, Mrs. M. C. Spalding, Miss May Hanley, Mrs. William C. Brooks, Jr. and Peter S. Jennings. Then, too, the members of the executive committee (Dr. Wolfgang A. Casper, Arthur E. Clemons, Mrs. William Bolton Cook, E. Irving Eldredge, Kelly Fox, Mrs. Clyde E. Holvenstot, Miss Emily Schweitzer and Clayton R. Webb) have special duties and rate praise for work well done.

The parent club acts as a clearing house for suggestions of the local clubs. It also maintains a central directory of several thousand Irish Setter owners, breeders and exhibitors in the United States, which is available for membership drives and publicity campaigns. The club has always provided information and assistance to Irish Setter fanciers everywhere. For those who would like to participate in work for the advancement of the Irish Setter on the bench, in the field, in obedience trials, and as an all-around companion, it is suggested that they apply for membership in the Irish Setter Club of America. The current president is Mr. Ivan Klapper, R.F.D., Gardiner, N.Y. 12525.

Bibliography

THE following bibliography has been compiled primarily for the use of the Irish Setter owner who may wish to assemble a well rounded, sporting dog library. The titles have been chosen from more than 3000 items with no attempt to make a complete list. Old classics, standard breed books and highly specialized volumes on various subjects have been included. Although many of the works are out of print (OP), every now and then some of them become available.

Another purpose of this bibliography is to indicate special sources of information on dog care, feeding, training, breeding and grooming.

American Field (weekly), started 1874.
   Field trial news. *Field Dog Stud Book* registrations.
   American Field Publishing Co., Chicago, Ill.
American Kennel Club: *Blue Book of Dogs* (1938)
   Foremost dogs of 1937.
   American Kennel Club, New York, N.Y.   OP
American Kennel Club: *Complete Dog Book* (1964)
   History & standards of dog breeds.
   American Kennel Club, New York, N.Y.

Dinner time.

American Kennel Gazette: *Pure-Bred Dogs* (monthly), started 1889.
    Bench, field & obedience reports.
    American Kennel Club, New York, N.Y.

Antunano, J. A. S.: *Practical Education of a Bird Dog* (1944)
    System for training shooting dogs.
    American Field Publishing Co., Chicago, Ill.

Arkwright, William: *The Pointer & His Predecessors* (1906)
    Classic work on the Pointer.
    Arthur L. Humphreys, London, Eng.   OP

Ash, Edward C.: *Dogs, Their History & Development* (1927), 2 vols.
    Comprehensive research on all breeds.
    Houghton Mifflin Co., Boston, Mass.   OP

Baird, Jack: *Pet Irish Setter* (1956)
    Small book of 63 pages.
    All-Pets Books, Inc., Fond du Lac, Wisc.

Becker, Bob: *Bob Becker's Dog Digest* (1947)
    E. M. Berolzheimer discusses Irish Setters.
    Paul, Richmond & Co., Chicago, Ill.

Bennett, Dr. Logan J.: *Training Grouse & Woodcock Dogs* (1948)
    Step by step training as the dog matures.
    G. P. Putnam's Sons, New York, N.Y.

Bepler, M. Inge & Ryan, C. W.: *Setters: Irish, English & Gordon* (1937)
    Mrs. Bepler owned Rheola Irish Setters.
    Our Dogs Publishing Co., Manchester, Eng.   OP

British Gordon Setter Club: *The Gordon Setter* (1939)
    Translation from Norwegian, Schilbred's *Pointer og Setter*.
    G & W Fraser, Aberdeen, Scotland.

Burges, Arnold: *American Kennel & Sporting Field* (1876)
    Early shows & trials. 332 sporting dog pedigrees.
    J. B. Ford & Co., New York, N.Y.   OP

Brown, William F.: *How to Train Hunting Dogs* (1942)
    Training Pointers, Spaniels & Retrievers.
    A. S. Barnes & Co., New York, N.Y.

Brown, William F.: *Field Trials* (1947)
    History, Management & Judging Standards.
    A. S. Barnes & Co., New York, N.Y.

Brown, W. F. & Buckingham, N.: *National Field Trial Champions* (1955)
    History of the National Championship, 1896–1955.
    Stackpole & Co., Harrisburg, Pa.

Calhoon, J. W. (M.D.): *Ch Milson O'Boy* (1965)
    Memorial to O'Boy.
    Popular Dogs Publishing Co., Philadelphia, Pa.

Connett, Eugene V. (editor): *American Sporting Dogs* (1948)
    Training, handling & breeding. Written by 26 authorities.
    D. Van Nostrand Co., New York, N.Y.

Cross, J. & Saunders, B.: *New Standard Book of Dog Care & Training* (1962)
    Down-to-earth handbook. 1001 questions answered.
    Howell Book House, New York, N.Y. Originally Greystone Press.

Litter by Ch. Hagginwood's Real McCoy ex Coolavin's Nanno.

Dalziel, Hugh: *British Dogs* (1888–1897), 3 vols.
　　Early development of various breeds.
　　L. Upcott Gill, London, Eng. OP

Daniel, Rev. W. B.: *Rural Sports* (1802–1813), 4 vols.
　　Hawking, Fowling, Shooting, Angling, Dogs, etc.
　　Longman, Hurst, Rees & Orme, London, Eng. OP

Davis, Henry P.: *Training Your Own Bird Dog* (1948)
　　Primarily for the amateur trainer.
　　G. P. Putnam's Sons, New York, N.Y.

Davis, Henry P. (editor): *Modern Dog Encyclopedia* (1949)
　　Variety of data pertaining to all breeds.
　　Stackpole & Heck, Harrisburg, Pa.

Denlinger, Milo G.: *Complete Irish Setter* (1949)
　　Brief history, standard, care & training.
　　Howell Book House, New York, N.Y. Originally Denlinger. OP

Dog News (monthly), started 1922.
　　All breed magazine with Irish Setter column.
　　Alice Rosenthal, Cincinnati, Ohio.

Dog World (monthly), started 1916.
　　All breed magazine, with Irish Setter column.
　　Dog World Magazine, Chicago, Ill.

Duncan, William C.: *Dog Training Made Easy* (1940)
　　Duncan was ISC of America delegate to AKC, 1925–1945.
　　Little, Brown & Co., Boston, Mass.

Foster, James C.: *Twentieth Century Dog Breeding* (1939)
　　Popular, basic book on breeding.
　　The Naylor Co., San Antonio, Tex. OP

Free, James L.: *Training Your Retriever* (1963)
　　Excellent book on retrieving.
　　Coward, McCann, New York, N.Y.

Graham, Joseph A.: *The Sporting Dog* (1904)
　　Interesting accounts of well known gun dogs.
　　The Macmillan Co., New York, N.Y. OP

Haberlein, Ed F.: *The Amateur Trainer* (1938)
　　Standard work in numerous editions.
　　Privately printed, McPherson, Kans.

Herbert, Henry W.: *Frank Forester's Field Sports of the U.S.* (1858), 2 vols.
　　Classic work of this prolific sporting writer.
　　W. A. Townsend, New York, N.Y. OP

Hochwalt, A. F.: *The Pointer & Setter in America* (1911)
　　Detailed, thorough history of field dogs.
　　Sportsmen's Review Publishing Co., Cincinnati, Ohio. OP

Hochwalt, A. F.: *The Modern Setter* (1923, 1935), 2 vols.
　　English, Irish & Gordon Setters in field trials.
　　A. F. Hochwalt Co., McLean, Va.

Holland, Ray P.: *My Gun Dogs* (1929)
　　Hunting stories.
　　Houghton Mifflin Co., Boston, Mass.

265

A basketful.

Howell, Denlinger & Merrick: *Howell Book of Dog Care & Training* (1963)
 Practical guide on dog keeping.
 Howell Book House, New York, N.Y.

Hubbard, Clifford L. B.: *Literature of British Dogs* (1949)
 Description of early day dog books.
 Privately printed, Ponterwyd, Wales.

Hutchinson, Walter (editor) : *Dog Encyclopedia* (1935), 3 vols.
 Comprehensive, well illustrated & unequalled.
 Hutchinson & Co., London, Eng.   OP

Johns, Rowland (editor): *Our Friend the Irish Setter* (1933)
 A general dog book.
 E. P. Dutton & Co., New York, N.Y.

Kennel Review (monthly) , started 1898.
 All breed magazine with Irish Setter column.
 B & E Publications, North Hollywood, Cal.

Kirmse, Marguerite: *Dogs in the Field* (1935)
 Limited edition with sketches of 300 dogs.
 Derrydale Press, New York, N.Y.   OP

Kjelgaard, Jim: *Big Red* (1945)
 Story of an Irish Setter & a boy. Famous as a movie.
 Holiday House, New York, N.Y.

Koehler, Wm. R.: *Koehler Method of Dog Training* (1962)
 Koehler trained Big Red for the movie.
 Howell Book House, New York, N.Y.

Laverack, Edward: *The Setter* (1872)
 First breed book on all setters. Collector's item.
 Longman's Green & Co., London, Eng.   OP

Lee, Rawdon B.: *Modern Dogs* (Sporting Division) (1897) , 2 vols.
 Interesting Irish Setter chapter.
 Horace Cox, London, Eng.   OP

Leighton, Robert: *New Book of the Dog* (1911), 2 vols.
 All breed book.
 Cassell & Co., London, Eng.   OP

Lloyd, Freeman: *All Setters* (1937)
 History, Rearing & Training.
 Privately printed, New York, N.Y.   OP

Lyon, McDowell: *The Dog in Action* (1963)
 Study of dog locomotion & confirmation.
 Howell Book House, New York, N.Y. Originally Orange Judd.

Lytle, Horace: *Breaking a Bird Dog* (1924)
 The Irish Setter field trial winner, Smada Byrd.
 D. Appleton & Co., New York, N.Y.   OP

Lytle, Horace: *Gun Dogs Afield* (1942)
 Collection of Hunting Stories.
 G. P. Putnam's Sons, New York, N.Y.

Lytle, Horace: *How to Train Your Bird Dog* (1946)
 For the amateur trainer.
 A. F. Hochwalt Co., Dayton, Ohio.

Litter by Pat Powers II ex Peggy Judy Law.

Lytle, Horace: *Simple Secrets of Dog Discipline* (1946)
  The best of Lytle's writings.
  G. P. Putnam's Sons, New York, N.Y.

Lytle, Horace: *How to Win Field Trials* (1950)
  Practical handbook of breeding & training.
  D. Van Nostrand Co., New York, N.Y.

Lytle, Horace: *Point!*
  Collection of hunting experiences.
  Stackpole Co., Harrisburg, Pa.

Mason, Charles H.: *Our Prize Dogs* (1888)
  Dog show winners of 1887.
  Forest & Stream Publishing Co., New York, N.Y.   OP

McCay, Clive: *Nutrition of the Dog* (1949)
  Scientific feeding of dogs.
  Comstock Publishing Co., Ithaca, N.Y.

Miller, Warren H.: *The American Hunting Dog* (1926)
  Modern strains of bird dogs.
  D. Appleton & Co., New York, N.Y.   OP

Millner, Col. J. K.: *The Irish Setter: Its History & Training* (1924)
  Early setters in Ireland.
  H. F. & G. Witherby, London, Eng.   OP

Moffit, Ella B.: *Elias Vail Trains Gun Dogs* (1937)
  Vail owned the Elcova Irish Setters.
  Howell Book House, New York, N.Y. Originally Orange Judd.

National Geographic Society: *Book of Dogs* (1958)
  342 illustrations of dogs of all breeds.
  National Geographic Society, Washington, D.C.

Naylor, Leonard E.: *The Irish Setter* (1932)
  History, Temperament and Training.
  H. F. & G. Witherby, London, Eng.   OP

Onstott, Kyle: *The New Art of Breeding Better Dogs* (1962)
  Revised by Professor Philip Onstott.
  Howell Book House, New York, N.Y. Originally Denlinger.

Pearce, Rev. Thomas (Idstone): *The Dog* (1872)
  Early day standard all-breed book.
  Cassell, Petter & Galpin, London, Eng.   OP

Pfaffenberger, Clarence: *New Knowledge of Dog Behaviour* (1963)
  A relatively new field of study.
  Howell Book House, New York, N.Y.

Pohl, Otto: *The Irish Setter* (1917)
  His Past Performances & His Present Possibilities.
  Privately printed, Fremont, Neb.   OP

Popular Dogs (monthly), started 1928.
  An all breed magazine with Irish Setter column.
  Popular Dogs Publishing Co., Philadelphia, Pa.

Redlich, Anna: *The Dogs of Ireland* (1949)
  The Irish red & white setter and the Irish red setter.
  Dundalgan Press, Dundalk, Ire.

Four Irishmen.

Russell, R. L.: *Whole Art of Setter Training* (1930)
    British work on training Irish Setters.
    The Field, London, Eng.   OP

Saunders, Blanche: *How to Trim, Groom & Show Your Dog* (1963)
    Instructions for setters included.
    Howell Book House, New York, N.Y.

Saunders, Blanche: *Complete Book of Dog Obedience* (1965)
    Basic work on obedience training
    Howell Book House, New York, N.Y. Originally Prentice-Hall.

Schilbred, Lt.-Col. Corn: *Pointer og Setter* (1924)
    Norwegian book. Author had setters for 40 years.
    H. Aschehough & Co., Oslo, Norway.

Shaw, Vero: *The Illustrated Book of the Dog* (1881)
    Standard all breed book.
    Cassell & Co., London, Eng.   OP

Shelley, Er M.: *Bird Dog Training, Today & Tomorrow* (1927)
    System for training shooting dogs.
    G. P. Putnam's Sons, New York, N.Y.

Shields, G. O.: *The American Book of the Dog* (1891)
    All breed classic with fine Irish Setter chapter.
    Rand McNally & Co., New York, N.Y.   OP

Stokes, G. Vernon: *The Drawing & Painting of Dogs* (1934)
    For amateur artist.
    Seeley, Service & Co., London, Eng.   OP

Taplin, William: *The Sportsman' Cabinet* (1803–4), 2 vols.
    Early sporting classic with wood engravings.
    J. Cundee, London, Eng.   OP

Taylor, J. M.: *Bench Show & Field Trial Records of Dogs in America* (1892)
    Tremendous compilation applying to sporting dogs.
    Rogers & Sherwood, New York, N.Y.   OP

Thompson, Lloyd: *King of Maple Dale* (1927)
    Irish Setter field trial story.
    D. Appleton & Co., New York, N.Y.   OP

Thompson, William C.: *Irish Setter in Word & Picture* (1954)
    Irish Setter breed book.
    Howell Book House, New York, N.Y. Originally Denlinger.   OP

Thompson, William C.: *100 Irish Setter Pedigrees* (1948)
    4-generation pedigrees from 1860 to 1948.
    E. W. Leach Publishing Co., Minneapolis, Minn.   OP

Thompson, William C.: *Irish Setter Champions & Obedience Title Winners* (1966)
    3000 dogs listed.
    Irish Setter Club of America, New York, N.Y.

Thompson, W. C. & Wallo, O.: *Irish Setter History* (1949)
    Translation from Schilbred's *Pointer og Setter.*
    Howell Book House, New York, N.Y.   OP

Tuck, D. H. & Howell, E. S.: *The New Complete English Setter* (1964)
    English Setter breed book.
    Howell Book House, New York, N.Y. Originally Denlinger.

Verwey, G. J.: *Setters en Pointers* (1949)
  Dutch book on gun dogs.
  A. J. G. Strengholt, Amsterdam, Holland.

Walsh, J. H. (Stonehenge): *The Dogs of the British Islands* (1878)
  All breed book with Irish Setter chapter.
  Horace Cox, London, Eng.   OP

Walsh, J. H.: *Dogs of Gt Britain, America & Other Countries* (1888)
  Standard all breed book.
  Orange Judd & Co., New York, N.Y.   OP

Watson, James: *The Dog Book* (1905), 2 vols.
  Thorough all-breed work with Irish Setter chapter.
  Doubleday Page & Co., New York, N.Y.   OP

Wehle, R. G.: *Wing & Shot* (1964)
  Development of the gun dog.
  The Country Press, Scottsville, N.Y.

Welch, Marie Louise: *Your Friend & Mine* (1934)
  Author was an Irish Setter breeder.
  Privately printed, Baltimore, Md.   OP

Western Kennel World (monthly), started 1912
  All breed periodical.
  Western Kennel World Publishing Co., San Francisco, Cal.

Whitford, C. B.: *Training the Bird Dog* (1928)
  Author was one of the old time professional trainers.
  The Macmillan Co., New York, N.Y.

Whitney, Dr. Leon F.: *How to Breed Dogs* (1949)
  Dog breeders' bible.
  Howell Book House, New York, N.Y., originally Orange Judd.

Wise, John S.: *Diomed* (1897)
  The Life, Travels & Observations of an English Setter.
  Lamson, Wolffe & Co., Boston, Mass.   OP

Wolters, Richard A.: *Gun Dog* (1961)
  Rapid method for training shooting dogs.
  E. P. Dutton & Co., New York, N.Y.